THEORY, PRACTICE, AND COMMUNITY DEVELOPMENT

For many scholars, the study of community and community development is at a crossroads. Previously dynamic theories appear not to have kept pace with the major social changes of our day. Given our constantly shifting social reality we need new ideas and research that pushes the boundaries of our extant community theories. *Theory, Practice, and Community Development* stretches the traditional boundaries and applications of well-established community development theory, and establishes new theoretical approaches rooted in new disciplines and new perspectives on community development.

Expanded from a special issue of the journal *Community Development*, *Theory, Practice, and Community Development* collects previously published and widely cited essays, as well as new theoretical and empirical research in community development. Compiled by the editors of *Community Development*, the essays feature topics as varied as placemaking, democratic theory, and rural organizing. *Theory, Practice, and Community Development* is vital for scholars and practitioners coming to grips with the rapidly changing definition of community.

Mark A. Brennan, PhD, is the UNESCO Chair in Rural Community, Leadership, and Youth Development and Professor of Leadership and Community Development in the Department of Agricultural Economics, Sociology, and Education at Penn State University. Dr Brennan's teaching, research, writing, and program development concentrates on the role of community and leadership development in the youth, community, and rural development process. In this context, much of his work has focused on community action, youth development, locally based natural resource management, economic development, and social justice. Dr Brennan's research and program development has been funded by a variety of government, foundation, and private sources, resulting in over 100 publications in leading peer-reviewed journals, books, Extension publications, and over 80 presentations at professional meetings. All research outputs have been translated into teaching and outreach curricula to facilitate the transfer of knowledge to a wider international audience. Included are over twenty outreach curricula designed for communities and youth to use in fostering community capacity building and local collective capacity.

Jeffrey C. Bridger, PhD, is Senior Scientist in the Department of Agricultural Economics, Sociology, and Education at Penn State University. He received his BS from George Mason University and his MS and PhD from Penn State University. His research and teaching interests include community theory, rural community development, the human dimensions of natural resource use, and university–community engagement. He currently teaches in the Community Environment and Development Program and in the Masters of Professional Studies Program in Community and Economic Development. His research has been supported by state, regional, national, and private agencies and has resulted in over 60 journal articles and book chapters. His most recent research focuses on the role of social capital in rural economic development and strategies for broadband deployment in rural America.

Theodore R. Alter, PhD, is a professor of agricultural, environmental, and regional economics and co-director of the Center for Economic and Community Development in Penn State's Department of Agricultural Economics, Sociology, and Education. He also serves as an Adjunct Research Fellow in the School of Law at the University of New England in Australia. His research and teaching focus on community and rural development, resource and environmental economics, public sector economics and policy, institutional and behavioral economics, and public scholarship and civic engagement in higher education. In recent years, Dr Alter has advanced his work to include the study of public and collective choice, democracy, and innovation, and how paradigms of public discourse have shaped complex societal issues from technology and communications development to entrepreneurship and public–private partnerships. Dr Alter has served as Penn State's associate vice president for outreach, associate and interim dean in the College of Agricultural Sciences, and director of Penn State Cooperative Extension.

The Community Development Research and Practice Series
Volume 1

Series Editor:
RHONDA G. PHILLIPS
Arizona State University, USA

Editorial Board:
MARK BRENNAN
Pennsylvania State University, USA

JAN FLORA
Iowa State University, USA

GARY P. GREEN
University of Wisconsin, USA

BRIAN McGRATH
National University of Ireland

NORMAN WALZER
Northern Illinois University, USA

This series serves community developers, planners, public administrators, and others involved in practice and policy making in the realm of community development. The series provides timely and applied information for researchers, students, and practitioners. Building on a 40-year history of publishing the Community Development Society's journal, *Community Development* (www.comm-dev.org), the book series contributes to a growing and rapidly changing knowledge base as a resource for practitioners and researchers alike.

For additional information please see the series page at www.routledge.com

THEORY, PRACTICE, AND COMMUNITY DEVELOPMENT

Edited by Mark A. Brennan, Jeffrey C. Bridger, and Theodore R. Alter

First edition published 2013
by Routledge

Simultaneously published in the USA and Canada
by Routledge
711 Third Avenue, New York, NY 10017

Routledge is an imprint of the Taylor & Francis Group, an informa business

© 2013 selection and editorial material, Mark A. Brennan, Jeffrey C. Bridger, Theodore R. Alter; individual chapters, the contributors

The right of Mark A. Brennan, Jeffrey C. Bridger, and Theodore R. Alter to be identified as authors of the editorial material, and of the individual authors as authors of their contributions, has been asserted in accordance with sections 77 and 78 of the Copyright, Designs and Patents Act 1988.

All rights reserved. No part of this book may be reprinted or reproduced or utilised in any form or by any electronic, mechanical, or other means, now known or hereafter invented, including photocopying and recording, or in any information storage or retrieval system, without permission in writing from the publishers.

Trademark notice: Product or corporate names may be trademarks or registered trademarks, and are used only for identification and explanation without intent to infringe.

British Library Cataloguing in Publication Data
A catalogue record for this book is available from the British Library.

Library of Congress Cataloging-in-Publication Data
Brennan, Mark A.
Theory, practice, and community development / Mark A. Brennan, Jeffrey C. Bridger, Theodore R. Alter. – 1st Edition.
pages cm. – (The community development research and practice series)
Includes bibliographical references and index.
1. Community development. I. Bridger, Jeffrey C. II. Alter, Theodore R. III. Title.
HN49.C6B74 2013
307.1'4–dc23   2012051064

ISBN13: 978-0-415-69413-1 (hbk)
ISBN13: 978-0-415-69414-8 (pbk)
ISBN13: 978-0-203-77371-0 (e-book)

Typeset in Bembo
by Cenveo Publisher Services

CONTENTS

List of Illustrations	ix
List of Tables	x
Acknowledgements	xi
Series Editor's Introduction	xiii

1   Introduction: Theory, Practice, and Community Development   1
*Mark A. Brennan, Paloma Z.C. Frumento,
Jeffrey C. Bridger, and Theodore R. Alter*

SECTION ONE
Defining and Understanding Community in Contemporary Society

2   The Post-Place Community: Contributions to the
Debate about the Definition of Community   11
Ted K. Bradshaw

3   Settling at the Margins: Exurbia and Community Sociology   25
Jeff S. Sharp and Jill K. Clark

4   Community Generalizing Structure Dimensions: Clarifying a
Fundamental Community Interaction Field Theory Concept   41
Peter F. Korsching and Cheryl Davidson

viii Contents

SECTION TWO
Community Dynamics

5 An Interactional Approach to Place-Based Rural Development   63
   Jeffrey C. Bridger and Theodore R. Alter

6 The Power of Community   78
   Mark A. Brennan and Glenn D. Israel

7 The Tamaqua Paradox: How History Shapes Social
   Capital and Local Economic Development Efforts   98
   Jeffrey C. Bridger, Paloma Z.C. Frumento, and Theodore R. Alter

SECTION THREE
Community, Local Decision Making, Democratic Participation, and Social Change

8 Populism, Power, and Rural Community Development   123
   Tony Varley and Chris Curtin

9 What Kind of Democracy Informs Community Development?   138
   David Mathews

10 The Basics: What's Essential about Theory for Community
    Development Practice?   163
    Ronald J. Hustedde and Jacek Ganowicz

11 A Framework for Thinking and Acting Critically in Community   180
    Jeffrey C. Bridger, Paloma Z. Frumento, Theodore R. Alter,
    and Mark A. Brennan

    Index   191

ILLUSTRATIONS

Figures

2.1	Proportion of People who Spend a Social Evening with Someone in Neighborhood and Elsewhere, Daily or Weekly, by Date of Survey	19
2.2	How Close Do You Feel to Places (Percent)	19
2.3	How Long Have You Lived in Your Community in Years (1996 Data)?	20
2.4	Would You Be Willing to Move to Another Place in Order to Improve Your Work or Living Condition?	20
3.1	Example of Ohio Government Geography	33
4.1	Perceptions of Community Generalizing Structure Dimensions among Business Proprietors in a small Midwestern Community	56
10.1	Three Key Concerns in the Community Development Field	165
10.2	Gidden's Modalities: The Link to Social Change at the Macro and Micro Levels	173

Map

3.1	Ohio's Metropolitan Areas (Central Counties Gray; Outlying Counties Striped) and Nonmetropolitan Areas (in White)	30

TABLES

2.1	Issues of Community from Different Perspectives	23
3.1	Ohio Population by Metropolitan Character, 2000 to 2010	31
3.2	Columbus Metropolitan Area, Population by Type of Place, 2000–2010	33
6.1	The Choice and Consequences of Power	88

ACKNOWLEDGEMENTS

The development of this edited volume would not have been possible without the tireless contributions of several important contributors.

First, and foremost, the editors wish to extend their most sincere gratitude to **Paloma Frumento**. While initially brought on to the project to assist with the logistics of producing this book, she contributed far more, and was invaluable to the entire project. Ultimately, Paloma co-authored three chapters, made sure the contributors submitted their manuscripts on time, coordinated the reviews, copy-edited many of the chapters, and managed the overall process of producing the book. She was also remarkable in immersing herself in the body of literature which was largely unfamiliar to her and developing a mastery of community theory. Through these efforts she brought a perspective and insight to the book that would not have otherwise been possible.

Kate Ortbal was invaluable in assisting with the various formatting of chapters, references, and content. As deadlines loomed, she untiringly assisted Paloma in finalizing the chapters and book structure.

Many of the chapters represent new contributions to community theory, and we called on several content **reviewers and subject matter experts** to provide reactions and suggestions, further improving the manuscripts. Their constructive contributions significantly contributed to the quality of the chapters ultimately produced.

Finally, this edited book originated out of a series of discussions and debates within the Community Development Society about the future of community theory. These discussions culminated in a special issue of *Community Development: Journal of the Community Development Society* in 2008. **Dr Rhonda Phillips**, Editor of *Community Development*, was a champion of this important and timely topic. Building on the success of this special issue, Rhonda encouraged the development of this book, which brings together select articles from the special issue, and

xii Acknowledgements

complements these with new theoretical contributions. Her contribution to the development of the book prospectus was immense, as were the significant suggestions of the Community Development Society Book Series review panel.

SERIES EDITOR'S INTRODUCTION

Community development as reflected in both theory and practice is continually evolving. This comes as no surprise as our communities and regions constantly change. As it is a practice-focused discipline, change is the only constant in the community development realm. The need to integrate theory, practice, research, teaching, and training is even more pressing now than ever, given uncertain and rapidly transforming economic, social, environmental, and cultural climates. Current and applicable information and insights about effective community development research and practice are needed.

In partnership with Routledge, the Community Development Society is delighted to present this new book series serving community developers, planners, public administrators, citizen activists, and others involved in community development practice, research, and policymaking. The series is designed to integrate innovative thinking on tools, strategies, experiences as a resource especially well-suited for bridging the gaps between theory, research, and practice. It is our intent that the series will provide timely and useful information for responding to the rapidly changing environment in which community development researchers and practitioners operate.

The Community Development Society was formed in 1970 as a professional association to serve the needs of both researchers and practitioners. That same year, the Society began publishing *Community Development*, its journal promoting exchange of ideas, experiences, and approaches between practice and research. *Theory, Practice, and Community Development* builds on this rich legacy of scholarship by offering contributions to the growing knowledge base.

The Community Development Society actively promotes the continued advancement of the practice and theory of community development. Fundamental to this mission is adherence to the following core principles of good practice. This new book series is a reflection of many of these core principles.

- Promote active and representative participation toward enabling all community members to meaningfully influence the decisions that affect their lives.
- Engage community members in learning about and understanding community issues, and the economic, social, environmental, political, psychological, and other impacts associated with alternative courses of action.
- Incorporate the diverse interest and cultures of the community in the community development process; and disengage from support of any effort that is likely to adversely affect the disadvantaged members of a community.
- Work actively to enhance the leadership capacity of community members, leaders, and groups within the community.
- Be open to using the full range of action strategies to work toward the long-term sustainability and well being of the community.

1

INTRODUCTION

Theory, Practice, and Community Development

Mark A. Brennan, Paloma Z.C. Frumento,
Jeffrey C. Bridger, and Theodore R. Alter

Over the past decade a variety of debates and discussions among community development professionals, academics, and practitioners concerning the current state of community theory have pointed to the need to explore the issue more systematically. In response, a special issue of *Community Development: Journal of the Community Development Society* was produced in 2009 (Volume 39, Issue 1) to bring together a wide range of theoretical and empirical articles that expand our theoretical understanding of community in contemporary life. This special issue proved widely popular, with articles being used extensively in both education and practice settings. More importantly, this special issue further ignited the call for the theoretical advances needed to understand our rapidly changing communities. These issues and concerns were the impetus for this book. Bringing together select articles from the special issue with newly commissioned work, the theoretical explorations presented in this book push forward our understanding of community and the various dynamics that contribute to its emergence and persistence.

The timing for this book is particularly relevant. For many scholars, the study of community and community development is at a crossroads. Previously, dynamic theories appear not to have kept pace with the major social, environmental, and technological changes of our day. Emerging perspectives, attempting to explain rapid social, environmental, and political changes, have often strayed from the logic and conceptualization essential to significant theoretical development. Given our constantly shifting social reality, we need new ideas and research that push the boundaries of extant community theories. Making such a claim does not necessarily mean a wholesale abandonment of existing theories and methods; it does, however, imply they must be adapted and further developed to meet new social realities. An ongoing and open discussion regarding the current state of community theory can only benefit community scholars and practitioners. It is particularly important to develop theoretical frameworks that are practically useful for applied efforts to enhance the well-being of our communities.

As is the case in any field of inquiry, this book also emerged out of the often contentious debates and provincialism that stem from our professional passions for our own theoretical perspectives. While debates are healthy, we must take care to ensure that they do not stifle and undermine our common dedication to enhancing and supporting community development. When certain theoretical perspectives become too institutionalized into a discipline, in essence becoming a de facto orthodoxy, they hinder progressive debates by inadvertently playing a gate-keeping function within our professional societies and journals. Equally important, their status often makes them off-limits for critical inquiry, leaving them open to failure in a rapidly changing world. This ossification is problematic in academic settings; it is devastating in applied practice. We must not lose sight of the fact that our development of theory is not an academic exercise, but is the cornerstone of effective practice on which communities and residents depend.

Thus, the book has two main goals: 1) to elucidate and stretch the traditional boundaries and applications of the well-established theories and 2) to catalyze discussion about how new and existing frameworks can be applied to the complex community settings where people live and work. To meet these goals the book is organized into three sections. The first section provides a context for defining and understanding community in contemporary society. The second section explores community dynamics in the broader geographical environments in which they are situated. The third, and final, section explores the importance of community for local decision making, democratic participation, and social change.

Current Perspectives, Future Theoretical Directions, and Calls to Action

Historically, one of the most prominent themes in the community literature has been the theoretical significance of place. Indeed, place has often been used interchangeably or synonymously with community. Over time, and particularly during the second half of the twentieth century, the connection between place and community became increasingly tenuous as advances in transportation and communication blurred the boundaries of once well-defined localities. Our social networks, service provision, employment, and other activities now occur in broader, more dispersed areas. The twenty-first century has brought technological advances that further confuse the distinction between community and place; physical or geographic constraints on social interaction are all but obsolete. The authors included in this book draw attention to the increasingly complicated relationship between place and community.

Section One begins with Ted Bradshaw's "The Post-Place Community: Contributions to the Debate about the Definition of Community," which raises and champions the issue of 'the post-place community'. With this concept, Bradshaw divorces place from the other traditional elements used to define community – solidarity, common identity, and shared norms – to argue for the continued relevance of Gemeinschaft-type relations. He draws empirical support from the University of Chicago General Social Survey by the National Opinion Research Center, which suggests that while people attribute increasing importance to social relations outside of their local communities, they still also remain attached to these local communities. For this reason, while place is no longer a necessary aspect of community, it may play a central role in structuring social relations in some communities. Bradshaw further explains that the relationship between community and place has become a more dynamic one; while place was previously seen to have a unidirectional influence on the formation of community, communities now may also influence place, given "that any place may be influenced by people having contacts at a local or global scale, and individuals at the global scale also participate at the local" (p.XX). This more nuanced conceptualization of community has important implications for policy; Bradshaw suggests that community developers should work to strengthen bridges between places and the larger social and economic networks with which residents may be involved as a means for generating civic engagement at "whatever scale makes sense for the common good" (p.XX).

Jeff S. Sharp and Jill K. Clark also tackle the relationship between place and community in their exploration of exurbia, or what is sometimes referred to as the rural-urban fringe, in "Settling at the Margins: Exurbia and Community Sociology." Some have suggested that this zone of settlement is too urban to attract the interest of rural social scientists and too rural to attract the attention of urban scholars. The authors argue that exurban research offers potential insights for both fields, given the questions that can be raised with regard to residential preference, land use and growth management, governance, and the possibility for the emergence of community. This last issue is particularly relevant to community theory as a whole, given the diversity of exurban residents, the relative absence of a shared history among newcomers and longtime local residents, and the diffused patterns of employment, service acquisition, and organizational membership.

The authors begin with a detailed literature review that considers defining and operationalizing exurbia, distinguishing the concept from suburbia, the role of the invasion/succession process in fostering conflict and shifting attitudes and cultures in previously rural areas, and the policy implications for land-use planning and growth management. To contextualize these themes, and to further illustrate the size of the population implicated in and impacted by exurban development, the authors use US Census data from Ohio. The remainder of the chapter focuses on three future directions for research based upon the themes identified earlier in the chapter and the authors' applied extension work in Ohio. In this section, they also consider the future of exurbia itself: the extent to which exurban development might return following the current economic downturn and whether the social trends that have given rise to exurbia are likely to change or evolve.

In "Community Generalizing Structure Dimensions: Clarifying Fundamental Community Interaction Field Theory Concept" Peter F. Korsching and Cheryl Davidson also seek to define and operationalize the essential linkages that hold community together. They consider what Wilkinson (1991) terms the 'generalizing structure' in his interactional field theory of community. This is a structure of linkages among individuals, organizations, and agencies that integrate, coordinate, reinforce, and mobilize the common elements of their differentiated special interests for the community's welfare. When local interaction occurs specifically for the benefit of the community, it builds a generalizing structure. Despite its importance to field theory, this remains a highly abstract concept that has not been adequately defined and clarified enough to be an analytically useful tool for understanding community organization and action, conducting community research, and implementing community development projects.

To operationalize the concept, the authors propose measureable dimensions of community generalizing structure. Building on Wilkinson (1991), they suggest that the dimensions of this generalizing structure are distributive justice, open communication, tolerance, collective action, and communication. These dimensions describe the nature of the relationship between the community and the social well-being of its population. The authors hypothesize that a strong generalizing community structure is perceived by residents as being a positive environment for both business and personal life. They conclude by discussing the results in terms of their implications for community interaction field theory and contributions to the literature on community attachment and participation.

Section Two of this book explores potential for community development action(s) in the broader geographical environments in which we live. This section begins with "An Interactional Approach to Place-Based Development." In this chapter, Jeffrey Bridger and Ted Alter note that globalization that has significantly reshaped and in some instances made obsolete the local social and economic structures that typified rural America through most of its history. Given this uncertain environment, economic development policies that may have worked in the past are no longer relevant. In their place is an emerging consensus that development must be more place-based and focused on enhancing regional and place competitiveness. The authors explore this strategy and identify some of its most serious shortcomings – especially for rural areas. The chapter proposes an interactional approach that integrates economic, environmental, and social well-being.

In "The Power of Community," Mark Brennan and Glenn Israel explore one of the most neglected facets in the community development literature: power. The authors provide a conceptual model for understanding the context and emergence of community power and the responses to power by local elites and stakeholders. While formally and informally recognized as being central to community action, research and theoretical literature provides little insight into the processes behind the emergence of community power. Power is usually presented in terms of a culmination of community actions that lead to its more equitable distribution. Less often considered are the processes and mechanisms through which civic engagement and capacity building activities enable citizens to gain power. The authors explore the ways in which power is conceptualized at this level, as a component of community development and social change. The authors provide a theoretical framework, based on an interactional field theoretical perspective, for better understanding the processes by which citizens gain entrée to power, as well as how they interact with elites that might otherwise limit the emergence of local capacity. The chapter concludes with a discussion of the implications for community development.

"The Tamaqua Paradox: How History Shapes Social Capital and Local Economic Development Efforts," by Jeffrey Bridger, Paloma Frumento, and Ted Alter, also focuses on the processes that structure community power and impact community action. Specifically, they examine the usefulness of social capital as a tool for understanding community action. As part of a larger USDA study considering six rural communities in the state, the authors trace the historical development of Tamaqua, a community located in the anthracite coal region of Pennsylvania. Despite evidence from interview data suggesting that Tamaqua had the highest levels of bridging social capital and economic development activeness of the communities included in the study, household survey data suggested that the community scored very low on both bonding and bridging social capital. In order to understand this paradox, the authors consider the historical context for contemporary social relations and community action. They conclude that social capital theory is inadequate for reconciling these conflicting views of local life. Instead, they argue, narrative analysis provides for a more nuanced consideration of the specific power relations that have resulted from a history of fractionalization and periodic collaboration.

The third, and final, section explores local decision making, democratic participation, and social change. The three chapters included in this section call to action citizens, scholars, and experts to take a more active role in these areas. This section begins with a chapter by Tony Varley and Chris Curtin, "Populism, Power, and Rural Community Development," which explores populism and what they term 'underdog' politics in a rural community development context. Underdog politics share two features of populism as it has traditionally been theorized and practiced. First, rural community interests are characterized as relatively powerless vis-à-vis external forces (often cities and the state). Second, advocates of populism argue that collective and state action can become forces of countervailing power capable of furthering rural interests. Varley and Curtin explore these two features with a view toward investigating the adequacy of 'populism' as a descriptive and interpretive category.

They begin by constructing a framework based on four oppositions describing urban power and rural powerlessness commonly associated with the term 'populism.' Here, they make a clear distinction between 'power over,' which describes Lukes's well-known second and third faces of power, and 'power to,' which describes the ability of collective action to support the interests of disadvantaged actors and generate structural change. The authors then describe two ideal-type scenarios through which collective and state actions may foster "populist and underdog community development and 'participative' forms of pro-community state intervention" (p.XX). These are the radical and the pragmatic approaches, which they frame using conflict and consensus models of social structure. Despite their differences, both approaches are similar in that claims to power, authority, and legitimacy are based in the conscious construction of an underdog, or disadvantaged, identity. The authors conclude with a frank assessment of the utility of 'populism' as a descriptive and interpretive term. They ultimately assert that the populist label is freighted with too much negative baggage to serve as a useful descriptive term. However, the framework of four oppositions that they construct could aid in its interpretive value.

In contrast to Varley and Curtin's emphasis on external actors representing community interests and initiating social change, David Mathews of the Kettering Foundation takes up the issue of local residents' self-representation through deliberative democracy. In "What Kind of Democracy Informs Community Development?" Mathews offers a unique insight that bridges academic and practice settings. He develops an ideal-type framework for the emergence of democracy at the community level based on the experience of the Kettering Foundation and the academic work it has sponsored. Unlike Bradshaw, Mathews argues for the continued, central relevance of place-based identities and communities: "... none of us lives in a petri dish divorced from place, physical, and human" (p.XX).

Mathews's conceptualization of democracy is structured by classical Greek theory and a deliberative model of participation. He argues that democratic practices involve citizens working together, driven by a common political will and set of values. These practices include identifying and naming problems, framing ways to deal with these problems, making decisions through deliberation, identifying and committing resources, organizing complementary acting, and public learning. According to Mathews, democratic practices can help to address many of the major issues that experts and practitioners identify as barriers to effective citizen participation. He illustrates this through the composite of Suggsville, based on work in more than 50 communities observed over 30 years. Through this model, Mathews addresses the potential for conflict that is inherent to settings marked by poverty and resource deprivation. He emphasizes the importance of creating processes for reaching consensus, while acknowledging that consensus is not always a realistic outcome. Mathews also suggests a more reflexive and equitable role for scholars, experts, practitioners, and citizens, one in which all of these actors work together to build better communities. Ultimately he asserts that, when employed in a holistic and context-relevant manner, democratic practices can be a positive force for both solidarity and agency even in the most challenged communities.

Solidarity and agency are also foundational to Ronald J. Hustedde and Jacek Ganowicz's approach to community development theory and practice. In "The Basics: What's Essential about Theory for Community Development Practice?," the authors provide an insightful overview of the often disconnected central strands of community theory, and argue that these theories have an important bearing on practice that has been widely overlooked. They contend that the multidisciplinary field of community development needs common theoretical concepts to help understand events and develop appropriate strategies and tools.

The authors argue that effective practice will take into account structure, power, and shared meaning. They relate these concerns to three classical theoretical frameworks: structural functionalism, conflict theory, and symbolic interactionism. These seemingly disparate theories can be brought together in a fruitful dialogue when viewed through the lens of Giddens' structuration theory, which links both macro and micro approaches through a meso-level analysis. Giddens describes the meso-level as modalities, or cultural patterns that actors use to structure and guide their behavior. Modalities are important because they can be used to influence the macro and micro levels of change. The potential for simultaneous stability and change at this level resolves the seemingly irreconcilable differences between structural functionalism and conflict theory, and the capacity for individual actors to influence modalities through their behaviors more clearly connects symbolic interactionism to each of these macro theories. Hustedde and Ganowicz view this model as particularly useful for practice because modalities can be mobilized to do everything from developing new structures to altering power relations and resolving local conflicts. By utilizing structuration theory, practitioners can identify local modalities and work with local people to use them for community development purposes.

Conclusion

The chapters in this book represent a continued refinement and advancement of our understanding of the theoretical basis of community and community development. Each author brings a unique perspective to these elusive concepts. Despite their differences, they also share a common interest in fostering the kind of community change that supports social well-being. Scholars and practitioners must continually reassess the norms and values that inform their research, teaching, and programs. As Bhattacharyya (2004, p. 10) notes, the type of theories that apply to community development are "… teleological – charters for action towards a goal, such as theories of democracy, freedom, equality, etc. where the purpose or the end reflexively enters the causal stream, urging, when necessary, modification of our action." If communities are to be adaptive, resilient, and sustainable, this conceptualization of theory and related actions is essential. It is our hope that this book will contribute to a more productive dialogue among scholars and practitioners as we move forward in addressing the needs and opportunities of communities in the twenty-first century.

References

Bhattacharyya, J. (2004). "Theorizing community development." *Journal of the Community Development Society*, 34(2), 5–34.

Wilkinson, K.P. (1991). *The community in rural America*. New York: Greenwood Press.

Section one
DEFINING AND UNDERSTANDING COMMUNITY IN CONTEMPORARY SOCIETY

2

THE POST-PLACE COMMUNITY

Contributions to the Debate about the Definition of Community

Ted K. Bradshaw

Tribute to Ted Bradshaw

Ted Bradshaw was a tireless disciple of community development and, especially, was concerned about the theory underlying its practice. Having worked on several projects with Ted over the years and served CDS in several roles together, as well as sharing a substantial number of hours of conversation on the topic, I knew Ted to be a serious scholar in a field that needs serious scholarship to support the tremendously important work being accomplished by practitioners. Many of Ted's early works primarily dealt with the "development" processes and principles. More recently Ted had begun to tackle the "community" part of the theory development challenge. This article represents some of his more recent thinking along these lines and is based on rather classical works from the sociological perspective. I think this is understandable since community is largely a sociological concept and the creation of community a social process. This article underscores this perspective and would constitute a basic starting point for anyone in the field of community development. The perspective here was to be Ted's starting point and he had asked me for comments and reactions only a couple of months before his tragic death. I have refrained from adding my own perspectives to this article as I wanted this to be representative of Ted's work rather than another's, but he has directly tackled one of the more pressing problems in community development – whether to concentrate on the development of places or of communities, wherever they may evidence themselves. Readers may not find this discussion satisfactory to their own way of thinking, but it should challenge all of us to think more systematically and clearly – as was characteristic of Ted's way of doing things – about this and other problems related to the theoretical basis for community development work.

Kenneth Pigg, University of Missouri

The Post-Place Community

In 1964 Melvin Webber published a short section of a book chapter on urban planning in which he coined the term "community without propinquity" (Webber, 1964).

12 T. Bradshaw

This concept of community gained notoriety among planning scholars who recognized it as a creative revision to the view that communities exist only among people in a bounded geographical area such as a small rural town, a neighborhood, or even a city. The traditional view that Webber challenged is that community is where one lives and consequently where one finds meaningful community interactions and social relations. His article, and a growing chorus of community scholars (Bhattacharyya, 2004), have argued that place, e.g. the spatial location of residence, needs to be decoupled from the essential characteristics of community – the social relations that bond people.

Places are not necessarily communities. Suburbs and gated developments (Blakely and Snyder, 1999) continue to be criticized for their lack of community – bedroom communities that lack social cohesion and generate alienation (Kunstler, 1996). Sprawling metropolitan regions are criticized for automobile-centered design that creates areas with minimal social interaction, rapid turnover of residents, no walkability, few community meeting places, and people with divided loyalties. For some, this is evidence of the loss of community (Salamon, 2005). However, in the modern metropolis with well-documented weak place identity, social relations are built around profession (scientific community), religion (Jewish community), sexual preference (gay community), or interest (stamp collecting, railroads, science fiction, music, art, environmentalism, or health – to list only a few examples), which are cited as evidence of community without propinquity.

Place communities such as rural small towns are typically heralded as model communities where social cohesion rules – strong patterns of social interaction based on long-lasting and deep personal relations. Place-based community continues to have strong advocates who argue that community is built around the formal institutions of a place such as government, economy, education, and religion. Moreover, place is important to government planners and developers who engage in programs such as community building, visioning, and conflict mitigation to help residents create identity and consensus within a geographical area and to improve well-being for residents facing some challenges.

The purpose of this paper is to balance these perspectives, arguing for a concept of post-place community in which the essential characteristics of community are the social relations (solidarity or bonds) between people. Community so defined has, historically, shared boundaries with one's geography of residence (town, neighborhood, city), but today the loss of place identity does not imply the loss of community since solidarity among people no longer needs to be tied to place. The purpose of this paper is to further the debate about decoupling the concept of community from place and to outline the theoretical and empirical foundations of a post-place theory of community.

Classical and Revised Concepts of Community

The classic concept of community is a story about the loss of community due to the processes of modernization. The best-known version of this is the ideal type that

The Post-Place Community **13**

Tonniës (2001) defined as Gemeinschaft and Gesellschaft (usually translated as community and society). The Gemeinschaft community is modeled on the historic village or small town which has inclusive social ties among members based on holistic views of individuals and families, sentiment, traditionalism, and stable or persistent social rankings that have developed over a long time. Trust and familiarity with others, and viewing people as total persons who are significant in their own right, provide a basis for core relationships in the community.

In contrast, Gesellschaft gets expressed in the urban or industrial city where people are interpersonally alienated, but are linked to their community by their roles and their mechanistic contribution to the working of the whole society. Rational will and legal contracts replace more sentimental bases for relationships, and status is not fixed but is fluid, based on achievements and role in the community. In developing the ideal type of Gesellschaft, Tonniës emphasized alienation and absence of strong social ties among people, criticisms more fully developed by Chicago sciologist Louis Wirth (1938) in his seminal paper, "Urbanism as a Way of Life." Tonniës (2002: 234) summarizes his typology:

> The whole movement, from its primary to its subsequent manifestations, can also be conceived as a transition from an original, simple, family communism, and village-town individualism based thereon, to an independent, universal, urban individualism and, determined thereby, a socialism of state and international type.

Family background and one's ascribed status are important in Gemeinschaft community, but in Gesellschaft members are freed of their family history and traditional community values, and are valued for their competitive market achievements and rational works. Robert Nisbet (1966) points out how this definition of community transformation due to industrialization has become a core unit-idea in sociology.

For Tonniës, the ideal type transformation from community to society takes place as people move from tight-knit towns to impersonal large urban cities lacking community. The potential of non-place community seems not to have figured into Tonniës's theory. Tonniës (2001: 52) says that "The theory of Gesellschaft takes as its starting point a group of people who, as in Gemeinschaft, live peacefully alongside one another ..." He also says that in urban areas some people have strong Gemeinschaft "left over from still lingering earlier conditions" (Tonniës, 2001: 252). However, he offers no additional insights into the potential for strong personal social ties occurring in non-place environments that are not based on traditional village social ties.

Parallel to the classic discussion of community, theories about the rural–urban continuum stress similar themes. Urban areas are modern while rural are not. There is ongoing debate about the validity of the rural–urban continuum, but it persists because, like the ideal types Tonniës describes, it provides a model that articulates some rural characteristics. However, it also suggests that rural communities are on a

14 T. Bradshaw

single track toward modernization and, with time, they will develop to be more urban-like small places. Others see the influence of urban modernity coexisting in rural communities, as was pointed out by Vidich and Bensman (1958) in their *Small Town in Mass Society* research. I reformulated this concept in rapid-growth rural areas as bifurcation, where advanced industrial patterns overlay the traditional small-town community but do not transform it. Community studies focusing on rural tend to be very place-oriented (Bradshaw, 1993).

Suburban communities have emerged as an attempt by residents to capture a bit of rural even while the urban remains dominant. The names of many typical suburban housing developments (e.g. Willowbrook, The Meadows) tend to emphasize this rural character, but wide streets, traffic congestion, and proximity to large shopping malls characteristic of suburbia today counter the rurality that is being sought. Salamon (2005) is the most recent in a series of studies that document how suburbanization undermines traditional community.

Non-Place Communities

Against this dominant perspective which equates community with place, scholars find increasing evidence that the concept of community is no longer useful unless it disentangles place and the institutions of place from the social relations that constitute community. In one form or another, those giving attention to non-place community argue that the process of modernization that produced Gesellschaft (typified by the industrial city) has continued (most significantly by cheap and rapid travel and communications) to create globally linked people with non-alienating social relations who happen to occasionally live in a place that is void of a significant amount of the social relations we think of as community. The industrial city is being displaced by global cities and mega-regions tied together not by the flow of materials and factories that characterized industrialization, but by freeways, airports, cell towers, and internet backbones. The global city (Sasson, 2001) makes it possible for most business transactions and social relations to be uncoupled from place since people are not hampered by the need to live close to others in order to have meaningful relations – they come together in the city for meetings to make deals, but do not live there.

Some of the evidence that is frequently mobilized to describe these non-place global communities shows that social relations associated with community work just as well across geographic boundaries as they do within. For example, Mel Webber, in his description of community without propinquity, illustrates his idea with a biological scientist who is part of a global community where he exchanges his most important social relations among people across several continents, but does not necessarily have community with his residential neighbors. Communities of interest or virtual communities based on intense relations developed via the internet (Rheingold, 1994) continue to be an example of the potential for important social experiences to be conducted without even face-to-face contact. Work situations that are trans-continental are illustrated by people who have houses both in Silicon

Valley and Taiwan (Chang, 2006). In a community without propinquity social control, values, status, and rewards are not tied to the reciprocal relations between people in a place but to a network of people who mostly live outside the place.

Suburbs are often considered the fullest expression of Gesellschaft, with high impersonal alienation and minimal involvement of people in things that matter to place – neighborliness, participation, common goals, and identity. However, it could be that although suburban communities are conducive to widespread social alienation between their residents, community there is taking a new form characterized by social relations liberated of place, and in these post-place communities the essence of community is the solidarity and social control that resides in overlapping virtual networks transcending time and place. Of course, even if the people in suburbs are not as isolated as Tonniës' Gesellschaft typology suggests, something is lost in places that are not also communities, especially collective action and bonding social capital. Ironically, many individuals having post-place community ties are far more networked than traditional residents of small towns. The local vacuum is not so much a lack of community as a lack of civic interaction.

A number of authors have tried to articulate the way contemporary communities differ from the ideal type Gesellschaft community. For instance, Bell's (1973) theme of the "post-industrial society" and Toffler's (1980) *Third Wave* are illustrations. Edge cities, as defined by Garreau (1991), show how traditional metropolitan regions get redefined when suburbs become employment centers. A review (not attempted here) of this large literature would agree with most of these definitional characteristics. What is key is that the processes of modernization that created community change and Gesellschaft are continuing in new forms.

Lyon (1999) catalogues different variations of "Post-Gesellschaft" thinking by different authors that capture some of the major differences and the explanations for them. He presents a chart that shows the transition from Gemeinschaft and Gesellschaft to what he calls "post-Gesellschaft." The chart summarizes change from community based on family and small town as the locus of most social interaction to social networks, the economic transition from agriculture to factories to an automated economy as a characteristic of post-gesellschaft community, and he notes that it is also identified with electronic communications and interurban (rather than rural–urban) transportation links. However, I interpret these largely economic and technological changes as being largely consistent with the social transformations that Tonniës theorized. This conceptualization would create the contractual and impersonal social relations of Gesellschaft. In other words, the concept of community in the Gemeinschaft – Gesellschaft tradition readily accommodates changes in economy, communications, transportation, and city form that are mentioned by Lyons and others. By themselves, these trends continue the process of modernization and do not fundamentally constitute a new conceptual dimension to community.

What really is different about many of the examples of communities tied to the high-technology world that extends the old models is that these new forms of community are not anchored in place. Post-place or non-place communities have a large following in the common descriptive language such as when we discuss the "scientific community," the "Jewish community," the "gay community," or even the network of family that came from a traditional community and now live all over the world. In a highly mobile society where people are linked by interest rather than traditional hometowns, it no longer makes sense to tie community to place. These post-place communities need to be taken seriously not as an aberration of language but as a potential conceptual insight into the essence of relations that constitute community.

Toward a Concept of Post-Place Community

The problem with proposing to define what constitutes a useful concept of community is that it is illusive – George Hillery (1955) identified some 94 definitions of community in his seminal categorization in *Rural Sociology*, and there are heated debates about definitions of community. My criteria for defining a concept like community is that it must be useful and distinguish things called community from other things that are not community. The reason for this effort is that place-based communities no longer encompass all the manifestations of community that we increasingly encounter when doing community development. What then is community?

Bhattacharyya (2004) identifies the essence of community as solidarity, which implies a common identity and set of shared norms and values. A common identity means that people need to be able to identify that they are part of a community or not, that becoming (or remaining) a member of a community is a significant act, and that others recognize the claim to membership. Community is typically associated with a sense of belonging (Webber, 1964: 108). Community identity is not permanent or exclusive, and individuals may have varying degrees of identification with their community.

Secondly, community has shared norms and values or some of the attributes of culture. Community involves a network of friendship (Wellman, 1999), or at least weak ties (Granovetter, 1973), where Tonniës's rational will can exercise itself. Community is about social control around these norms, involving shared values and beliefs about some things that are important to the maintenance of the community. Shared tolerance for diversity is as important as shared commonalities. A large group of people at a community event do not constitute a community because, outside of civility and good manners, the group does not enforce values and norms. A large group of employees or followers of a faith might participate in a similar event as a community because they are not strangers to each other and they share normative structures that shape involvement and behavior. A group of people that form a community is stronger when that group of people shares multiple areas of interest and norms, rather than single ones. While people in a community do not need to like each other, they do need to be bonded in a common enterprise.

Kempers (2001: 8) summarizes a useful concept of community, describing it as the "sum total of how, why, when, under what conditions, and with what consequences people bond together." That is another way of saying the essence of community is solidarity. If bonding or solidarity are keys to community, it is clear that bonding can take place in any space. Propinquity was necessary for bonding when travel and communications were slow and costly, but today this has been opened to vast distances between groups of people sharing a common bond. Community is now separate from place.

Bonding is clearly reciprocal and networked. Many studies of community look at the individual and their feeling of involvement and participation in a community, but few of these studies look at how the community reciprocates the feeling. A community is more than the sum of its parts, in the same way that social capital is a generalized characteristic of a group of people (usually a community) that changes the group as people become more trusting and reciprocal with each other. When most individuals trust each other (there is a lot of social capital) it changes the dynamics of a group because an individual can assume that their community participation will be reciprocated, but in groups with low social capital, feelings of distrust and suspicion lead to corruption or conflict. Bridging and bonding social capital (Putnam, 2000) are valuable extensions of this concept, showing how these similar processes can both focus on internal links to a group or place, or link the group or place externally.

Multiple Communities in Virtual Time-Space

People participate in multiple communities. While a person usually belongs to only one residentially based place-community at a time, one can easily belong to many regional and international post-place communities. For example, people can be active in their neighborhood community, but also be a fully involved member of regional communities trying to protect a wildland, or state-wide communities of alumni from one's college, or national/international communities based on profession or special interests such as a particular musical style or artist (e.g., Dead Heads).

The virtual communities of the internet provide a fascinating case study of an extreme non-place community. From early stories of the first internet community in California – the Well (Rheingold, 1994) – people became very intense participants in sharing and responding to crisis and success, even developing romanticized relationships with a group of people who had never met face-to-face.

Webber conceptualized community without propinquity schematically as a set of local places, laid out along a horizontal axis representing where people find community. Many people are involved in only their local community, which is represented by dots or short dashes as a first horizontal line. Other people have community at a regional scale, represented by longer dashes on another horizontal line lying above the first. Gradually, some people have state interests which are longer, or national interests which span most of the graphic or international interests, which become a solid line across the whole spectrum of local interests. People may participate at more than one level at a time and do not have to be involved in all the local places as they move in global circles. What this illustrates is that any place may be influenced by people having contacts at a local or global scale, and individuals at the global scale also participate at the local.

18 T. Bradshaw

Evidence of involvement in multiple communities is well documented. For example, immigration studies have shown that migrants participate in multiple communities – both in the community where they now live and in the community they left, often sending large remittances and participating in hometown associations in the US that are linked to community activities in Mexico. The transnational experience is one of community involvement in several places and, according to Smith and Guarnizo (1997), involves participating in organizations explicitly designed to recruit immigrants and keep them linked to their sending community.

A fascinating version of living in multiple communities is the trans-Pacific commuters studied by Chang (2006). Executives and electronic engineers from Taiwan and Silicon Valley are able to live in both places by recreating nearly identical house forms, landscape types, and even shopping centers, where they move between continents with unbelievable frequency. Within this community, which continuously bounces back and forth across thousands of miles of ocean and vastly different ethnic cultures, a transnational identity is formed in which one's cultural memories, norms, and social relationships might be:

> changed, rearranged, reformed, or completely transformed in interaction with the one other or many other cultures that these commuters experience in their "go-between lives." (Chang, 2006: 168)

In Taiwan, for example, suburbs for high-technology commuters have been built with Silicon Valley style shopping centers and stores, all with blatant symbolic copies of what they value. In California, the commuters seek suburban homes that have easy access to shopping centers where they can get Chinese food, novels, and services. Describing the commuters, she says:

> Inevitably, their residential experiences from the two places blend together. They enjoy their Hsinchu Science Park homes because, when they are there, they feel as if they are in their suburban American homes. They apply their specific Taiwanese habits when running daily errands at the Ranch 99 market in Silicon Valley. Moreover they encounter the same friends at both locations, while their individual family lives remain separate on the two sides of the Pacific.

This case is so interesting because it is clear that these trans-Pacific commuters share a common culture but place has become irrelevant as interpersonal relations, status, and symbol get transplanted, adapted and reshaped, separated by 12-hour flights. This is not alienating cultural homogenization, but it is community building at a global scale.

Survey Data Show Strength of Post-Place Communities

To get a sense of the strength of post-place communities I obtained data from the University of Chicago General Social Survey by the National Opinion Research

Center. These data from national surveys have been collected since the 1970s and include some relevant questions that provide background to the discussion of the social foundations of community. While these data do not fully amplify the questions we address in this paper, they provide useful data to frame the issue and support the solid examples from experience and literature.

Figure 2.1 shows clearly that people are socializing over a broader geographical area. In this figure, the data show the proportion of people who spend social evenings with people in their neighborhood daily or weekly, up to several times a month over time. The same question was asked at different periods of time, and the data show that neighborhood visits are declining while those outside the neighborhood are increasing.

Figure 2.2 shows that people have a weaker sense of place through their neighborhood while they feel stronger toward their city and state. This question asked how close they feel to their neighborhood and more distant places. Interestingly, over 40 percent of the respondents indicated that they were not close to their neighborhood but showed greater closeness as they broadened the scale of placeness (data from 1996 survey, 1537 respondents).

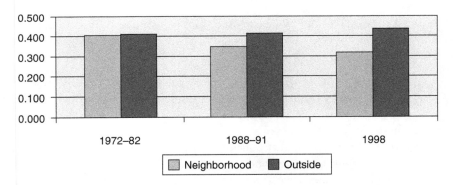

FIGURE 2.1 Proportion of People Who Spend a Social Evening with Someone in Neighborhood and Elsewhere, Daily or Weekly, by Date of Survey

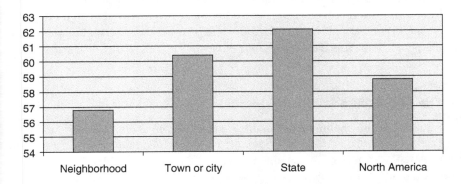

FIGURE 2.2 How Close Do You Feel to Places (Percent)

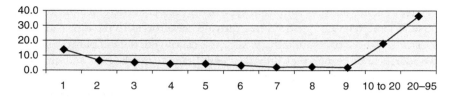

FIGURE 2.3 How Long Have You Lived in Your Community in Years (1996 Data)?

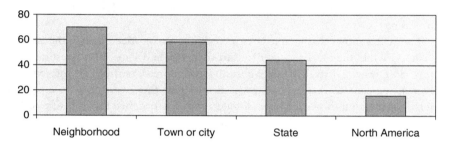

FIGURE 2.4 Would You Be Willing to Move to Another Place in Order to Improve Your Work or Living Condition?

Respondents to the general social survey for the most part are fairly long-term residents, as shown by Figure 2.3. While there is some mobility of people in the first few years, the majority of US residents are fairly stable and have lived in their communities for ten or more years.

Figure 2.4 finally shows that a majority of people would be glad to move to improve their work or living conditions but most want to stay where they are, presumably because they have social networks and have built work opportunities that would be difficult to transplant. However, still 45 percent were willing to move outside their state.

In sum, the data show that people are well rooted in their place, do not want to leave it, and are generally happy, but that they feel increasingly close to people who are not in that place. Place is useful for people because it solves their housing needs, but people look at greater and greater distances for the social closeness that is the core of the post-place community.

The Social Foundations of Community

The essence of community, based on the examples given above, is not local Gemeinschaft, but is in the wider networks of friendship extending beyond neighborhood. It is useful therefore to separate place as a geographical concept from community as the basis for social networks in which solidarity or bonding is characteristic. In post-place communities, people find that a growing proportion of their social relations of solidarity involve them in a network stretching outside their place of residence.

A key way to understand the social relations in community is through network analysis. Networks track acquaintance as well as types and intensity of relationships. Granovetter (1973) gave emphasis to the importance of weak ties in these networks, and one could argue that there has been a steady growth in weak ties spread over a larger area as communication and transportation have increased. The notion of a network is that not all people are connected to all others, but the connections are at a high density with multiple and varied connections, or the network may be uniform and relatively sparse.

A key feature of the solidarity-based community as opposed to the place-based community is that community becomes a concept that is variable rather than either or. If we define community on the basis of physical boundaries, then a resident is either in or out. If we define community in terms of social ties characteristic of solidarity, then it can scale from low to high. The question is not whether you are in a community but how much community you have (Brown et al., 2000). Consequently, from a community development perspective, community solidarity (identity and norms) can be nurtured, protected, and increased. Community identity and norms can be built around place, and place can be built around a common gathering place for people who share common identities and norms, but this relationship is variable and researchable, not assumed.

Community solidarity may not directly lead people to act collaboratively or even to congregate as a whole. In traditional communities people feel compelled to do many collective things such as attend parades and help at barn raisings because of their involvement in place. However, these community actions diminished with modernization, leading to concerns of alienation and isolation. In the non-place community solidarity is less often demonstrated collectively through attendance at something and more in communication or virtual celebrations. Sharing pictures of one's grandchildren over the internet may be replacing a baby shower. Another example might be the communication leading up to a dog breeder's convention when one of the members has a particularly exceptional litter. Tenure, or becoming a member of the Academy of Sciences, generates academic communications expressing solidarity through the internet nearly as warmly as a celebration at the faculty club. In short, our traditional measures of community have a hard time reflecting the bonding of a post-place community even though these social bonds are just as strong.

Place Matters: The Conundrum of Post-Place Communities

The previous sections have made a case for taking post-place communities seriously and for arguing that propinquity is not necessary for the formation and sustenance of communities not linked to residential area. However, I do not want to overstate the case. There is overwhelming evidence that propinquity counts, perhaps especially in those cases where the greatest post-place networking takes place – high technology clusters such as Silicon Valley. There, organizations such as Joint Venture

Silicon Valley are powerful examples of social action to increase the public good through the creation of public spaces and programs that protect the commons. Collective action in communities transforms them from alienating to attractive places to live. Indeed, Richard Florida's (2004) Creative Class includes people who congregate in certain creative areas because it provides a hospitable place to base their international interests. Creative cities and regions are the motors for change and stand out as the economic engines with new technologies and firms.

Similarly, research in economic development has stressed the importance of industrial clusters for regional growth and wellbeing (Bradshaw et al., 1999; Blakely and Bradshaw, 2002). Geographically based clusters of concentrated and competitive firms that are interdependent with specialized suppliers and infrastructure show strong growth and employment. For example, the firms in Silicon Valley benefit from the competition and sharing that takes place due to the proximity of related firms, as well as the direct ease of working with specialized suppliers and specialized infrastructure, including universities, that supply the technology supported by a density of venture capitalists, product lawyers, and marketing programs. The cluster idea suggests that place-community matters.

So the conundrum of the post-place community is that at the same time as community is more frequently defined in terms of non-place orientation, places may have huge advantages because of the collective action that gives them a reputation. In these places people are part of expansive international networks, yet they also need a place to be centrally located where certain transactions can take place or where they will have the highest chance of reducing some transaction costs because of propinquity. I argue that these special places are not equivalent to historic small-town communities, but exist because of the post-place community of which the place itself is a node.

Network concepts and complexity theory can help us resolve this conceptual problem. If we think of a community as a densely connected (but potentially widely dispersed) network of people organized around shared identities, norms, and bonding, then we know that these networks tend to generate nodes such as Silicon Valley. Or, to use complexity theory, networks self-organize into moderately sized clusters. If the concentrations get too large then the system tends to stagnate, and if it is too diffuse it tends to fall apart. Silicon Valley and creative cities are nodes in the post-place world where relations tend to organize but remain fluid as the rest of the network comes to the nodes from time to time to bring in new resources and ideas and to take away new opportunities.

The key issue in terms of community is that the creative people or leaders in the electronics industry occupy a non-place network that is a prototype post-place community. In the electronics industry case it includes firms in Singapore, factories in Ireland, software developers in India, and marketing offices in Europe. The electronics industry, probably better than any other, is known for its networked and non-place capacity to be effective. Many people in the industry live and work outside of Silicon Valley and they move frequently around the world as part of a community of engineers and specialists who constitute a global community. However, Silicon Valley is the most important hub in a far-flung network. The community really is not local but the valley is important because it is such an important hub.

Conclusion

Douglas Henton and his colleagues (1997) have championed an idea of the civic entrepreneur. The civic entrepreneur is a bridge maker in the way we have been discussing. The role of the civic entrepreneur is to connect the resources and capacities of economic systems and the various competencies in the community that support community and economic values, and to help them act to improve the community quality of life. The civic entrepreneur is engaged at a regional level to make place, not by defining the place in a geographically limited way but by making the place the must-visit part of the node of very interconnected individuals who can make a difference (Table 2.1).

Community developers as civic entrepreneurs work effectively in a post-place environment. Their main function is brokering and networking to link those whose community links extend no further than their neighborhood with others who work on a national and regional scale. Finding commonality and creating the context for identity around whatever scale makes sense for the common good remains a high priority for the maintenance of community.

TABLE 2.1 Issues of Community from Different Perspectives

Dimension of Community	Gemeinshaft	Gesellschaft	Post-Place Communities
Issues of Place			
Geography	Rural and small town	Urban neighborhoods	Virtual and global
Participation	One community	Larger community	Many communities
Stability/change	Stable	Transitional	Fluid/dynamic transformative
Issues of Social Relations			
Bonding/bridging social capital	Strong ties/bonding social capital	Mixture of strong and weak ties	Weak ties/bridging social capital
Community structure	Individual/family	Group	Network
Interaction	Face to face; propinquity	Usually face to face supported by mail and phone	Largely electronic with occasional face to face; propinquity not necessary
Identity	Residence/place	Residence and work	Relationships in networks

References

Bell, D. (1973). *The Coming of Post Industrial Society*. New York: Basic Books.

Bhattacharyya, J.T.C.D.V. (2004). Theorizing Community Development. *Journal of the Community Development Society*, 34(2).

Blakely, E.J., & Bradshaw, T.K. (2002). *Planning Local Economic Development* (3rd ed.). Thousand Oaks: Sage.

Blakely, E.J., & Snyder, M.G. (1999). *Fortress America: Gated Communities in the United States*. Washington, DC: Brookings Institute.

Bradshaw, T.K. (1993). In the shadow of urban growth: Bifurcation in rural California communities. In T.A. Lyson & W.W. Falk (Eds.), *Forgotten Places: Uneven Development in Rural America* (pp. 218–256). Lawrence: University Press of Kansas.

Bradshaw, T.K., King, J.R., & Walstrom, S. (1999). Catching on to clusters. *Planning*, 65(6), 18–21.

Brown, R.B., Xu, X., Barfield, M.B., & King, B.G. (2000). "Community Experience and the Conceptual Distinctness of Rural Community Attachment and Satisfaction." In *Research in Community Sociology*, Vol. 10, by D. Chekki (ed.) (pp. 427–446). Stamford, CT: JAI Press.

Chang, S. (2006). *The Global Silicon Valley Home*. Stanford: Stanford University Press.

Florida, R. (2004). *The Rise of the Creative Class: And How It's Transforming Work, Leisure, Community and Everyday Life*. New York: Basic Books.

Garreau, J. (1991). *Edge City*. New York: Doubleday.

Granovetter, M. (1973). The strength of weak ties. *American Journal of Sociology*, 78(6), 1360–1380.

Henton, D., Melville, J., & Walesh, K. (1997). *Grassroots Leaders For A New Economy*. San Francisco: Jossey Bass.

Hillery, G. (1955). Definitions of community: Areas of agreement. *Rural Sociology*, 20, 791–799.

Kempers, M. (2001). *Community Matters: An Exploration Of Theory And Practice*. Chicago: Burnham Inc.

Kunstler, J.H. (1996). *Home from nowhere: Remaking our everyday world for the 21st century*. New York: Simon and Schuster.

Lyon, L. (1999). *The Community In Urban Society*. Prospect Heights, IL: Waveland Press.

Nisbet, R. (1966). *The Sociological Tradition*. New York: Basic Books.

Putnam, R. (2000). *Bowling Alone*. New York: Simon and Schuster.

Rheingold, H. (1994). *The Virtual Community*. New York: Harper.

Salamon, S. (2005). From hometown to nontown: Rural community effects of suburbanization. *Rural Sociology*, 68(1), 1–24.

Sassen, S. (2001). *The Global City: New York, London, Tokyo*. Princeton, NJ: Princeton University Press.

Smith, M.P., & Guarnizo, L. (1997). *Transnationalism From Below*. Princeton, NJ: Transaction Press.

Toffler, A. (1980). *Third wave*. New York: Morrow.

Tonniës, F. (1957). *Community and Society*. East Lansing, MI: Michigan State University Press.

Tonniës, F. (2001). *Community and Civil Society* (J. Harris & M. Hollis, Trans.). Cambridge: Cambridge University Press.

Tonniës, F. (2002). *Community and Society* (C.P. Loomis, Trans.). Mineola, NY: Dover.

Vidich, A., & Bensman, J. (1958). *Small town in mass society*. Princeton, NJ: Princeton University Press.

Webber, M. (1964). Urban place and the nonplace realm. In M. Webber et al. (Eds.), *Explorations into urban structure*. Philadelphia, PA: University of Pennsylvania Press.

Wellman, B. (1999). *Networks in the global village*. Boulder, CO: Westview.

Wirth, L. (1938). Urbanism as a way of life. *American Journal of Sociology*, 44, 8–20.

3

SETTLING AT THE MARGINS

Exurbia and Community Sociology

Jeff S. Sharp and Jill K. Clark

Introduction

While the condition and evolution of urban places and rural areas have consistently garnered the attention of community sociologists, the places located at the intersection of the urban and rural have received more modest and sporadic attention. The rural–urban fringe, or what is increasingly referred to as exurbia, has attracted interest in recent years due to the relatively rapid population growth and land-use change occurring there. In addition, the purported impact of exurbanite voters on recent US elections has also contributed to greater public awareness of these locations (Brooks, 2004; Lyman, 2005; Mahler, 2005). A limiting factor in the development of a coherent body of knowledge regarding the rural–urban fringe, though, may be the fact that it "is too urban to attract traditional rural researchers and too rural to incite urban scholarly inquiry" (Audirac, 1999, p. 7). In this chapter we seek to introduce community scholars to the exurban research tradition and then offer some ideas for future research. We provide some statistics related to exurban Ohio to illustrate the significance of this area and draw on our own experience to explain why we believe this settlement zone merits additional scholarly attention. Finally, we offer some potential future directions for exurban research.

Defining the Exurbs

Many approaches to defining and characterizing the exurbs draw on ecological traditions of community sociology, in which the spatial organization of communities is a central focus, including attention to the processes of land-use and community change and a focus on the particular characteristics of the population residing in a spatially defined area (Lyon, 1989). While there is a consistent focus on the settlement patterns and population characteristics of the exurbs, one problem with locating and reviewing the academic literature related to exurbia is the existence of several different labels[1] referring to, and definitions of, this settlement zone (Audirac, 1999; Berube et al., 2006). Berube et al. (2006, p. 1) describes the exurbs as

> somewhere beyond the suburbs. At the urban–rural periphery, outer suburbs bleed into small-town community with an agricultural heritage. Not yet full-fledged suburbs, but no longer wholly rural in nature, these exurban areas are reportedly undergoing rapid change in population, land use and economic function.

This description of the exurbs echoes Kurtz and Eicher's (1958, pp. 36–37) description of the rural–urban fringe as a

> location beyond the limits of the legal city, in the 'agricultural hinterland' exhibiting characteristics of mixed land use, with no consistent pattern of farm and nonfarm dwellings. The residents are involved in rural and urban occupations. The area is unincorporated, relatively lax zoning regulations exist, and few, if any municipal services are provided. The area shows potentialities for population growth and increasing density ratios. Present density ratios are intermediate between urban and rural.

In many ways the terms are interchangeable, with the rural–urban fringe having a longer history of use among demographers and sociologists (Kurtz and Eicher, 1958; Pryor, 1968; Shyrock and Siegel, 1980) and exurbs being more popular among some planners (Nelson, 1992; Nelson and Sanchez, 1997) and those writing for the wider public (Brooks, 2004). While we primarily use the term exurbia in this chapter, we (and others) have also used the term rural–urban fringe (Sharp and Clark, 2006).[2]

Exurban Research Themes

In our reviews of the academic literature, we have identified four research themes related to exurbia or the rural–urban fringe that seem particularly salient to community sociologists. The first area of work concerns definitions: what (or where) are the exurbs? The follow-up problem is how one operationalizes the chosen definition, given the available data.[3] The influences of classic ecological approaches to community, such as concentric zone models (Lyon, 1989), are obvious in much of this work. Audirac (1999) does a nice job of summarizing several definitions and models that have appeared in the literature through the late 1990s,[4] and Pryor's (1968) work provides substantial background from an earlier era. Berube et al. (2006) outline many of the more recent empirical approaches to this question, and Taylor (2011) brings us up to date with her own review that covers a great deal of material from the 2000s. One challenge of developing and applying the exurban concept, particularly among planners, is the need to both identify the existence of low-density settlements just beyond the urban edge and also account for the process of exurbanization by which these low-density areas become more settled and are incorporated into an adjoining urban-area sphere of influence.

While the exact definition one chooses to define the exurbs (or the process of exurbanization) will be influenced by the research question or practical problem to be examined, there are similarities among definitions despite no consensus regarding an official definition. Most definitions begin by focusing on the phenomenon of lower density areas that are in close proximity to an urbanized area. Defining what constitutes "close proximity" can be highly variable, with some suggesting particular distances beyond the edge of large urbanized areas (sometimes even scaling up the distance according to the size of the urbanized area). Some have even made distinctions within exurban areas, often based on proximity to the central urbanized areas, to suggest there are inner and outer exurban areas (Audirac, 1999; Ilbery, 1985; Lamb, 1983; Sharp and Clark, 2006). Some definitions rely on density, defining exurban as the low-density settlement areas within a metropolitan statistical area (MSA) (see Berube et al., 2006 for a summary of many popular approaches). What the appropriate density threshold is, though, can be debated (e.g. Besussi and Chin, 2003).

A second theme of the literature that naturally follows from the definitional question is whether the exurbs are a distinct settlement form or simply an early stage in the process of becoming a suburb. Findings are mixed. Some researchers find many similarities between exurban and suburban residents (Davis, 1993; Nelson and Sanchez, 1999; Patel, 1980), leading to the conclusion that the exurbs are not distinct but a suburban variant (the suburbs of the suburbs). Others, though, have identified the existence of differences, primarily arising from locational attributes (such as higher average commuting distances for exurban residents compared to suburban residents) (Lessinger, 1986). In our own work (Sharp and Clark, 2006), we consider exurban distinctiveness by approaching the problem in relation to classic explorations of the rural–urban continuum that focus on occupational, socio-cultural, and ecological characteristics of a particular population (Pahl, 1966; Willits and Bealer, 1967; Willits et al., 1982). Unlike much of the research focusing on exurban residents relative to suburban and urban ones, we include contrasts with rural residents as well. We find that fringe residents occupy a middle position between rural and urban in terms of demographic and occupational characteristics (for instance, less occupational reliance on agriculture or natural resources than more rural residents but more reliance than suburban and urban residents). But there were also several similarities between exurbanites and suburbanites (particularly in terms of household income – exurban income was higher than in urban or rural – and poverty levels – which were lower among exurbanites compared to urban and rural populations). We found the exurban residents to be markedly different from urban and suburban residents and more similar to rural residents in terms of their views of agriculture, the environment and their social connections to agriculture. We also observed differences among exurban residents who reside in small towns and villages versus those residing in the open country. In regard to this latter finding, rural community sociologists have not been particularly attentive to investigating the variability between small-town and open-country residents (Galpin, 1915 being an interesting exception), perhaps because historically the distinctive agricultural character of most rural open-country residents and their strong social connections to the small-town central place did not require any special considerations. Our work suggests, though, that the exurban open-country residents differ from their small-town neighbors as well as the historic rural, open-country residents and thus warrant further investigation. We will discuss this matter in greater detail in a later section.

A third exurban research tradition includes the ethnographic community studies that investigate the values, attitudes and culture of exurbia, with examples in both the popular press (Brooks, 2004; Spectrosky, 1955) and academic outlets (Bell, 1992; Salamon, 2003). In the popular press, exurbia has garnered attention from journalists who have used the exurbs as a setting to critically (and often humorously) discuss a changing America and the evolving pursuit of the American Dream (Brooks, 2004; Spectrosky, 1955). A common interest of academics coming out of the rural community tradition has been investigation of the invasion/succession process associated with the settlement of newcomers into previously rural areas. The focus has been on the tensions arising from the intermixing of a new class of residents among a longstanding rural population. These more qualitative or case-study approaches have examined such questions as the varying experiences of community attachment or involvement or the variable views of nature or agriculture (Bell, 1992; Friedland, 2002; Salamon, 2003) between contrasting sets of exurban residents.

A fourth theme concerns the practical matters of land-use planning and growth management, which are quite real challenges in many urban fringe communities experiencing extensive nonfarm development and an influx of new residents. Daniels (1999; Daniels and Bowers, 1997) has authored several reference books on the subject and has reported on case studies and provided conceptual outlines of possible strategies for managing growth, preserving farmland and maintaining the rural character (Daniels, 2000; Daniels and Lapping, 2005). In addition to discussions related to metropolitan and exurban "smart growth" strategies, substantial interest exists in the challenge of preserving farmland in the face of nonfarm growth and development (Bunce, 1998; Olson and Lyson, 1999). Besides focusing on the available tools for managing exurban growth and change and the strategies for retaining farmland, some scholars have taken a more conflict-oriented approach by investigating why land-use planning and community governance are the way they are, who are the winners and losers of such planning and governance, and how might future efforts to manage change account for these findings (Cadieux and Hurley, 2011; Pfeffer and Lapping, 1994; Rudel et al., 2011). Some of these more recent avenues of inquiry also consider the global dimensions of exurbanization, looking at the ties between rural landscape consumption and global processes, and at the complexity of individual actions within the social, cultural, economic, and

Settling at the Margins **29**

political infrastructure that enables (and sometimes encourages) exurbanization (Cadieux and Hurley, 2011).

This outline of the key themes and the variety of research is neither exhaustive nor complete, but it does provide a starting point for exploring this body of literature. The review does show how exurban scholarship has largely followed in the ecological tradition of community research, although ethnographic investigations of exurban culture and conflict-oriented investigations of power and the distribution of costs and benefits of exurban development exist as well. While we have organized the review according to thematic questions that have been explored, one feature of the exurban or rural–urban fringe literature that is not obvious from this organizational structure is how exurban scholarship has attracted considerable interest and then faded several times over the last 60 years. In the 1950s, during the postwar boom, there first emerged acknowledgements of the interconnection between lightly settled rural regions and more urban areas (e.g. Kurtz and Eicher, 1958; Spectrosky, 1955). Interest spiked during the 1970s into the beginning of the 1980s (e.g. Ilbery, 1985; Lamb, 1983) but faded as the pace of exurban growth moderated substantially in conjuction with a slowdown in the economy. Interest in exurban growth and land-use planning reemerged in the late 1990s into the 2000s as growth and development accelerated in these exurban areas (e.g. Audirac, 1999; Berube et al., 2006; Brooks, 2004; Daniels and Lapping, 2005). One of the questions that we have concerns the consequences of the housing bust that started around 2008 on both exurban development and scholarly/policy interest in this settlement area. While we cannot speak for other scholars, we argue that exurbia requires sustained consideration by academics not only to understand the historical and ongoing processes of community growth and change, but also to understand the challenges that are independent of whether there is growth and development. In the next section, we report some current statistics to illuminate characteristics of the exurban population and settlement area that we believe justify sustained consideration.

Exurban Change and Significance in Ohio

As we have previously noted, there are a number of different ways to examine the population or spatial characteristics of the exurbs. Some scholars rely on sophisticated spatial analysis of census block groups or tracts at varying distances from densely populated urbanized areas, while others utilize existing geopolitical boundaries, such as counties, cities, townships and metropolitan areas, to parse up the population into urban, suburban, exurban and rural categories. We adopt the latter approach to provide some basic understanding of the ecological characteristics of one state's (Ohio's) exurban population. We argue that Ohio is a good case study given the highly exurbanized nature of the state and conditions that result in disaggregated decision making over land use. Ohio now has more people living in unincorporated townships than in cities or villages (Partridge and Clark, 2008), and Ohio ranks third in the total population living in exurbs, according to a Brookings Institution ranking (Berube et al., 2006). While the scale of exurban development is great in Ohio, many other states of the Midwest and South have similar exurban conditions (Berube et al., 2006); in addition, the Midwest and South also have some of the least restrictive land-use regulations (Gyourko et al., 2008).

Our analysis relies on US Census of Population data from 2000 and 2010. We report total population counts for 2000 and 2010 as well as rural population counts from the 2000 census (rural population counts from the 2010 census are not yet available). We utilize several different units of political geography, including county metropolitan character and county subdivisions such as townships (unincorporated areas), villages (incorporated areas with a population of less than 5,000 in the state of Ohio), and cities (incorporated areas with a population greater than 5,000). Ohio's 1,309 townships range in resident population from 86 to 60,958 residents.[5]

To efficiently approximate what is exurban, we consider the population residing outside the core urbanized area (which includes the central city and the adjoining

MAP 3.1 Ohio's Metropolitan Areas (Central Counties Gray; Outlying Counties Striped) and Nonmetropolitan Areas (in White)

suburbs) of a metropolitan area as exurban (a variant of this approach was reported in Sharp and Clark, 2006). We find this approach to be effective since what constitutes a metropolitan area includes not only counties containing the densely populated urban areas but also a large number of less densely populated counties that have few urban areas but which are still closely tied to the urban core of the metropolitan area via commuting patterns. Following the population census, we label counties where at least half the population resides inside a large urban area as core counties. Outlying counties of the metropolitan area that do not meet the core requirement but are closely connected to the central counties via commuting we label as fringe counties. Bearing in mind the fact that Ohio contains all or parts of a great many metropolitan areas ($N = 16$), with three especially large ones (Columbus, Cleveland, and Cincinnati), we further distinguish among counties associated with one of these three large metropolitan areas (classed as either large core or large fringe) versus counties associated with one of the other 13 metropolitan areas (small core or small fringe).

In addition to the distinction between fringe and core within the metropolitan area, the US Census of Population rural designation is helpful for enumerating the number of persons within the metropolitan area who reside in relatively sparsely populated areas (at least relative to the core urban area). The census defines people as urban if they reside in a core census block or a block group with a population density of 1,000 per square mile or greater. In addition, the census blocks adjoining urban areas are considered "urban" if they have a density of 500 people per square mile or greater. Individuals who are not classified as urban are defined as rural. In 2000, just under 23 percent of Ohio's population was designated rural, or nearly 2.6 million people (of 11.3 million residents). While many states have a higher proportion of their total population designated as rural, Ohio had the fourth largest rural population in the US in 2000 (with Texas, North Carolina and Pennsylvania having larger rural populations). While many might think of rural as persons residing quite far from the city, it ends up that a majority of Ohio's rural population resides inside of metropolitan areas (over 1.3 million) (Table 3.1). There were 1.2 million

TABLE 3.1 Ohio Population by Metropolitan Character, 2000 to 2010

Metro Character (Counties)	Total Pop. 2000	Total Pop. 2010	% Change 2000–10	Rural Pop. 2000	% Rural Pop. 2000
Nonmetro (40)	**2,212,334**	**2,237,079**	**1.1**	**1,215,499**	**54.9**
Metro (48)	**9,140,806**	**9,299,425**	**1.7**	**1,355,312**	**14.8**
Large Core (10)	4,556,916	4,694,072	3.0	338,315	7.4
Large Fringe (8)	760,676	845,110	11.1	280,723	36.9
Small Core (18)	3,668,972	3,605,011	-1.7	636,000	17.3
Small Fringe (9)	154,242	155,232	0.6	100,274	65.0
Total All Counties	**11,353,140**	**11,536,504**	**1.6**	**2,570,811**	**22.6**

Ohioans defined as rural and residing in nonmetropolitan areas of the state in 2000. As one might expect, when looking more closely at the state's metropolitan counties, we find that a substantial proportion of the population in some of these counties is rural. For instance, over a quarter million rural residents resided in one of the eight Ohio fringe metropolitan counties adjacent to a large core metropolitan county, or more than 1 in 3 residents of these counties in 2000. There are over 600,000 rural residents residing in one of the 18 small core metropolitan counties (just over 17 percent of the total population of these counties). In the fringe counties of these small metropolitan areas, there are just over 100,000 rural residents (or 65% of their total population).

The point of noting these statistics is to reveal the sheer number of people living just beyond the edges of large cities in a state like Ohio, which is not unique in this regard as similar patterns can be found in states such as Georgia, Pennsylvania, Florida, North Carolina, etc. Returning to the Audirac (1999) observation we quoted at the start of this chapter, it is easy to imagine how these exurban residents might be overlooked as rural community scholars attend to the large population of rural residents and communities located in the nonmetropolitan areas and the urban scholars attend to the 85 percent of Ohio metropolitan residents who are urban as identified in our example.

One exurban feature that has received attention, a theme we noted earlier, is the land-use, planning and growth management challenges of fringe metropolitan counties. Our data provide some insight as to why this is the case. In Ohio, while overall state population growth was a tepid 1.6% between 2000 and 2010, the population residing in the state's largest fringe metropolitan counties grew 11.1 percent (Table 3.1). Through our own university extension work we can attest to the fact that urban and regional planners as well as many traditional "rural" landscape stakeholders have been very interested in understanding how to best manage these changes. The Ohio media have been quite attentive as well (e.g. the Columbus Dispatch year-long study that resulted in a five-day series entitled "The Price of Progress" running September 8th through September 12th, 1996).

But while land-use planning and growth management might be the most mediaworthy element of exurbia in the 2000s, there are many features of these communities that remain unexamined. To begin to appreciate this fact, we report some data from the Columbus Metropolitan Area, which we are most familiar with. Within the metropolitan area, we distinguish between cities, villages, and townships. Figure 3.1 provides an illustration of how these various geopolitical units fit together within a county. What is interesting is that local governance related to these sets of population is quite different. In Ohio, the Ohio Code recognizes two types of incorporated places, cities (with population of 5,000 or more) and villages (population less than 5,000 residents). These places can exercise all powers of self-government (also known as "home rule"), including growth management, as long as their actions do not conflict with Ohio law. In contrast, townships are unincorporated units of state government and sub-territories of counties, and are only able to exercise powers provided them by the state through the Ohio Revised Code. This results in limited authority to manage their local area.

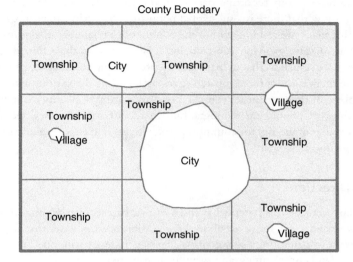

FIGURE 3.1 Example of Ohio Government Geography

According to the 2010 census, the Columbus MA is home to over 1.8 million persons. While 71% of those residents reside in the many cities of this eight-county region (the largest proportion in Columbus and its adjoining suburbs – an estimated 1,230,221 from the 2010 American Community Survey), about 24 percent of the region's residents reside in townships (Table 3.2). In addition, the population residing in townships grew nearly 16 percent, compared to just over 13 percent growth in the cities and villages across the state. Further, one challenge of tracking change across times with this level of geography is that cities and villages can annex townships and realize population growth through the addition of land area (while townships would experience population declines as a result of land area loss). So, the aggregate increase of township population residing within the 2000 township land area was greater than what is derived from subtracting 2000 from 2010 figures. The fact that the political geography can easily change contributes to some of the data problems that challenge exurban researchers.

TABLE 3.2 Columbus Metropolitan Area, Population by Type of Place, 2000–2010

	Total Pop. 2000	Total Pop. 2010	% Change, 2000–2010	% of 2010 MA Pop.
Villages (64)	98,929	99,658	0.7	5.4
Townships (132)	373,619	432,341	15.7	23.5
Totals	**1,612,694**	**1,836,536**	**13.9**	**100.0**

The purpose of our reporting data from the last decade in Ohio and Central Ohio is to show that there is a substantial population living in exurban regions and to show that many are residing within the confines of a relatively rural form of local government despite growing substantially. The story that the Ohio data reveal would be quite similar to that in many other states and metropolitan areas across the US. While there is room for comparative research among the various state contexts that enable, constrain or impact exurban population growth, we turn our attention from analysis of population demographics to identifying what we see as some broader avenues of inquiry for community sociologists that explore exurban growth and change more generally.

Future Directions

We've alluded to several potential avenues of exurban scholarship and in this final section we elaborate in more detail on three possible areas of work that are particularly relevant to community sociologists. These include: 1) continued examination of exurban land-use planning and growth management, especially with a greater sensitivity to the political economy of exurban growth as well as the ecological question of agricultural adaptation to increased population densities and civic agricultural development; 2) greater attention to the exurban social system, including attention to matters of institutional governance as well as attention to the character of community organizational and individual interaction; and finally there are 3) the questions related to the social impacts and legacy of the boom/bust cycle that seems to be a historical characteristic of urban edge growth.

We previously identified land-use planning and growth management as a longstanding theme of exurban research, but there is a need for additional work in this area. Examination of the tools of planning and growth management has received the majority of attention (Daniels, 1999; Daniels and Lapping, 2005) as many communities have sought to assert some control over exurban development, either before it occurs or at the early stages, to preserve local quality of life and desired amenities in addition to minimizing the loss of farmland or open space. Recent work has begun to go beyond enumerating and evaluating the tools and their effect to beginning to understand why tools are implemented as they are and to whose benefit (Cadieux and Hurley, 2011; Rudel et al., 2011), and there are opportunities to further explore the political economy of exurban land-use change.

Another opportunity is to move beyond the farmland preservation focus of many land-use policies and begin to explore policy strategies that support farm enterprise adaptation as well as the development of new farms in response to changing opportunities and structures of farming. With the growing public interest in local food systems (Lyson, 2004; Lyson et al., 2008), coupled with the economic downturn, some exurban governments and development organizations are especially motivated to support increased economic activity in the agricultural sector as the housing and construction sector has cooled off. We and others have reported that there is a substantial amount of farming occurring in exurban areas despite the urban pressure (Jackson-Smith and Sharp, 2008; Thomas and Howell, 2003), and in some of our recent field research we identify a large cadre of small and medium size farms adapting and expanding to meet consumer demand; we also identify the emergence of first-generation farmers creating businesses to serve these markets (Clark et al., 2010; Inwood and Sharp, 2012). Analysis of policies that are effective in supporting local farm growth and development would be of great use to exurban economic development efforts.

But analysis of exurban agriculture need not only focus on the economic development dimension. A particularly exciting aspect of the exurban and agriculture/food system nexus is the opportunity to explore extensions of Lyson's (2004) idea of civic agriculture that builds on the classic Goldschmidt (1978) tradition of farm community studies. What we are proposing is the investigation of several related ideas, including: how does the structure of exurban agriculture, such as the existence or even growth of small and medium scale farms in the locality, impact the well-being of the community? how do the non-farming public's views of agriculture and their willingness to support local food systems contribute to a more vital small and medium scale farm culture? and finally, how does the existence of a more "civic" agriculture (that is a place where there is a mutual interaction and support between the farmers and nonfarming public) impact other social indicators of wellbeing as identified by Goldschmidt and studied by others?

A second broad area of potential exurban research is a focus on exurban community, government and capacity. The exurbs are an interesting community form in that they are closely linked to nearby urban areas and are often nested in complex regional governance structures. In essence, the exurbs are part of a complex social system that is easily recognized but not well studied. Further complicating the matter is that exurban governance structures can be quite variable. In one of our earlier works (Sharp and Clark, 2006), we argued that it is important to distinguish among the various types of exurban places by the primary local governments. In Ohio, this means attention to the role and distinctions among counties, cities, villages and townships (this arrangement will vary according to the state). Further, exurban government officials, such as township trustees and village elected officials, often have to grapple with urban land-use problems with outdated rural planning and governance tools. Past research does indicate that, as communities grow, they adopt more land-use controls (Broussard et al., 2008; Pratt and Rogers, 1986) as they transition from managing typical rural issues (like maintenance of local cemeteries) to managing much larger populations and the associated challenges of: traffic congestion, farmer and nonfarmer conflicts, and the overarching goal of preserving the rural "character." Unfortunately, many local governments who struggled to manage the substantial growth in the 2000s with limited resources are now experiencing budget reductions in the 2010s as a result of the economic downturn, further reducing their capacity to respond to increased demands.

In Ohio, and in other states, the challenge of local governance is further complicated by the fact that the state-level response to diminished resources is to advocate government consolidation. In Ohio, the very existence of townships and other forms of local government are being questioned by the state's Commission on Local Government Reform and Collaboration. While no action has been taken to eliminate townships, the state has substantially reduced funds that support local government operation as a result of lower state tax revenues while also encouraging local governments to share services and collaborate on infrastructure development to achieve greater efficiency. The irony is that many of these exurban locales had insufficient resources to meet local needs and now they are being asked to find ways to address these needs with even fewer resources.

In our applied outreach work, we have consistently heard township trustees and village officials voice frustration for not being heard or understood in the larger processes of regional planning. As we have worked with these exurban officials, we recognize a real need for systematic exploration of the challenges faced by these small rural and exurban governments. Neither political science nor planning has been particularly attentive to understanding these governments, but the growth in many exurban areas across the US means that there are quite real challenges these governments face and a great need to develop the capacity of these governments to govern and manage these challenges.

In addition to a need to focus on exurban governance challenges, there are also some fundamental questions about the internal workings of the exurban community social system that need attention. Some ethnographic case studies do exist (Bell, 1992; Salamon, 2003), and we have also attempted to examine patterns of interaction among exurban farmers and nonfarmers (Sharp and Smith, 2004), but the extent to which the social interactions that can give rise to a viable exurban community social system capable of engaging in community action (Wilkinson, 1999) has largely been unexplored. Examination of the extent to which community-oriented individual and organizational interaction has developed among the long-time and relatively new residents logically leads to additional questions regarding the extent to which the more or less developed community fields of exurbia improve local capacity to manage growth or improve local quality of life. Salamon's (2003) ethnographic work reveals quite varied patterns of social interaction arising from exurban change, and further work of this sort in exurban locales across the US is warranted.

A third area of future exurban exploration that could approach the problem from a variety of theoretical directions (including ecological, social system or political economy perspectives) concerns what may be the defining exurban issue of the 2010s: what are the long-term social and community impacts of the housing boom and subsequent bust? Problems associated with exurban homeowners unable to sell their homes, the high rates of foreclosure in some exurban locations, declining property values and the associated decline in local tax revenue, and the impact of higher transportation fuel costs all contribute to an uncertain future for whatever exurbia might look like between now and the mid-21st century. Popular media and some researchers are reporting that we are unlikely to see exurban growth like that of the 1990s and early 2000s for the foreseeable future (Leinberger, 2008; USEPA, 2010). Some exurban scholars are even going the next step, such as Arthur Nelson, to speculate that the exurbs may be the future slums of America. He forecasts a future surplus of 22 million large-lot homes (houses built on one-sixth of an acre or more) by 2025 – which is roughly 40 percent of the large-lot homes in existence today (Leinberger, 2008). While his prediction (and the similar ones of Kunstler, 2005) might be extreme, it does raise questions about how to manage the existing, overbuilt and often permanent, exurban infrastructure, even as growth moderates or stops. While it is too early to tell whether the exurban residential "experiment" has failed, the legacy of this era of growth and development and the subsequent efforts to maintain and develop both the physical and social aspects of communities are rich and needed areas of exploration for community sociologists.

Conclusions

In conclusion, we have attempted to provide an overview of the state of our knowledge of the exurbs in the US. If the last era (1970s into the early 1980s) of relatively large population growth at the rural–urban interface provides any insights regarding where community research will go in relation to the exurbs, then we might expect a steady tapering off of interest in this settlement area as growth subsides (which was true during the 1980s). What we have attempted to do, though, is to outline why this settlement area is important to understand regardless of whether there is growth and development. We also believe the exurbs provide a very interesting context for exploring community planning tools, agricultural adaptation and development, local governments, community interactional structures and community responses to economic decline. In fact, we think the ongoing evolution of the exurbs provides a great opportunity to continue the more public conversation facilitated by popular writers such as Spectrosky (1955) and Brooks (2004) regarding what the exurbs say about the human condition, the nature of community and society, and the sustainability of our residential settlement patterns.

Notes

1   Many other terms aside from exurbia and rural–urban fringe have been used to describe the region in question, including metropolitan orbit (Blumenfeld, 1983), extended urban area (Wolman et al., 2005), and urban shadow (Ilbery, 1985).
2   In the natural resource management field, particularly among those studying forests and fires, there is also the term wildland–urban interface, which also encompasses the idea of urban or residential development into or near wildlands and does not necessarily stress the importance of adjacency to large, urbanized areas.
3   Available data can present some challenges, because the concept of exurbia transcends the common data aggregation boundaries such as metropolitan, nonmetropolitan, urban and rural. Additional data manipulations are often necessary to reveal exurban characteristics (Theobald, 2001).
4   Audirac (1999) presents many figures revealing the spatial location of the exurbs relative to more urban and rural locations that are largely refinements of the classic Chicago school representations of urban communities and their various zones (Lyon, 1989).
5   Townships, in general, are an important form of local government in Ohio, as well as in many other Midwestern and Northeastern states. Townships offer an array of services,

from mandated road maintenance to fire and police protection to zoning. However, when it comes to land-use decision making, Ohio has a unique governance structure. In most states, the county is responsible for planning and zoning in unincorporated areas. In Ohio, townships are responsible for zoning, with the assistance of the county. This condition further exacerbates exurbanization, as previous research has found that the density of local governments making land-use decisions, or governmental fragmentation, increases urban sprawl (Carruthers and Ulfarsson, 2002).

References

Audirac, I. (1999). Unsettled views about the fringe: Rural–urban or urban–rural frontiers. In J.F. Owen & M.B. Lapping (Eds.), *Contested countryside: The rural urban fringe in North America* (pp. 7–32). Brookfield, VT: Ashgate Publishing Company.

Bell, M.M. (1992). The fruit of difference: The rural–urban continuum as a system of identity. *Rural Sociology*, 57(1), 65–82.

Berube, A., Singer, A., Wilson, J.H., & Frey, W.H. (2006). Finding exurbia: America's fast-growing communities at the metropolitan fringe. *Living Cities Census Series*. Washington, DC: Brookings Institution.

Besussi, E., & Chin, N. (2003). Identifying and measuring urban sprawl. In P.A. Longley & M. Batty (Eds.), *Advanced spatial analysis: the CASA book of GIS*. Redlands, CA: ESRI.

Blumenfeld, H. (1983). Metropolis extended. *Journal of the American Planning Association*, 52(3), 346–348.

Brooks, D. (2004). *On paradise drive: How we live now (and always have) in the future tense*. New York: Simon and Schuster.

Broussard, Shorna R., Washington-Ottombre, C., & Miller, B.K. (2008). Attitudes toward policies to protect open space: A comparative study of government planning officials and the general public. *Landscape and Urban Planning,* 86, 1–24.

Bunce, M. (1998). Thirty years of farmland preservation in North America: Discourses and ideologies of a movement. *Journal of Rural Studies*, 14(2), 233–247.

Cadieux, Valentin, K., & Hurley, P.T. (2011). Amenity migration, exurbia, and emerging rural landscapes: global natural amenity as place and as process. *GeoJournal*, 76, 297–302.

Carruthers, J., & Ulfarsson, G. (2002). Fragmentation and sprawl: evidence from interregional analysis. *Growth and Change*, 33, 312–340.

Clark, J.K., Munroe, D.K., & Mansfield, B. (2010). What counts as farming: How classification limits regionalization of the food system. *Cambridge Journal of Regions, Economy and Society*, 3(2), 245–259.

Daniels, T., & Bowers, D. (1997). Holding our ground: protecting America's farms and farmland. Washington, DC: Island Press.

Daniels, T.L. (1999). When city and country collide: Managing growth in the metropolitan fringe. Washington, DC: Island Press.

Daniels, T.L. (2000). Integrated working landscape protection: The case of Lancaster County, Pennsylvania. *Society & Natural Resources*, 13(3), 261–271.

Daniels, T., & Lapping, M. (2005). Land preservation: An essential ingredient in smart growth. *Journal of Planning Literature*, 19, 316–329.

Davis, J.S. (1993). The commuting of exurban homebuyers. *Urban Geography*, 14(1), 7–29.

Friedland, W.H. (2002). Agriculture and rurality: Beginning the 'final separation'? *Rural Sociology*, 67(3), 350–371.

Galpin, C.J. (1915). *The social anatomy of an agricultural community*. Madison, WI: Agricultural Experiment State of the University of Wisconsin.

Goldschmidt, G. (1978). *As you sow*. Harcourt, NY: Brace & Co.

Gyourko, J., Saiz, A., & Summers, A. (2008). A new measure of the local regulatory environment for housing markets: The Wharton residential land use regulatory index. *Urban Studies*, 45(3), 693–729.

Ilbery, B.W. (1985). *Agricultural geography: a social and economic analysis*. New York, NY: Oxford University Press.

Inwood, S.M., & Sharp, J.S. (2012). Farm persistence and adaptation at the rural urban interface: Succession and farm adjustment. *Rural Studies*, 28(1), 107–117.

Jackson-Smith, D., & Sharp, J. (2008). Farming in the urban shadow: Supporting agriculture at the rural–urban interface. *Rural Realities*, 2(4), 1–12.

Kunstler, H.J. (2005). *The long emergency*. New York, NY: Atlantic Monthly Press.

Kurtz, R.A., & Eicher, J.B. (1958). Fringe and suburb: A confusion of concepts. *Social Forces*, 37(1), 32–37.

Lamb, R.F. (1983). The extent and form of exurban sprawl. *Growth and Change*, 14(1), 40–48.

Leinberger, C.B. (2008, March). The next slum? *Atlantic Monthly*. http://www.theatlantic.com

Lessinger, J. (1986). *Regions of opportunity: A bold new strategy for real estate investment with forecasts to the year 2010*. New York, NY: Times Book.

Lyman, R. (2005, August 15). Living large, by design, in the middle of nowhere. *New York Times*. www.nytimes.com

Lyon, L. (1989). *The community in urban society*. Lexington, MA: Lexington Books.

Lyson, T.A. (2004). *Civic agriculture: Reconnecting farm, food, and community*. Medford, MA: Tufts University Press.

Lyson, T.A., Stevenson, G.W., & Welsh, R. (2008). *Food and the mid-level farm: Renewing an agriculture of the middle*. Cambridge, MA: MIT Press.

Mahler, J. (2005, March 27). The soul of the new exurb. *New York Times*. www.nytimes.com

Nelson, A.C. (1992). Characterizing exurbia. *Journal of Planning Literature*, 6(4), 350–368.

Nelson, A.C., & Sanchez, T.W. (1997). Exurban and suburban households: A departure from traditional location theory? *Journal of Housing Research*, 8(2), 249–276.

Nelson, A.C., & Sanchez, T.W. (1999). Debunking the exurban myth: A comparison of suburban households. *Housing Policy Debate*, 10(3), 689–709.

Olson, R.K., & Lyson, T.A. (1999). *Under the blade: The conversion of agricultural landscapes*. Boulder, CO: Westview Press.

Pahl, R.E. (1966). The rural urban continuum. *Sociologia Ruralis*, 6(3), 299–329.

Partridge, M., & Clark, J.K. (2008). *Our joint future: Rural–urban interdependence in 21st century Ohio*. Washington, DC: The Brookings Institution.

Patel, D.I. (1980). *Exurbs: Urban residential developments in the countryside*. Washington, DC: University Press of America.

Pfeffer, M.J., & Lapping, M.B. (1994). Farmland preservation, development rights and the theory of the growth machine: The views of planners. *Journal of Rural Studies*, 10(3), 233–248.

Pratt, S.R., & Rogers, D.L. (1986). Correlates of the adoption of land use controls. *Rural Sociology*, 51(3), 354–362.

Pryor, R.J. (1968). Defining the rural–urban fringe. *Social Forces*, 47, 202–215.

Rudel, T.K., O'Neill, K., Gottlieb, P., McDermott, M., & Hatfield, C. (2011). From middle to upper class sprawl? Land use controls and changing patterns of real estate development in northern New Jersey. *Annals of the Association of American Geographers*, 101(3), 609–624.

Salamon, S. (2003). *Newcomers to old towns: Suburbanization of the heartland*. Chicago, IL: The University of Chicago Press.

Sharp, J.S., & Clark, J.K. (2006). Between the country and the concrete: Rediscovering the rural–urban fringe. *City & Community*, 7(1), 61–79.

Sharp, J.S., & Smith, M.B. (2004). Farm operator adjustments and neighboring at the rural–urban interface. *Journal of Sustainable Agriculture*, 23(4), 111–131.

Shyrock, H.S., & Siegel, J.S. (1980). *The methods and materials of demography: Volume 1.* Washington, DC: US Government Printing Office.

Spectrosky, A.C. (1955). *The exurbanites.* Philadelphia, PA: Lippincott.

Taylor, L. (2011). No boundaries: Exurbia and the study of contemporary urban dispersion. *GeoJournal*, 76, 323–339.

Theobald, D.M. (2001). Land-use dynamics beyond the American urban fringe. *Geographical Review*, 91(3), 544–565.

Thomas, J.K., & Howell, F.M. (2003). Metropolitan proximity and U.S. agricultural productivity, 1978–1997. *Rural Sociology*, 68(3), 366–386.

United States Environmental Protection Agency (USEPA) (2010). *Residential construction trends in America's metropolitan regions.* Retrieved from http://www.epa.gov/dced/pdf/metro_res_const_trends_10.pdf

Wilkinson, K.P. (1999). *The community in rural America. Classic studies in rural sociology series.* Middleton, WI: Social Ecology Press.

Willits, F.K., & Bealer, R.C. (1967). Evaluation of a composite definition of 'rurality'. *Rural Sociology*, 32(2), 165–177.

Willits, F.K., Bealer, R.C., & Crider, D.M. (1982). The persistence of rural–urban differences. In D. Dillman & D. Hobbs (Eds.), *Rural Society: Issues for the 1980s* (pp. 69–76). Boulder, CO: Westview Press.

Wolman, H., Galster, G., Hanson, R., Ratcliffe, M., Furdell, K., & Sarzynski, A. (2005). The fundamental challenge in measuring sprawl: Which land should be considered? *The Professional Geographer*, 57(1), 94–105.

4

COMMUNITY GENERALIZING STRUCTURE DIMENSIONS

Clarifying a Fundamental Community Interaction Field Theory Concept

Peter F. Korsching and Cheryl Davidson

Introduction

Interaction theory is a major theoretical approach for examining and understanding the structure and organization of community. The basic tenet of this theory is that community is defined by the regular and sustained interaction of individuals who share a common geographic area with an interest in the welfare of the locality. Over time such interaction becomes structured, individuals identify with the locality, and they develop ties among those with whom they interact. A community interaction field emerges.

First introduced by Harold Kaufman (1959), community interaction field theory was elaborated and refined by Kaufman's student, Kenneth Wilkinson, and further amplified by Wilkinson's students and colleagues. A comprehensive statement of the theory is found in Wilkinson's (1991) *The Community in Rural America*. In relation to community development, the two primary processes are: structure building, strengthening the relationships within the community to increase its problem solving capacity; and task accomplishment, achieving goals of infrastructure and economic improvement. Over the years community interaction field theory scholars applied the theory to a wide range of substantive issues. A sampling of these studies includes flood insurance participation (Luloff and Wilkinson, 1979), local participation in the federal grant system (Martin and Wilkinson, 1984), rural manufacturing development (Lloyd and Wilkinson, 1985), rural crime (Wilkinson, 1990), community leadership (Israel and Beaulieu, 1990), sustainable development (Bridger and Luloff, 1999; 2001), technology adoption by telephone companies (Korsching et al., 2003), and rural entrepreneurship (Korsching and Allen, 2004a; 2004b). Other recent restatements of the theory have attempted to demonstrate its relevance to the solution of problems and issues faced by rural communities in today's global economy (Bridger et al., 2002; Luloff, 1990; Luloff and Bridger, 2003; Swanson and Luloff, 1990).

42 P. Korsching and C. Davidson

At the heart of community interaction field theory is the concept of "generalizing structure." According to Wilkinson (1991), it is the generalizing structure that provides the foundation upon which the community field is built. The generalizing structure concept is central in and crucial to the understanding of community as a geographically based social organization. Unfortunately, in all the statements, restatements, and applications of community interaction field theory by Wilkinson and his students in research and practice, generalizing structure is never explicitly identified, defined, and used as a variable. Its importance may be discussed in the theoretical section of research reports, but it is then ignored in the operationalization of the research. Although examples can be found (Korsching and Allen, 2004a; 2004b), the literature demonstrating its use as an organizing principle in applied programs is also exceedingly rare. In referring to the community action continuum of structure building and task accomplishment, Wilkinson (1991, p. 96) states that little attention has been given to this important element of community action. Despite its importance to community interaction field theory, the concept remains abstract and indeterminate.

In this chapter we seek to further define and explicate the generalizing structure concept to increase its utility and, in turn, the utility of community interaction field theory for community research and community development practice. We suggest that the body of Wilkinson's work already includes the fundamental elements necessary for clarification and development of the concept in the five major characteristics or dimensions he identifies as conditions of the relationship between community and social well-being of the local people. The five dimensions are: distributive justice, open communication, tolerance, collective action, and communion. The purpose of this chapter is to theoretically integrate these five conditions of community social well-being into the community generalizing structure concept, resulting in a construct that provides greater analytical insight into the community development process. We explore the relevance and role of the construct's five dimensions in the mutually reinforcing processes of structure building and task accomplishment.

Community Interaction Field Theory

According to Wilkinson (1991), we should study the community as a field of interaction among individuals, groups, and organizations. Community is a dynamic entity that emerges from interaction among actors in a locality. Interaction fields can emerge and evolve around any issue or interest of the local population. The character of the locality is determined by the properties or characteristics of individuals, groups, and organizations involved in the interaction fields, and by the outcome of their interaction. "Social interaction delineates a territory as the community locale; it provides the associations that comprise the local society; it gives structure and direction to processes of collective action; and it is the source of community identity" (Wilkinson, 1991, p. 13). Any number of interaction fields can exist in a locality, but most cannot be considered community interaction fields.

What differentiates the community interaction field from other fields of interaction is the interests of the actors. Community interaction fields are defined by the actors' interests in the welfare of their locality, which, in turn, determine the goals and objectives of their actions. Actions based on their shared interest for the welfare of the locality that they physically share creates the community interaction field. "Locality orientation is the hallmark of community action" (Wilkinson, 1991, p. 84).

Frequent and sustained interaction among individuals, groups, and organizations in any situation results in the emergence of a social structure that to some degree creates expectations of appropriate behavior among the actors and provides order to continued interaction. Thus, when actors in a common geographic locality regularly interact, a social structure emerges. But it is only when they interact specifically for the welfare of that locality that the social processes initiate the emergence of a community generalizing structure. It is a *community* structure because the interaction is for the betterment and benefit of the locality. And it is a *generalizing* structure because it transcends the specific private interests of any individual or group involved in the interaction. Individuals' and groups' actions and interactions that are specifically oriented toward improving their ability to address and resolve community needs, issues, and problems reinforce and energize the linkages among the actors in the generalizing structure and, in turn, strengthen the community interaction field.

This emerging, evolving, and strengthening of the community field is community development. Community development is a process consisting of "... a deliberate and substantial attempt to strengthen the horizontal pattern of a community" (Warren, 1978, p. 325). As an outcome of the community interaction field, community development has the following characteristics: "Community development is always purposive ... expresses a purpose that always is positive ... exists in the efforts of people and not necessarily in goal achievement ... therefore, community development is structure oriented" (Wilkinson, 1991, pp. 93–94). In other words, community development lies in the efforts and activities of improvement that increase people's willingness and capacity to come together and act to improve their lives and the community. Whether or not the actions are guided by concrete goals, and whether or not those goals are achieved, is secondary. Community development is the purposeful interaction that results in building and strengthening the community's generalizing structure, not necessarily the improvement of its physical facilities or services, or the creation of jobs and income. From the community interaction field theory perspective, community development is development *of* the community, that is, development of the community's generalizing structure – the community's capability to identify, address, and resolve problems and issues related to the welfare of its residents. It is the development of community agency – the ability to act and adapt to its changing environment. Improvement of the physical facilities and services is development *in* the community.

In his consideration of the community development literature Wilkinson (1991) asserts that inordinate attention has been given to the action processes of achieving goals. Much of the literature focuses on application of the theory to the analysis of specific problems or issues (Bridger et al., 2011). A major theme in much community development research is examination of the action process of task accomplishment of the local population, from initially recognizing a problem or need through the planning, organizing, and taking action to address the issue (Wilkinson, 1970). It is useful to understand the action process of task accomplishment, but, Wilkinson insists, it is equally useful and perhaps more critical to understand the structure building process to ensure long-term community development sustainability. "Less attention has been given to the crucial but necessarily more abstract analysis of the structure building dimension of community action" (Wilkinson, 1991, p. 96).

Although structure building – development of the community – has primacy in community interaction field theory's conceptualization of community development, payoff from community development activities for the community and its residents necessarily also comes from the mobilization of the structure in task accomplishment – actions toward achieving specific desired goals. The residents of a locality may or may not appreciate the importance of an organizational structure to address their problems or needs, but they do have expectations about progress toward resolving those issues. Without some tangible progress toward resolving issues, that is, unless the community development process also results in development *in* the community, community residents may weary of the work, let action lapse, and let the generalizing structure degenerate (Korsching and Allen, 2004a; Warner and Monk, 1979). In their definition of community development Christenson and Robinson (1989, p. 14) basically agree with Wilkinson on the need for structural development, but they go on to state that the process is important to a local population when it leads to community action "... to change their economic, social, cultural, or environmental situation." Unless people are organized, goals are set, and there is some task accomplishment toward those goals – some sense among the participants that their efforts have made a difference to the well-being of the community – the participants may become disenchanted or weary of the process. Claude et al. (2000) found that the residents of a highly active community actually reported relatively low levels of community well-being, which they attributed to pessimism over repeated failures in economic development ventures. Over time, enthusiasm wanes and activity ceases, and whatever structure was developed eventually atrophies or disintegrates. The community's generalizing structure and action efforts are mutually reinforcing. Ultimately, the role of the generalizing structure is to help the community achieve its goals, and task accomplishment, in turn, results in feelings of achievement and reinforces the commitment to decisions and actions devoted to structure building.

As Wilkinson (1991) states, considerable work has been devoted to understanding the task accomplishment process, with far less attention directed to the more abstract but critical process of building the generalizing structure. But what is this generalizing structure, and what is its relationship to task accomplishment? As social scientists – theoreticians, researchers, and practitioners – how do we identify, define, measure, analyze, evaluate, and use it? What are its dimensions? Are the dimensions of development *of* the community also related to success in development *in* the community, and if so, how?

The literature provides little direction for making this concept more analytically and practically useful. Wilkinson (1991) discusses the concept at length but leaves it fairly amorphous. In an earlier work he defines community structure "... in terms of its generality or comprehensiveness of interest scope" (Wilkinson, 1972, p. 48). Fortunately, a close reading of his works does provide insight into potential further refinement of the community generalizing structure concept. Drawing on Wilkinson's work which demonstrates an evolving theory of community generalizing structure, making some assumptions about the role of the generalizing structure within his larger community theory, and bringing in the work of another community scholar – Roland Warren – allows us to identify and explicate the generalizing structure's dimensions. These dimensions provide the key to clarification and amplification of the nature of community generalizing structure and serve to increase its usefulness to community action and development research and practice.

Community Generalizing Structure and Community Context

In a locality, the community interaction field is only one of several (perhaps many) interaction fields. The community field is distinguished from the others in that its interaction pursues the interest of the general community rather than any single or more specific and selfish interests of actors who share these fields. Furthermore, the community field functions as an interstitial system that links together relevant community-oriented components of other local interaction fields. Its field provides the structure for the essence of community and seeks to link and coordinate the actions and interactions in the other local fields so that they might contribute to the community's well-being. "The structural interest in the community field is expressed through linking, coordinating actions, actions that identify and reinforce the commonality that permeates the differentiated special interest fields in a community" (Wilkinson, 1991, p. 90). The community field initially emerges from the action in the other fields, but then assumes its own reality. It is "... an abstraction from other fields of community action, and its contribution is that of articulating and enforcing linkages among other fields" (Wilkinson, 1991, p. 90). Because actors (individuals, organizations, and agencies) and the purpose and scope of their actions and interactions are constantly changing, the community field also is in a continuous state of flux. Strengthening the community field helps generate positive effects for the community from the actions occurring within the locality. Thus, strengthening the community field is community development, which is "... *purposive* [italics original] efforts to build the generalized structure that characterizes a community field. People try to build the community field, and that process of trying constitutes community development" (Wilkinson, 1991, p. 91).

Roland Warren (1978) agrees with Wilkinson that community development is strengthening the horizontal pattern (generalizing structure) of the community. But Warren goes on to argue that communities often face a dilemma in attempting to strengthen the horizontal pattern. Communities also have specific goals they want to accomplish, and to what degree can communities do both in the same action process, that is, achieve the goal of some tangible improvement in the community and also strengthen the community's horizontal pattern – the generalizing structure? Furthermore, even though most professional community developers may stress the need for process, outside organizations and agencies involved with the projects, especially those providing resources such as funding, may be more interested in, and indeed demand, tangible goal achievement for continued support (Lumb, 1990).

In discussing community action toward task accomplishment and community development, Warren (1978, p. 336) states: "The two are inseparable except in abstract analysis." Yet, he also goes to great pains to elaborate on this difficulty of achieving both ends in the same action course. Whereas initially community leaders may attempt to build the generalizing structure by promoting broad community participation in planning, decision making, and implementation, the impetus for seeing the project through to completion often falls to a small group of leaders. The long-term goal of strengthening the generalizing structure is rationally usurped by the more immediate and demanding goal of the specific project, or the demands of external organizations that control needed resources such as funding for the project. "The process of encouraging people to make their own decisions about what is good for them gives way to the process of convincing them of what a change agent or a small group of leaders think is good for them" (Warren, 1978, p. 331).

The danger of the decision making passing from broad community participation to a small group of leaders is that the will of the community may be co-opted to reflect the will of special interests (Molotch, 1976). Just as there are many action fields in a locality, not all of which are community action fields, so there also is a potential for many leaders in a community, not all of whom are community leaders or always act as community leaders. Leaders who support and promote specific community projects or goals may be considered community leaders only if, in their efforts with these activities, they also consciously attend to the development of the generalizing structure (Wilkinson, 1991). In other words, in their actions community leaders support and promote the public interests of the community over personal interests.

Because local leaders' ostensible community actions may be more apparent than real, the community public should be wary when local leaders promote projects or activities that are allegedly in the "public interest." Although the promoted projects certainly may be in the public interest, in reality there are few community projects on which everyone will agree. Depending on the political or economic clout of those in disagreement, that is, their power in the community, they may be forced to set aside their interests in preference to what seems best for the community (Brennan and Israel, 2008). A large body of literature exists on community power and its role in community decision making, action, and welfare, but Wilkinson (1991) does not address the issue of community power and its impact other than a brief discussion of the nature and role of community leadership in community development. Wilkinson contends that community interaction that is dominated by outside interests or a powerful elite will fall short of providing conditions needed for social well-being (Bridger et al., 2011).

Literature on power strongly suggests that those with power will not relinquish it to those without power (Warren, 1978, p. 388):

1. Collaboration strategies will result only in programs and policies that the existing power configuration finds acceptable.
2. Power will not voluntarily be given up by elites.
3. Attempts by the [powerless] ... to participate in community decision-making often will not be resisted as long as they do not pose threats to the well-being of those in power, or threats to change the power configuration.
4. Where such threats are posed ... participants will be co-opted, controlled, or fiercely attacked by those in power.

"Most community change theory is based on the often fallacious assumption that there is a public interest and that people can find it and agree on it" (Warren, 1978, p. 377). The seeming consensus the public reaches on defining community problems and issues and their solutions may be illusory. It may simply be a case of ritualized agency – no alternate choice available, or, more likely, abandoned agency – acquiescence or complacency because those who disagree assume the power holders are legitimate and act in the best interest of the public whether in reality they do or do not (Brennan and Israel, 2008). The ritualized or abandoned agency results in a superficial consensus on issues, and this superficial consensus is facilitated by a more fundamental but potentially pernicious consensus "... on the manner in which the issue is to be resolved, the way in which the contest is to be conducted, and there is consensus on the legitimacy of the final outcome" (Warren, 1978, p. 389).

Community Generalizing Structure Dimensions

Community development or development *of* the community is positive purposive action that builds and strengthens the community generalizing structure. To achieve community development requires local actors who must place the welfare of the community above their own personal interests for the purpose of striving for the illusive "public interest." The ability to work toward and achieve goals that truly reflect the broad community public interest can vary across communities for a number of reasons, including social and structural characteristics of the community. Some communities have characteristics that are more facilitative of organized action toward community goals (Brennan and Israel, 2008; Warren, 1978). They have a generalizing structure that is more developed to support community actions toward goals that serve the public interest. But what, specifically, are the elements, characteristics, or dimensions of the generalizing structure that facilitate or support community action?

Warren (1970, p. 15) suggested a number of characteristics that a good community should have "... for citizens working to improve their own communities, or for professional community development workers, to operate effectively." Other community scholars have followed up with their own lists of characteristics necessary for community development such as the components of an entrepreneurial social infrastructure (Flora and Flora, 1990; 1993), elements of community fields that provide the capacity to take action on behalf of the wider community (Sharp, 2001), characteristics of a sustainable community (Bridger and Luloff, 1999), and the resource base or assets upon which a community can build (Green and Haines, 2012). Although each of these lists differs somewhat on the inclusion of specific characteristics or elements, there are more similarities than differences in the concepts underlying each list's characteristics. These lists of community characteristics also strongly correspond with Wilkinson's (1991, p. 73) five community characteristics (he terms them conditions) that are dimensions of social well-being and "...can be used to elaborate the relationship between community and social well-being."

According to Wilkinson (1991), the interactional community has three essential properties: 1) the local ecology, which is the organization of local life for meeting daily needs and adapting to changes; 2) a comprehensive interactional structure which expresses the common needs and interests of local residents; and 3) a bond of local solidarity expressed in community action. The first essential property, local ecology, is instrumental in ensuring the physical well-being of the population in a locality by providing the sustenance or economic and service development needs. Sustenance needs include jobs, income, housing, medical care, education, and municipal services, among others. Meeting the sustenance needs, however, is only the means to the ends and not the ends themselves. The ends are higher-level needs and relate to the social well-being of the local population. Wilkinson (1979) states that social well-being, defined as self actualization, is located in interpersonal dynamics (the interactional structure) and is a quality of social interaction. "Self actualization is assumed to be a natural tendency in people but one which can be suppressed either by deficits in meeting primary needs such as for food and shelter, or by sociocultural patterns which discourage its expression" (Wilkinson, 1979, p. 7). He stresses that it would be presumptuous to conclude that certain social conditions cause individual well-being, but they can play an important role. Social conditions that permit and even facilitate and promote social well-being "... produce minimum interference with accurate personal and interpersonal response" (Wilkinson, 1973, p. 162). Wilkinson (1991, p. 73) suggests five conditions "... as the social dimensions or elements of social well-being, and these can be used to elaborate the relationship between the community and social well-being." The five conditions or dimensions are (Wilkinson, 1991, pp. 73–75):

Distributive justice – In its simplest form, distributive justice refers to equity-in-exchange as part of the normative system, but in a broader sense it endorses human equality and promotes actions that deliberately eliminate inequality.

Open communication – For constructive interaction toward community support and improvement to occur, open communication is an absolute necessity. Communication improves with efficiency of channels and honesty, completeness, and authenticity of exchanges.

Tolerance – Acceptance and respect of differences and diversity among people in a community improves interaction among them.

Collective action – People within a common locality work together on common interests to achieve common goals related to the welfare and betterment of the community. This builds social relationships and provides the basis for the local social infrastructure.

Communion – Communion is the willful, sincere, and selfless participation in community activity so that "Communication in the true sense represents an opening of consciousness and of the emotional life of a people ... and common, shared purpose becomes a factor in subsequent social interaction."

These five dimensions of community social well-being are the foundation of the community generalizing structure, and they are the second essential property of the interactional community, the comprehensive network of individual and organizational relationships that expresses the common needs and interests of local residents. The generalizing structure is a direct result of interaction in the community field. Wilkinson's (1991) definitions of the five social well-being dimensions reflect the inclusion of interaction in each dimension; that is, the community achieves higher levels of well-being through interaction that normatively embodies these dimensions. Unless the community normative structure embraces, enhances, and actualizes these five dimensions, the "generalizing" descriptor of generalizing structure will be difficult, if not impossible, to achieve. It is only through the norms embodied in these five dimensions that the generalizing structure evolves to serve broad community interests rather than specific individual or group interests, and thereby builds the capacity of the community for positive, purposive community action.

Linking the components of social well-being to the community generalizing structure as dimensions of the structure also follows logically from Wilkinson's work. In his early writing, Wilkinson (1979) had not yet adopted the "generalizing structure" term, but simply referred to the concept as the community field. He actually identified four different types of community field, the first three being fields in different community sectors that act independently, fields where interests are in opposition, and fields based on functional interdependence. Only one type of community field fits the characteristics of the concept he would later call the generalizing structure. "A fourth type of community field is one in which social fields are linked through a sense of communal identity among participants. Local residents identify various problems as parts of a collective concern and undertake concerted action that is generalized because of the shared sentiment" (Wilkinson, 1979, p. 12). The shared sentiment relates to the third essential property of the interactive community – the bond of local solidarity. He continued, stating that such a community field, reflecting comprehensive linkages, cooperation, and shared commitment, will be more facilitative and supportive of social well-being. The organizational structure of such a community field, built through concerted generalized action, is the generalizing structure with a foundation consisting of the five conditions of social well-being.

Structure Dimensions and Community Action

Ultimately, the role of the generalizing structure is to help the community achieve its specific goals: development in the community facilitated by a generalizing structure with strength in all five of its dimensions. From an interactional perspective, it is the interaction of individuals in and for a locality that defines the community. When residents of a community then act collectively to pursue a commonly valued goal, the activity transcends a simple aggregation of their individual actions and emerges as a community action (Luloff, 1990; Luloff and Swanson, 1995). The ability of communities to act is community agency, and "... such agency is more than the sum of its parts" (Luloff and Swanson, 1995).

Luloff and Swanson (1995) assume a positive relationship between the quality of community agency and the effective mobilization of resources for general well-being of the community. Effective community development programs require the incorporation of community agency. All community action, of course, is an interplay between volition of the community to achieve its goals and structural factors that can either hinder or facilitate community action. Warren (1978) has been criticized for making a too-strong case for loss of local autonomy at the community level, yet communities, in their vertical relationships with state and federal governments, non-governmental organizations, and businesses, and even in many of their horizontal relationships with local entities, do face structural barriers that limit their actions. There often is a great deal of latitude within those barriers, however, that provides opportunities for local action (Richards, 1984). Community agency "... assumes that people make choices, even though the range of choices may be greatly (but not exclusively) shaped by structural factors" (Luloff and Swanson, 1995, p. 357).

To facilitate and promote the community's ability or capacity to make choices and act on those choices, in other words, to have the potential for agency, requires social infrastructure or capacity, which includes intangible factors such as local culture, innovativeness, quality social interaction, leadership, and also more tangible characteristics such as social stratification, political and economic power, and social equality (Swanson, 1996). The essence of each of these social infrastructure elements is captured in the five dimensions or conditions of the community generalizing structure. In turn, a community with a generalizing structure that embodies those five elements also embodies the social infrastructure or social capacity necessary for community agency.

To summarize, a comprehensive community generalizing structure is necessary, although in itself not sufficient, to ensure community agency. Community development – development *of* the community that, in turn, facilitates development *in* the community – can therefore be achieved through strengthening each of the five dimensions of the community generalizing structure. The community development literature demonstrates the importance of each of the five dimensions in facilitating community development.

- *Distributive justice:* Higher levels of distributive justice mean broader representation and participation in community planning and decision making, resulting in widely distributed benefits and costs from the activities (Dolan, 2008). There is no development without change, and change usually results in redistribution of goods and resources (Christenson and Robinson, 1989). If participation in the democratic process is not encouraged for all members of a group, then the potential for activity may be impeded or the outcomes may be subverted (Pateman, 1970). However, "... leadership programs, if designed to capitalize on the enfranchisement of new skills to a segment of the population not included could foster a redistributive effect of community development activities" (Luloff, 1990, p. 266). Policy makers, beginning with publicly elected and appointed officials in local government, have a responsibility to create a level playing field in all the functions of local government (Lowe and Harris, 2011).

- *Open communication:* Communication is essential for any human activity and it is the basis for community capacity building (Brennan and Israel, 2008). "Community has always been based on communication. The traditional 'little community,' working-class urban communities, migrant communities, and neighborhoods have all been organized through communicative ties ..." (Delanty, 2003). Open communication makes certain that interaction can be directed toward outcomes that benefit the group (Sager, 1995). Readily accessible and efficient communication channels are especially important for the introduction of new ideas into a group (Rogers, 2003) and to provide knowledge of and access to external resources for accomplishing community goals (Garkovich, 1989).

- *Tolerance:* A higher degree of tolerance of diversity can gain benefits for the community through consideration of a greater variety of new ideas and approaches for handling problems, as well as avoiding long-term costs of overlooking important issues of disenfranchised groups (Bridger and Luloff, 1999). Whether by race, class, or other criteria, segregation undermines the democratic process and creates barriers to participation in community activities and decision making (Green and Haines, 2012). Flora and Flora (1993) state that to achieve inclusiveness as an approach to diversity requires actively working to bring disenfranchised groups into the decision-making process. Sharp and Flora (1999) found that communities having success using self-development economic development strategies engaged a greater diversity of local actors. In promotion and support of entrepreneurship, rural communities with large, broadly-based networks are more successful than communities with small, closely-knit networks (Korsching and Allen, 2004b).

- *Collective action:* Collective action toward common goals strengthens social relationships and develops the social infrastructure. Strengthening social relationships and developing the social infrastructure is the ultimate goal of one of the major paradigms of community development practice – the "self-help" approach (Littrell and Hobbs, 1989). Community action builds the capacity for subsequent community action as it creates networks, roles, and a pool of shared experience (Wilkinson, 1992). Community development, development of the generalizing structure, occurs when community residents take action to address

52 P. Korsching and C. Davidson

common issues (Bridger and Luloff, 2001; Bridger and Luloff, 1999; 2003). The body of research by Wilkinson and colleagues indicates that active communities were more successful in participating in national flood insurance programs (Luloff and Wilkinson, 1979), obtaining community development funds through government grants (Martin and Wilkinson, 1984), promoting rural manufacturing development (Lloyd and Wilkinson, 1985), and taking actions to resolve community issues (Zekeri et al., 1994). "Without deep participatory roots in community life, interest group politics seem destined to perpetual conflict over relatively narrowly defined issues while our ... communities stagnate" (Warren, 1998, p. 90).

- *Communion*, the common shared purpose of local residents, results in actions for the benefit of the group. Zekeri et al. (1994) found that in a sample of Pennsylvania communities, solidarity, which he defined as the capability of a group to act as one through local horizontal ties that facilitate and encourage collective action, was related to success in local development efforts. In research on the impact of urban newcomers to rural Illinois communities, Salamon (2003, p. 71) found that community adaptation to change was facilitated by "... strong community identity and tight connectedness ... cultural traits associated with an agrarian covenant: priority given to communitarian ideals for group welfare." Similarly, Schmidt et al. (2002), in their restudy of Landaff, New Hampshire, found that both old-timers and newcomers had a strong affection and commitment to the locality with an overarching interest in limiting unchecked development and maintaining the rural setting binding them together.

Development of and Development in the Community

Success and permanency of any program of local development hinges upon building problem-solving capacity through a structure of local relationships and networks. Warner and Monk (1979) studied the development process in 54 Appalachian Kentucky communities. These communities, located in ten northeast Kentucky counties, had the social, economic, and infrastructure problems typically associated with the Appalachian coal mining region, not the least of which was a lack of social infrastructure to initiate and conduct development activities. Warner and Monk (1979) found that successful communities demonstrating program longevity and tangible accomplishments began with small-scale, largely expressive activities (structure building) such as community recreation, celebration, or entertainment events, then, having achieved success in these smaller projects, moved on to exceedingly longer and more complex largely instrumental (task accomplishment) activities, eventually to include parks, playgrounds, community centers, fire departments, and water systems.

Warner and Monk (1979) demonstrate two relevant points. First, the building of a generalizing structure is vital to the success and longevity of community development programs. Second, unless community residents are able to achieve some of the goals they set, in the long run the program is likely to fail, and, more importantly, whatever structure has been developed also may decline or even disappear. Warren

(1978) insisted that community structure building and task accomplishment are inseparable, and, similarly, Wilkinson (1972) noted that few acts in a community are exclusively oriented to structure building. Although development in the community can and does occur without thought to structure building, development of the community is seldom the sole purpose of community action; rather, it is part of a broader effort of development in the community. Even when initiating activities in a community with little or no experience in community organizing or social infrastructure to support the effort, which was the condition of many of the communities in the Warner and Monk (1979) research, there invariably also needs to be an instrumental element in community action. The key is to ensure that the development program is based on and enhances the generalizing structure's five dimensions, but also that the implementation of activity is successful in achieving at least some of its goals. "It is important that the group identify common goals and celebrate milestone accomplishments to keep collaboration efforts moving forward. ... Acting on short-term, high-visibility projects while more complex issues are being considered will motivate people to continue working together" (Ayres and Silvis Heinz, 2011, p. 164).

Ayres and Silvis Heinz (2011) provide a case-study example demonstrating the importance of both structure building and goal achievement for long-term development program sustainability. Carroll County, Indiana, initiated a local development effort in 2004 beginning with structure building through county-wide forums, organization of a steering committee, and community seminars. The effort was highly successful, resulting in achievement of concrete goals and also continued structure building with spin-off organizations and activities. In 2009, to maintain momentum, the project's collaborative effort was reinvigorated through celebrating the successes, identifying new issues, and reengaging the local population (Ayres and Silvis Heinz, 2011).

Practical Application

As demonstrated in the detailed discussion of the five dimensions, community and community development literature generally provides support to the existence of relationships linking community action to variables that reflect each of the five dimensions. What has been lacking in community interaction field theory is a more comprehensive framework that incorporates the dimensions into the theory. The elaboration of community generalizing structure as a construct that incorporates the five dimensions presented here provides that comprehensive framework, resulting in increased utility of the theory.

First, there is theoretical grounding in community interaction field theory for predicting the nature of the relationships between each of the five dimensions and their effect on organizing and conducting community action and community development. Having a common theoretical base for various measurements of the dimensions and interpretation of research results will facilitate one of the goals of the scientific process – building a cumulative body of knowledge.

Second, the theory provides guidance for variables that could or should be included in research exploring the nature of community development and factors related to successful development projects. One of the striking commonalities of many empirically based research reports using community interaction field theory is that the primary explanatory variable related to development activity success is one of the generalizing structure dimensions, the level of past or current community action or activeness. Although this is an important finding, the depth of understanding of community processes might have been increased had one or more of the other generalizing structure dimensions been included as variables in the research. The theory and past research suggest the other variables also are important and should have an impact apart from or in addition to community activeness.

A third and closely related point is that of potential interaction effects among the five dimensions in community development activities. Similar to community agency, which transcends the simple aggregation of the actions of individuals (Luloff and Swanson, 1995), the combined effect of two or more dimensions might be considerably different from the impacts of the dimensions considered individually.

Fourth, a community generalizing structure robust in all five dimensions should go far toward assuring that community development activities will serve the community public interest, not just the interest of a select few or a small community sector. Assurance that the public interest is served is usually achieved through community participation techniques. A deep and wide participatory process in community activities might be the ideal, but, aside from the smallest of communities, such a process logistically cannot involve everyone (Cornwall, 2008). The goal should be optimum participation with a balance between depth and inclusion, plus ascertaining that those involved in the process do indeed have voice. Although Warren (1978) casts grave doubt on the efficacy of collaborative strategies in determining a community's future, the definitions of the five dimensions all suggest that a community robust in each dimension will be open to, and indeed actively seek, participation from all parts of the community.

Community developers already have available strategies based on community interaction field theory that involve collaborative participation of all parts of a community, thereby facilitating creation and growth of a generalizing structure. One strategy, "whole community organizing," operates under a framework that specifies that: 1) everyone, not only local leaders and elites, should be involved; 2) including the whole community means breaking down social barriers between groups that traditionally have either been ignored or have not worked together; and 3) the formation of new relationships expands existing and creates new networks with the potential for access to previously unknown or unavailable resources (Aigner et al., 2002). The issue of distribution of community power thwarting collaborative efforts, a major concern of Warren (1978), is specifically addressed by another strategy, the "collaborative problem-solving framework." In this strategy power is not viewed as a zero-sum entity, but rather as an infinite resource that can be created and expanded through working together (Ayres and Silvis Heinz, 2011). In a collaborative effort, through pooling knowledge, creativity, and problem-solving ability, the group has increasing emergent power. Bringing together the diverse elements of community in these collaborative strategies to create the generalizing structure is the role of community leadership. Community leadership and community emerge together through mutually influencing relationships focused on a common purpose. Leaders are distinguished from followers by their ability to exercise more influence and thereby to "… transform individual private interests into common purposes that carry greater meaning… including reciprocity and mutuality as features of the interactional structure" (Pigg, 1999, p. 201).

Employing strategies such as whole community development and collaborative problem solving, the community development practitioner need not be concerned with making determinations about what projects qualify as being in the public interest. Adherence to the principles and processes built into these strategies guarantees broad participation and input with results that serve the community's public interest. The primary roles of the community developer are to facilitate implementation of the process and assist the community in creating and enhancing community leadership and the generalizing structure.

The presence of a generalizing structure robust in all five of its dimensions can help ensure that no relevant community stakeholders are overlooked or ignored in decision making, and that activities and projects selected, planned, and implemented serve the public interest. An expansive generalizing structure helps provide the social capacity necessary for community agency. "Where relationships between different and varying segments of a local society can be established and maintained, agency and increments of local adaptive capacity emerge" (Brennan and Luloff, 2007, p. 54). Determining the strength of that adaptive capacity has been the objective of several scholars (e.g. Laverack, 2005; Magis, 2010). They suggest that concepts such as community capacity or community resilience are really constructs composed of several different dimensions, and those constructs can be measured through each of their dimensions to determine a community's overall adaptive capacity. Extending that logic, a community's ability for agency and adaptive capacity can be assessed through the five dimensions of the community generalizing structure construct. By assessing the strength of each of the generalizing structure's dimensions, the practitioner has a tool to determine where to focus effort and resources to strengthen the weaker dimensions and help ensure the efficacy of the collaborative strategies.

A survey conducted in a small, Midwestern town to examine the support received by business proprietors from local sources illustrates the utility of this tool. Local business proprietors often have multiple roles in the community (residents, business owners, organization members, community leaders), and the diverse interactions through these multiple roles give them insight into community culture and social structure. The survey included questions on the proprietor's perceptions of each of the five dimensions of the local generalizing structure. Two Likert-type items were included for each dimension. Indicators for each dimension were developed after reviewing the definitions and survey instruments used by other researchers. The items were scored one through five from strongly disagree to strongly agree, and for each dimension the two scores were summed and divided by

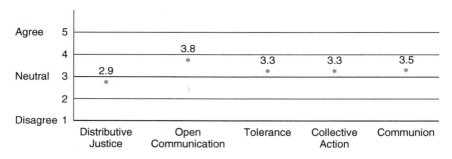

FIGURE 4.1 Perceptions of Community Generalizing Structure Dimensions among Business Proprietors in a Small Midwestern Community

two, except for open communication. The two open communication items did not scale, so the item deemed most representative of the concept was used. Figure 4.1 contains the results.

A community development practitioner working with this community could conclude that the community is not particularly strong in any of the dimensions, although open communication seems to be a stronger asset than the others. Furthermore, the data show that a primary need and focus for structure building, at least from the perspective of the business proprietors, is to establish greater equity in decision making and distribution of resources. Comments from the respondents supported this conclusion by expressing dissatisfaction with the operations of the Chamber of Commerce. The data also seem to indicate that collaborative strategies would be suitable for development activities.

These responses are, of course, from the perspective of the local residents, and a narrow sector of the residents at that, and thus reflect their interests and biases. The community development practitioner certainly must keep that in mind by supplementing survey results with additional data, including newspaper articles, reports on public meetings, and personal observations, and interpret the results with caution. Nevertheless, beliefs of community residents, even inaccurate beliefs, can become real in their consequences, and the issues of equity, tolerance, and inclusion addressed through the generalizing structure dimensions are often overlooked in community resources and needs assessments. If the community survey is sufficiently large and randomly distributed, the data can be analyzed to determine whether perceptions differ across community sectors.

Conclusion

This chapter has addressed Wilkinson's concern that too little attention has been given to the extremely important but abstract structure-building dimension of community action and development. Specific focus was on community generalizing structure, a concept that is central to community interaction field theory but largely ignored in theory and research literature. A critical review of Wilkinson's works revealed the evolution of the concept and a source and rationale for expansion and elaboration through its five dimensions – distributive justice, open communication, tolerance, collective action, and communion. The dimensions of community generalizing structure become particularly relevant to community goal achievement by assisting community development practitioners in selecting the appropriate strategy for the community and working toward achieving projects that qualify as being in the public interest. What is needed now is research to determine the impact of the dimensions, both individually and collectively, in community development activities and related areas such as community satisfaction, community attachment, and community participation and leadership.

References

Aigner, S., Raymond, V.J., & Smidt, L.J. (2002). 'Whole community organizing' for the 21st century. *Journal of the Community Development Society*, 33, 86–106.

Ayres, J., & Silvas, Heinz A. (2011). Principles of working together: Developing relationships that support community development initiatives. In J.W. Robinson, Jr., & G.P. Green (Eds.), *Introduction to community development* (pp. 155–168). Thousand Oaks, CA: Sage.

Brennan, M.A., & Israel, G.D. (2008). The power of community. *Community Development: Journal of the Community Development Society*, 39, 82–98.

Brennan, M.A., & Luloff, A.E. (2007). Exploring rural community agency differences in Ireland and Pennsylvania. *Journal of Rural Studies*, 23, 52–61.

Bridger, J.C., & Luloff, A.E. (1999). Toward an interactional approach to sustainable community development. *Journal of Rural Studies*, 15, 377–387.

Bridger, J.C., & Luloff, A.E. (2001). Building the sustainable community: Is social capital the answer? *Sociological Inquiry*, 71, 458–472.

Bridger, J.C., Brennan, M.A., & Luloff, A.E. (2011). The interactional approach to community." In J.W. Robinson, Jr., & G.P. Green (Eds.), *Introduction to community development* (pp. 85–100). Thousand Oaks, CA: Sage.

Bridger, J.C., Luloff, A.E., & Krannich, R.S. (2002). Community change and community theory. In A.E. Luloff & R.S. Krannich (Eds.), *Persistence and change in rural communities: A 50-year follow-up to six classic studies* (pp. 9–21). New York: CABI Publishing.

Christenson, J.A., & Robinson, J.W., Jr. (1989). Community development. In J.A. Christenson & J.W. Robinson, Jr. (Eds.), *Community development in perspective* (pp. 3–25). Ames, IA: Iowa State University Press.

Claude, L.P., Bridger, J.C., & Luloff A.E. (2000). Community well-being and local activeness. In P.V. Schaeffer & S. Loveridge (Eds.), *Small town and rural economic development* (pp. 39–45). Westport, CT: Praeger.

Cornwall, A. (2008). Unpacking 'participation': Models, meanings and practices. *Community Development Journal*, 43, 269–383.

Delanty, G. (2003). *Community*. London: Routledge.

Dolan, P. (2008). Social support, social justice, and social capital: A tentative theoretical triad for community development. *Community Development: Journal of the Community Development Society*, 39, 112–119.

Flora, C.B., & Flora, J.L. (1990). Developing entrepreneurial communities. *Sociological Practice*, 8, 197–207.

Flora, C.B., & Flora, J.L. (1993). Entrepreneurial social infrastructure: A necessary ingredient. *Annals*, 529, 48–58.

Garkovich, L.E. (1989). Local organizations and leadership in community development. In J.A. Christenson & J.W. Robinson, Jr. (Eds.), *Community development in perspective* (pp. 196–218). Ames, IA: Iowa State University Press.

Green, G.P., & Haines, A. (2012). *Asset building and community development* (2nd ed.). Thousand Oaks, CA: Sage.

Israel, G.D., & Beaulieu, L.J. (1990). Community leadership. In A.E. Luloff & L.E. Swanson (Eds.), *American Rural Communities* (pp. 181–202). Boulder, CO: Westview.

Kaufman, H.F. (1959). Toward an interactional conception of community. *Social Forces*, 38, 8–17.

Korsching, P.F., & Allen, J.C. (2004a). Locality based entrepreneurship: A strategy for community economic vitality. *Community Development Journal*, 39, 385–400.

Korsching, P.F., & Allen, J.C. (2004b). Local entrepreneurship: A development model based on community interaction field theory. *Journal of the Community Development Society*, 35, 25–43.

Korsching, P.F., Sapp, S.G., & El-Ghamrini, S. (2003). Rural telephone company adoption of service innovations: A community field theory approach. *Rural Sociology*, 68, 387–409.

Laverack, G. (2005). Evaluating community capacity: Visual representation and interpretation. *Community Development Journal*, 41, 266–276.

Littrell, D.W., & Hobbs, D. (1989). The self-help approach. In J.A. Christenson & J.W. Robinson, Jr. (Eds.), *Community Development in Perspective* (pp. 48–68). Ames, IA: Iowa State University Press.

Lloyd, R.C., & Wilkinson, K.P. (1985). Community factors in rural manufacturing development. *Rural Sociology*, 5, 27–37.

Lowe, J.S., & Harris, W.M. (2011). Community development challenges in inner-city neighborhoods. In J.W. Robinson, Jr., & G.P. Green (Eds.), *Introduction to community development* (pp. 193–208). Thousand Oaks, CA: Sage.

Luloff, A.E. (1990). Commmunity and social change: How do small communities act? In A.E. Luloff & L.E. Swanson (Eds.), *American rural communities* (pp. 214–227). Boulder, CO: Westview.

Luloff, A.E., & Bridger, J.C. (2003). Community agency and local development. In D.L. Brown & L.E. Swanson (Eds.), *Challenges for rural America in the twenty-first century* (pp. 203–214). University Park, PA: Pennsylvania State University Press.

Luloff, A.E., & Swanson, L.E. (1995). Community agency and disaffection: Enhancing collective resources. In L.J. Beaulieu & D. Mulkey (Eds.), *Investing in people: The human capital needs of rural America* (pp. 351–372). Boulder, CO: Westview.

Luloff, A.E., & Wilkinson, K.P. (1979). Participation in the national flood insurance program. *Rural Sociology*, 44, 137–152.

Lumb, R. (1990). Rural community development: Process versus product. In Henry Buller & Susan Wright (Eds.), *Rural development: Problems and practices* (pp. 177–190). Aldershot, England: Avebury.

Magis, K. (2010). Community resilience: An indicator of social sustainability. *Society and Natural Resources*, 23, 401–416.

Martin, K.E., & Wilkinson, K.P. (1984). Local participation in the federal grant system. *Rural Sociology*, 49, 374–388.

Molotch, H. (1976). The city as a growth machine: Toward a political economy of place. *American Journal of Sociology*, 82, 309–332.

Pateman, C. (1970). *Participation and democratic theory*. Cambridge: Cambridge University Press.

Pigg, K.E. (1999). Community leadership and community theory: A practical synthesis. *Journal of the Community Development Society*, 30, 196–212.

Richards, R.O. (1984). When even bad news is not so bad: Local control over outside forces in community development. *Journal of the Community Development Society*, 15, 75–85.

Rogers, E.M. (2003). *Diffusion of innovations*. New York: Free Press.

Salamon, S. (2003). *Newcomers to old towns: Suburbanization of the heartland*. Chicago: University of Chicago Press.

Schmidt, F., Skinner, E., Ploch, L.A., & Krannich, R.S. (2002). Community change and persistence: Landaff, NewHampshire. In A.E. Luloff and R.S. Krannich (Eds.), *Persistence and change in rural communities: A 50-year follow-up to six classic studies* (pp. 95–116). New York: CABI Publishing.

Sharp, J.S. (2001). Locating the community field: A study of interorganizational network-structure and capacity for community action. *Rural Sociology*, 66, 403–424.

Sharp, J.S., & Flora, J.L. (1999). Entrepreneurial social infrastructure and growth machine characteristics associated with industrial-recruitment and self-development strategies in nonmetropolitan communities. *Journal of the Community Development Society*, 30, 131–153.

Swanson, L.E. (1996). Social structure and economic development. In T.D. Rowley, D.W. Sears, G.L. Nelson, N. Reid & M.J. Yetley (Eds.), *Rural development research: A foundation for policy* (pp. 103–119). Westport, CT: Greenwood.

Swanson, L.E., & Luloff. A.E. (1990). Barriers and opportunities for community development: A summary. In A.E. Luloff and L.E. Swanson (Eds.), *American rural communities* (pp. 228–234). Boulder, CO: Westview.

Warren, M. (1998). Community building and political power: A community organizing approach to democratic renewal. *American Behavioral Scientist*, 42, 78–92.

Warner, P., & Monk, P.M. (1979). The formulation and testing of a process model for community development. *Journal of the Community Development Society*, 10, 17–27.

Warren, R. (1970). The good community – What would it be? *Journal of the Community Development Society*, 1, 14–24.

Warren, R. (1978). *The community in America* (3rd ed.). Chicago, IL: Rand McNally.

Wilkinson, K.P. (1970). Phases and roles in community action. *Rural Sociology*, 35, 54–68.

Wilkinson, K.P. (1972). A field-theory perspective for community development research. *Rural Sociology*, 37, 43–52.

Wilkinson, K.P. (1973). Sociological concepts of social well-being: framework for evaluation of water resource projects. In W.H. Andrews, R.J. Burdge, H.R. Capener, W.K. Warner & K.P. Wilkinson (Eds.), *The social well-being and quality of life dimension in water resource planning and development* (pp. 160–170). Logan, UT: Utah State University.

Wilkinson, K.P. (1979). Social well-being and community. *Journal of the Community Development Society*, 10, 5–16.

Wilkinson, K.P. (1990). Crime and community. In A.E. Luloff and L.E. Swanson (Eds.), *American Rural Communities* (pp. 151–168). Boulder, CO: Westview.

Wilkinson, K.P. (1991). *The community in rural America*. Westport, CT: Greenwood.

Wilkinson, K.P. (1992). The process of emergence of multicommunity collaboration. In P.F. Korsching, T.O. Borich & J. Stewart (Eds.), *Multicommunity collaboration: An evolving rural revitalization strategy* (pp. 259–264). Ames, IA: North Central Regional Center for Rural Development.

Zekeri, A.A., Wilkinson, K.P., & Humphrey, C.R. (1994). Past activeness, solidarity, andlocal development. *Rural Sociology*, 59, 216–255.

Section two
COMMUNITY DYNAMICS

5

AN INTERACTIONAL APPROACH TO PLACE-BASED RURAL DEVELOPMENT

Jeffrey C. Bridger and Theodore R. Alter

Introduction

Rural America is in the midst of the most far-reaching and rapid transformation in our history. Globalization is fundamentally altering the economic landscape and erasing many of the better sources of income and employment. Manufacturing, which is still the most important economic sector, has declined markedly in recent years. In 2005, manufacturing accounted for approximately 12 percent of all jobs in nonmetropolitan counties. This represents a sharp drop from 1976, when almost 19 percent of the rural workforce was employed in manufacturing (USDA, 2006). And although manufacturing has stabilized over the last two years, the picture varies considerably by region and industry. Parts of the northwest, for instance, are continuing to shed jobs in timber and other natural resource industries (Whitener and Parker, 2007).

Many agriculturally dependent communities have also fallen on hard times. Small farms have been disappearing for decades, but losses have been accelerated by changes in the structure of US agriculture, especially the decisive shift away "… from the production of commodities to finely graded products and a shift from spot and futures markets to contracts" (Drabenstott, 2001:10). Instead of producing generic commodities for sale on the open market, many farmers have become the first link in vertically integrated supply chains which coordinate production, processing, marketing, and consumption (Buttel, 2003). As this consolidation continues, more and more farms will be forced out of business. Nowhere can this be seen better than in the pork industry, which experts estimate will be dominated by fewer than forty supply chains in just a few years. Only a small fraction of the nation's 100,000 hog farmers will receive production contracts (Drabenstott, 2001). The remainder will be forced to shift to another commodity or seek alternative sources of income and employment.

Supply chains are also changing the geography of US agriculture. Because it is more efficient to reduce the distance between production and processing, farms are increasingly locating near processing facilities. The poultry industry, for instance, is concentrated around processing facilities in the South, the mid-Atlantic, and the upper Midwest. As this process gains momentum, clusters of agricultural production will replace the dispersed settlement pattern that has historically characterized agriculturally dependent rural areas. In fact, as the declining number of farm-dependent counties indicates, geographic reorganization is already occurring. In 1990, 618 of the nearly 2,000 nonmetropolitan counties were farm-dependent. By 2000, only 420 nonmetropolitan counties were still relying on agriculture for 15 percent or more of earnings (Ghelfi and McGranahan, 2004). As these counties have lost their farms, they have also lost banks and other businesses. And in many historically farm-dependent counties, matters have been made worse by a lack of alternative employment opportunities (Ghelfi and McGranahan, 2004).

Even in those rural locations where jobs are available, they tend to pay less than in urban areas. And the wage gap between rural and urban America has widened in recent years. In 2006, median weekly earnings for rural workers were only 84 percent of the average for their metropolitan counterparts (Whitener and Parker, 2007). In some sectors of the rural economy, wages are actually declining. For instance, workers in the meat packing and processing industry have seen their wages fall by 30 to 40 percent since 1990 (Drabenstott, 2001; Brueggemann and Brown, 2003). This trend is particularly troubling because meat packing and processing is the largest employer in the rural manufacturing sector.

Figures from the 2000 census underscore the economic problems facing rural America. Between 1990 and 2000, 25 percent of nonmetropolitan counties lost population. Remote, agriculturally dependent counties were most likely to lose people, especially young people. Over half of these counties had fewer people in 2000 than in 1990, and in over a third of these places the loss exceeded 5 percent (McGranahan and Beale, 2002). During the same period, many rural counties with natural amenities or within commuting distance to metropolitan areas experienced moderate growth. These divergent population trends reflect a pattern of uneven development that is fostering increasing spatial inequality and threatening the security of many rural communities (Harvey, 1996; Falk and Labao, 2003; Drabenstott, 2001).

In such a dynamic and uncertain environment, economic development has become more important and more complicated than ever. Unfortunately, rural policies have not kept pace with the changes described above. At the federal level, we have never had a coherent policy for rural America. Instead, we have implicitly equated rural with agriculture and relied on agricultural subsidies and selective infrastructure investments that ultimately benefit a small segment of the population. At the state and local levels, a variety of industrial recruitment and retention strategies continue to dominate efforts to stimulate rural economies. The problem with these approaches is that in a global economy, rural America no longer has the competitive advantage it once had. In the past, abundant natural resources, low-cost land, and relatively cheap labor gave rural areas an edge over their metropolitan counterparts. Today, corporations can search the globe for the most profitable place to do business. In this context, it is both expensive and risky to offer tax breaks and other incentives to lure footloose industries that can easily relocate to lower-cost foreign locations (Drabenstott, 2001).

Although no single strategy has emerged to replace traditional approaches to economic development, there is an emerging consensus that enhancing community or regional competitiveness will be key to the future of rural America:

> More and more policy experts agree that rural policy in the 21st century must center on enhancing the competitiveness of places. In short, rural America needs a policy focused on geography, supporting economic development in defined geographic areas. Place policy supports a community's ability to compete in the new economy by highlighting and accentuating community attributes that are attractive to households and firms. The attributes are sources of strength from which a community provides economic opportunity and value. Put another way, these strengths define a place's competitive advantage.
> (Johnson, 2001:2)

In this paper, we begin by describing place-based economic development in more detail. Following this, we examine some of the problems associated with place competitiveness. Finally, we draw on an interactional approach to social organization (Wilkinson, 1991; Bridger et al., 2002; Luloff and Bridger, 2003) to create a more comprehensive place-based policy framework that integrates economic, environmental, and social well-being.

Place Competitiveness as Rural Development

Economists have not traditionally paid much attention to why certain activities happen in certain places, preferring instead to develop models where locations are portrayed, in Krugman's (1991:2) words, as "… dimensionless points within which factors of production can be instantly and costlessly moved from one activity to another." The reality, of course, is not so simple. Location clearly does matter. Consider, for example, the case of Dalton, Georgia (Krugman, 1991). In 1895, a teenager named Catherine Evans made a bedspread as a wedding gift. But this was no ordinary bedspread. It utilized a technique called tufting. Over the next few years, Miss Evans made several of these bedspreads, and in 1900, she perfected a technique for locking the tufts into the backing. After this discovery, she began to sell the bedspreads, and a local handicraft industry sprang up in the area. For the next few decades, tufting was done exclusively by hand. But after World War II, a machine was developed for producing tufted carpets, which were much cheaper than the woven carpets commonly in use at the time. With its workforce skilled in tufting, Dalton was able to capitalize on this advance and soon many small carpet manufacturers popped up in the area, together with supporting businesses that specialized in

66 J. Bridger and T. Alter

dyes and carpet backings. Over the next several decades, Dalton emerged as the carpet capital of America.

Until recently, economic development policy has for the most part ignored the experience of places like Dalton where some unique characteristic has been the key to their success. In fact, policy has been designed largely to flatten the landscape. While investments in education, infrastructure improvements, and industrial sectors might be targeted at different locations, the actual intent is to minimize the differences between places and create a system in which individuals (rather than places) have the maximum chance for success (Johnson, 2001).

Now, policy analysts are focusing on the features that distinguish places from one another and asking how these differences might be harnessed to foster more sustained growth and development (Johnson, 2001). Obviously, places differ from one another in myriad ways. At the most basic level, there are attributes there are largely "given" and beyond the control of local leaders or residents. These include physical qualities such as distance from other communities, climate, scenery, and natural resource endowments. They also include previous developments such as highways, railroads, and other infrastructure investments. Finally, population characteristics (age structure, educational attainment, and ethnicity) can be features that are difficult to change over the short run.

In addition to these more or less fixed attributes, there are other characteristics which can be modified. Leadership capacity and local governance, for instance, can be strengthened in ways that enhance competitiveness. Workforce development can be aligned with emerging market opportunities, polluted environments can be remediated, and new infrastructure investments can be made. And in many places, unique historical and cultural attributes can be mobilized for development efforts:

> The communities have a history and culture that may not be fully expressed. This history and culture as well affects what the community or region can be or how it can change. The idea here is path dependence, where we are and will be is a function of where we have been ... what a community can and will be is with the wisdom and culture of the local people and reflective of what has occurred in the past. ... Much of this wisdom and the cultural uniqueness of places is resident in the local people – a part of the social capital of the community.
>
> (Johnson, 2001:3)

Proponents of place-based development argue that the key to success hinges on making the most of "... the unique package of differentiating factors that add value to the region or community or its products" (Johnson, 2001:3). This process involves a number of steps. First, both fixed and malleable assets must be identified. These assets must then be analyzed with an eye toward identifying how they truly differentiate a place. The idea is to create strategies that build on local uniqueness in ways that enable places to carve out an economic niche in the global market. Ideally, places will sort themselves out in a way that results in a more diverse and economically stable landscape. Instead of competing for the same pool of manufacturing jobs, for instance, places will be offering unique products or services matched to local assets.

This approach to economic development differs dramatically from previous strategies. Instead of trying to level the playing field, a place-based approach must by definition be specific to a community and/or region. In short, this kind of development is an "inside job" by local actors and organizations (Wilkinson, 1991). External resources will be needed, but the real work will have to be done at the local level.

Barriers to Place-Based Competitiveness

In theory, a place-competitive approach to rural development seems viable – especially in light of the economic trends described above. In practice, there are a number of potential obstacles that must be overcome. First, it is doubtful that capitalizing on local uniqueness will remedy past patterns of uneven development. While regional/place-based approaches to rural development may foster a more equitable distribution of jobs and income, there is no guarantee that they will. In fact, a narrow focus on place competitiveness may reinforce or exacerbate existing patterns of uneven development. Historically, this has certainly been the case:

> Small, pre-existing differences, be it in natural resources or socially constructed endowments, get magnified and consolidated rather than eroded by free market competition. The coercive laws of competition push capitalists to relocate production to more advantageous sites and the special requirements of particular forms of commodity production push capitalists into territorial specialization. … Agglomeration economies … generate a locational dynamic in which new production tends to be drawn to existing production locations.
> (Harvey, 2006:98)

In other words, places that are already in a privileged position because of geography, natural resource endowments, infrastructure, proximity to transportation routes, or a variety of other factors, tend to prosper while their less well-endowed counterparts fall behind. And, as Harvey (2006:109) points out, the landscape that results from this process is marked by a "… hierarchy of power and interests such that the richer regions grow richer and the poor languish in indebtedness."

Matters are further complicated by differences in local capacity for action. Every element of a place competitiveness strategy, from identifying an economic niche to retraining the workforce, to creating complementary clusters of firms, places heavy demands on local institutions. To take just one example, consider the level of technical expertise needed to identify a potential economic niche. At the very least, this requires a thorough understanding of regional economic assets and trends and how these relate to emerging opportunities in the global market. And once a potential niche is identified, a host of additional issues must be addressed, ranging from workforce development to infrastructure requirements, to financing strategies. Few communities – especially rural communities – have the resources or leadership to undertake such a complicated venture. Once again, it is the places that are already most developed that are likely to be in a position to most successfully leverage local assets.

Even so seemingly a straightforward task as drawing on local history and cultural traditions in ways that add value to the region raises complicated issues that are not adequately addressed in much of the recent writing on place competitiveness. One of the biggest problems is that places do not have just one history or one culture. Consider, for instance, the case of Lancaster County in Pennsylvania's historic "Dutch Country." The story most people know of Lancaster County revolves around the Amish and their simple, agrarian lifestyle. But there are other stories that can be told about this place, including one in which the county is a bastion of growth and entrepreneurial capitalism. As one local reporter explained, "Lancaster is a community with a dual personality. ... One personality glorifies capitalism. ... There are few communities in Pennsylvania, perhaps in the U.S., that match Lancaster Countians in their belief in free enterprise, the preeminence of the businessman and economic growth. The other half of the split personality longs for preservation, old-fashioned things and quaint ways. This is the homeland of the plain people, a conservative sect that gets about in horses and buggies in the supersonic age" (Klimuska, 1988:14).

Most communities have these kinds of competing heritage narratives, which are best defined as selective representations of the past that feed into and are partially driven by the sentiments and interests of contemporary residents (Bridger, 1996). And, for this reason, heritage narratives are never politically neutral. In fact, they are frequently mobilized to position different groups to support lines of action that result in an inequitable distribution of costs and benefits. In Lancaster County, the Amish story has been pitted against the entrepreneurial narrative in a protracted struggle over land use and economic development strategies that has helped shape the region's developmental trajectory (Bridger, 1996).

As this example illustrates, local history does not necessarily provide guidance for place differentiation. Place construction (and reconstruction) is a cumulative and messy process that involves material, discursive, and symbolic practices in ways that are unpredictable and fraught with deep-seated conflicts over the inter-pretation of history, culture, and identity (Bridger, 1996; Harvey, 1996; Molotch et al., 2000).

Over time, all of these elements interact to create physical and cultural environments that affect current and future possibilities. Even places like Santa Barbara and Ventura California that have similar climates, environmental assets, and demographic characteristics, can proceed along very different trajectories that leave them with very different options for future economic development opportunities (Molotch et al., 2000). Santa Barbara has come to approximate "... development experts' ideal – a "learning community" on the forefront of information, technology, and leisure services ...," while Ventura "... more nearly typifies the qualities that preoc-cupy critics of U.S. urban places" (Molotch et al., 2000:797). What the experiences of these two communities suggest is that even when places have similar assets, a

Place-Based Rural Development **69**

variety of forces, ranging from local power structures to historical accidents, affect the ability to capitalize on them.

Place and Social Well-Being

While the emphasis on place is a welcome shift, the problems identified above point to the need for a more holistic framework. And perhaps more importantly, a broader perspective is needed because place competition, as currently conceived, does not adequately address the non-economic factors that impact the local quality of life. In our view, place competitiveness has a role to play but only as one component of a multi-faceted strategy. As a first step in sketching such an approach, it is important to specify the relationship between place and individual and social well-being because this underlies the rationale for an alternative policy.

As many observers (Leach, 1999; Zukin, 1991; Meyrowitz, 1985) have noted, the role of place in social life has become increasingly uncertain in the wake of globalization and the rapid changes it has spawned. Places that once seemed invincible suddenly find themselves vulnerable to economic, financial, and physical shifts over which they have no control. The stability and permanence we associate with specific places have been fundamentally undermined. Zukin (1991:8) likens this change to the "Great Transformation" that happened in England during the 18th and 19th centuries (Polyani, 1957). In her view, abstract market forces have both separated people from social institutions and "... have overpowered specific forces of attachment identified with place" (Zukin, 1991:4). Meyrowitz (1985) goes so far as to argue that place no longer matters in today's world. And Leach (1999:8) writes of a placeless society – a world in which "we live longer but emptier, without those nurturing habitats or places which remind us where we came from and, therefore, who we are."

Despite this alarmist rhetoric, there is reason to doubt that place has become less important. The meaning of place may have changed, and our relationship to specific places may have become more contingent and complicated (Bridger and Alter, 2006). But, as Agnew (1987:33) argues, for most people, place continues to play an important role in the social construction of meaning:

> The strongest forms of bonding are still local: a village or a town, particular valleys or mountain. ... Common experiences engendered by the forces of "nationalization" and "globalization" are still mediated by local ones. Most people still follow well-worn paths in their daily existence. Though "national" or "global" issues have increased in number and significance relative to local ones, they take on meaning as they relate to local agendas ... all issues, whatever their source or pervasiveness, are meaningful or important only in the context of outlooks derived from everyday life.

In short, place, and experience in place, are fundamentally implicated in our understanding of the world. As Casey (1993:307) puts it, "Where we are has a great deal to do with who and what we are. ... Where something or someone is, far from being a casual qualification, is one of its determining properties. As to the *who*, it is evident that our innermost sense of personal identity ... deeply reflects our implacement." To be more specific, our experience of place, and the interactions that occur in specific places, affect individual and social well-being in important ways.

The first and most fundamental connection between place and well-being stems from the simple fact that the locality is where the individual and society intersect. The family, of course, is the first point of contact between the child and the larger world. But this is a sharply limited form of contact, and one that "... screens and conveys selected information and selected demands from the outside world" (Wilkinson, 1991:77). The local society, by contrast, provides the opportunity to experience a wider range of people and institutions, and thus represents a tangible manifestation of the larger social order. This is important for well-being because the quantity and quality of available interpersonal contacts provide the raw material for social interaction. And, as Wilkinson (1991) argues, it is a truism that well-being depends crucially on the ability to interact with a broad range of other people.

To fully appreciate this relationship, consider the opportunity structure for interaction in rural localities. Many of our rural communities lack a complete table of social organization. Consequently, people must travel to different places to meet many of their daily needs. In such a situation, the locality becomes primarily a place of residence only, "... as relatives and neighbors who are strongly tied to one another have few mutual contacts in their separate involvements outside the place of residence" (Wilkinson, 1991:114). Available contacts tend to be repeated and become what Granovetter (1973) calls "strong ties." On the surface, the prevalence of strong ties would seem to foster well-being because they promote solidarity and can be a source of financial and other resources. But, at the same time, the lack of weak ties among a population makes it difficult to create linkages between clusters of strong ties. Without these linkages, it is difficult to create a holistic local society and develop the range of relationships that foster well-being.

There is also evidence to suggest that because living in a rural location creates an opportunity structure for certain forms of contact, it fosters a unique set of social problems. The idea here is that different kinds of social disruptions tend to be associated with different types of interpersonal contacts (Wilkinson, 1991). Robberies and other violent crimes tend to be committed by strangers or non-intimates. Homicides, on the other hand, are more likely to be committed by an intimate associate of the victim (Paulozzi et al., 2002). Other problems such as suicide and child abuse are frequently associated with isolation from social networks (Paulozzi et al., 2002; De Leo and Spathonis, 2004). And while it is difficult to say for sure that rurality is at the root of these problems, it does appear that the fragmented social structure of many rural areas contributes to certain forms of social disruption. Among white males, for instance, suicide rates are consistently higher in rural areas (Kaplan and Geling, 1998).

These interpersonal issues point to another important way in which locality-based interaction affects well-being: it is the setting for the emergence and development of the self. As Mead (1934) argued long ago, the self does not exist as an entity lodged within the isolated individual; selves take on meaning only through the relationships in which we are embedded: "It is the social process itself that is responsible for the appearance of the self; it is not there as a self apart from this type of experience" (Mead, 1934:142).

In Mead's framework, the self first arises in interactions with specific others. Later, as we come into contact with a wider range of people and groups, our concept of self is influenced by these interactions as well. Mead (1934:155) calls this the generalized other and claims that this "... social process influences the behavior of the individuals involved in it and carrying it on ... for it is in this form that the social process or community enters as a determining factor into the individual's thinking." In the course of this process, we develop bonds with specific and generalized others, and, by taking the role of the other, we become aware of the role we play in social interaction and what it means to be a social being. Hence, the self, as it arises out of social interaction, connects the individual with society by creating a bond of shared meaning. Or, as Mead (1934:162) puts it, "There are certain common responses which each individual has toward certain common things, and in so far as those common responses are awakened in the individual when he is affecting other persons he arouses his own self. The structure, then, on which the self is built is this response to all, for one has to be a member of a community to be a self."

Mead's theory of the self was not explicitly tied to place. The generalized other, for instance, simply refers to social processes and activities within which specific interactions occur, regardless of location. In today's world, there are many ways to interact with other people across vast distances, and these interactions obviously also affect the on-going construction of the self. At the same time, the vast majority of people continue to have most of their being and existence in specific geographic locales. People who share a common territory tend to interact with one another, even as they participate in more far-flung networks (Bernard, 1973; Wilkinson, 1991; Bridger et al., 2002; Oldenburg, 1999). And these patterns of interaction have a profound effect on how we understand and relate to one another. Duncan (1999:193) provides a powerful example of this in her description of how the class structure and social stratification in parts of the rural South have undermined civic culture and constrained social mobility:

> The structure of daily life that takes shape over time is taken for granted. Because new ideas and new resources rarely penetrate this environment that the powerful have deliberately kept closed off – worlds apart – from the larger society, people form their cultural tool kit in the context of the relationships and norms they know. Their immediate social context shapes who they become and how they see their options, both as individuals and as a community.

For better or worse, place, social interaction, and well-being are inextricably linked together. In fact, they are mutually dependent on one another.

As Gieryn (2000:467) argues, "... place stands in a recursive relationship to other social and cultural entities: places are made through human practices and institutions even as they make those practices and institutions. ... Place mediates social life; it is something more than just another independent variable."

The Interactional Approach to Development

This conceptualization of the relationship between place, social interaction, and well-being suggests a unique approach to development. In addition to focusing on jobs and income, development must facilitate other conditions that support individual and social well-being. From an interactional perspective (Wilkinson, 1991; Bridger and Luloff, 1999; Bridger et al., 2002; Luloff and Bridger, 2003; Bridger and Alter, 2006) this is best accomplished by enhancing the capacity of residents to create a holistic local society by strengthening the political, economic, social, and environmental dimensions of the places where they live – and the connections between them.

In contrast to human ecology and systems approaches to social organization, the interactional perspective views local life in more fluid and processual terms. The various actors that give form and texture to places are more or less organized as unbounded fields of interaction (Bridger et al., 2002). In most localities, for example, it is possible to identify a number of social fields that are concerned with different issues ranging from environmental protection to social services to workforce development.

In order for a place to "hang together" as a local society, there must be some mechanism that connects the acts that occur in these special interest fields into a discernable whole. This is accomplished by a broader, more inclusive "community" field, which like other social fields comprises actors, agencies, and associations. The key difference is that the community field does not pursue a single or narrow set of interests. Instead, it creates linkages between the actions and interests of other social fields:

> The community field cuts across organized groups and across other interaction fields in a local population. It abstracts and combines the locality-relevant aspects of the specialized interest fields, and integrates the other fields into a generalized whole. It does this by creating and maintaining linkages among fields that are otherwise directed toward more limited interests. As this community field arises out of the various special interest fields in a locality, it in turn influences those special interest fields and asserts the community interest in the various spheres of local social activity.
>
> (Wilkinson, 1991:36)

The actors and actions that comprise the community field coordinate the more limited and more narrowly focused actions that occur in other social fields. The community field is a linking device that covers many substantive areas and harbors "... memory traces ... through which something like a social structure can transpose

Place-Based Rural Development **73**

tself from one time or institutional realm to the next." The community field helps to bridge "... the somewhat ineffable 'betweenness' of people's subjective experiences and the objective realities of locale" (Molotch et al., 2000:794). In the course of this process, the community field creates a larger whole – one that is unbounded, dynamic, and emergent. As it builds linkages across different domains of local life, the community field provides the interactional milieu upon which individual and social well-being depend. And as these relationships are strengthened, they simultaneously enhance the capacity of local residents to address common issues and problems that inevitably cut across interest fields.

Because of the important role the community field plays in well-being, from the interactional perspective it is *the* primary focus of development efforts. Indeed, the entire process of development can be viewed as a process of developing the community field (Wilkinson, 1991; Bridger and Luloff, 1999; Luloff and Bridger, 2003). Obviously, the interactional processes that give rise to, and that are subsequently shaped by, the community field are in a continuous state of change. This means that the community field is also in constant flux as actors and organizations come and go, different interests arise and assert themselves, and outside forces impinge on local life. Thus, the community field is variable over time; at one moment it may be strong, at a later date it may be weak. But regardless of its state at a particular time, the main goal of development is to strengthen and institutionalize the community field by building from more narrowly focused fields of interaction to find points of intersection that can be used to enhance local capacity to solve problems.

It is important to note that from this perspective development does not depend on objective measures of success. Indeed, trying to accomplish some goal is enough to qualify as development. To require success not only ignores the fact that many forces other than purposive actions contribute to change, it also misses the point that "... development is a process rather than an outcome of social interaction. ... Development exists in the action that is undertaken with positive purpose" (Wilkinson, 1991:94). Indeed, the mere fact that people have taken an action to improve local life contributes to local capacity and enhances well-being because the action itself helps to build the linkages that are the essence of the community field.

Recent research supports this assertion. In a study of four small communities in Pennsylvania, Claude et al. (2000) found that in those places that displayed high levels of activeness, residents rated community well-being higher than residents in communities that were less active. This relationship held even when levels of success were not high. Indeed, residents of communities that had high levels of activeness and low levels of success rated community well-being higher than their counterparts in communities with high levels of success but low levels of activeness.

Conclusion: Toward a Holistic Place-Based Development Policy

Taking this as a general description of the development process, we are now able to more clearly specify what an interactional approach to place-based development

74 J. Bridger and T. Alter

would entail. First, and most obviously, there must be an explicit focus on building linkages between interactional fields in ways that contribute to individual and social well-being. In practical terms, this means strengthening the relationships between the economic, social, environmental, and political dimensions of local life. To take just a couple of examples, workforce development should be closely tied to emerging economic trends and job opportunities, and safe, affordable child care should be provided to enable low-income workers to participate fully in economy. In short, an effective place-based policy will identify relationships between a wide range of issues and interests and develop plans that build on these connections to create balanced and healthy communities.

Achieving this kind of balance also requires that such activities as innovation, entrepreneurship, job creation, infrastructure improvement, and business retention are tied to the broader process of developing the community field. Here it is useful to draw a distinction between development *in* the community and development *of* community. Job creation and the other instrumental activities listed above are examples of development in the community. In contrast, development of community is oriented toward building the structure of the community field by creating connections between special interest fields and enhancing problem-solving capacities.

In many communities, there is an obvious need for better jobs and higher incomes. At the same time, though, focusing too heavily on these sustenance issues misses the important contribution that development of community makes to well-being. Moreover, when growth is pursued as *the* answer to rural problems, without careful consideration of how it affects other aspects of life, the results are often environmentally and socially disruptive (Wilkinson, 1991; Bridger, 1996). Effective development is a broad and multi-faceted process that requires both development of community and development in the community.

Leadership is crucial to achieving this goal. Unfortunately, leadership development programs do not always promote the common good. In many instances, leadership skills contribute more to the lives and careers of individuals than they do to the local capacity to solve problems. And when leadership programs focus heavily on specific issues and topics, they may actually hinder broad development efforts (Bridger and Alter, 2006). By including insights from the interactional perspective in leadership development curricula, it is possible to build individual skills while fostering local capacity to address issues and problems. For instance, leadership development can focus on building the skills needed to identify potential connections between interactional fields, promoting actions that provide mutual benefits across fields, and facilitating concerted actions across groups and organizations. Participants could also learn about the phases and roles associated with community actions and how these provide opportunities to strengthen lines of communication and build capacity (Wilkinson, 1991).

Currently, there are no development policies in the US that are capable of easily incorporating the interactional perspective – primarily because they are preoccupied with economic growth. In contrast, the latest framework for rural development under the common agricultural policy (CAP) in the European Union (EU) explicitly considers many of the issues raised in this article. One component of this policy, which was initiated in the 1990s, presented disadvantaged rural areas with an opportunity to establish Local Action Groups and collaborate "... in order to construct a territorial identity that would meet their own needs as well as those of the policy controllers (the EU), and the political agendas of any regional or national government intermediaries" (Ray, 1999:260). In other words, it actively encouraged residents to build the linkages that contribute to the development of the community field.

CAP rural development policy further strengthens the community field through four strategically interdependent initiatives (European Union, 2006). The first focuses on ensuring the competitiveness of agriculture through increased efficiency, strengthening orientation toward markets, and taking advantage of opportunities for economic diversification. The second set of activities fosters sustainable management and use of agricultural lands and forests, ensuring the preservation and enhancement of natural resources, landscapes, and associated amenities and services. The third focuses on strengthening the broader economy to promote environmentally sustainable employment opportunities and a better quality of life. Finally, the Leader Community Initiative works to enhance local leadership, emphasizing the importance of building capacity and encouraging community action within and across the other arenas of activity to update and create new, locally driven development plans.

Obviously, the EU rural development policy cannot simply be imported to the US – rural Europe and rural America are different in many ways. But what is applicable to the American experience is the emphasis on local participation, empowerment, and strengthening the community field. Incorporating these elements into place-based rural development policy will require a major shift in our thinking. For too long, we have ignored the relationship between place and well-being, focusing instead on constantly generating wealth with little concern for the physical and social settings in which we live. Indeed, there has been an implicit assumption that economic growth will simply translate into all sorts of other benefits. And up to a certain level this is probably true. Indeed, for most of human history, more did mean better. As McKibben (2007:45) puts it, "When More and Better shared a branch, we could kill two birds with one stone." Now, there is mounting evidence that the unmediated pursuit of economic growth can reach a point of diminishing returns and undermine the very conditions that are essential for ecological, individual, and social well-being (Wilkinson, 1991; Bridger and Luloff, 1999; McKibben, 2007).

If we hope to create better places, our state and federal policies must provide rural areas with the incentives and the resources to create more holistic local societies – societies which provide the interactional opportunities that are crucial to individual and social well-being. In some instances, this might entail the creation of more local jobs. But it will also require building new institutions and strengthening the connections between organizations and social fields (Alter et al., 2007). And while this will ultimately depend on the efforts of local people, we need a coordinated and comprehensive rural policy framework – at the federal, state, and local levels – that removes barriers to effective local action.

References

Agnew, J.A. (1987). *Place and Politics*. Winchester, MA: Allan and Unwin.

Alter, T.R., J.C. Bridger, J. Findeis, T.W. Kelsey, A.E. Luloff, D.K. McLaughlin, & W.C. Shuffstall (2007). *Strengthening Rural Pennsylvania: A Rural Policy Agenda for the Commonwealth*. Report to the Brookings Institution.

Bernard, J. (1973). *The Sociology of Community*. Glenview, IL: Scott, Foresman and Company.

Bridger, J.C. (1996). Community imagery and the built environment. *Sociological Quarterly* 32(3):353–374.

Bridger, J.C., & A.E. Luloff (1999). Toward an interactional approach to sustainable community development. *Journal of Rural Studies* 15(4):377–387.

Bridger, J.C., & T.R. Alter (2006). Place, community development and social capital. *Community Development* 37(1):5–18.

Bridger, J.C., A.E. Luloff, & R.S. Krannich (2002). Community Change and Community Theory. pp. 9–22 in A.E. Luloff & R.S. Krannich (eds.), *Persistence and Change in Rural Communities*. New York: CABI Publishing.

Brueggeman, J., & C. Brown (2003). The decline of industrial unionism in the meatpacking industry. *Work and Occupations* 30(3):327–360.

Buttel, F.H. (2003). Continuities and Disjunctures in the Transformation of the U.S. Agro-Food System. pp. 177–189 in D.L. Brown & L.E. Swanson (eds.), *Challenges for Rural America in the Twenty-First Century*. University Park, PA: Penn State University Press.

Casey, E.S. (1993). *Getting Back Into Place: Toward a Renewed Understanding of the Place-World*. Bloomington, IN: Indiana University Press.

Claude, L.P., J.C. Bridger, & A.E. Luloff (2000). Community Well-Being and Local Activeness. pp. 39–45 in P.V. Schaeffer & S. Loveridge (eds.), *Small Town and Rural Economic Development: A Case Study Approach*. Westport, CT: Praeger Publishers.

De Leo, D., & K. Spathonis (2004). Culture and suicide in late life. *Psychiatric Times,* Vol. XX [electronic version], retrieved 12/2/05 from www.psychiatrictimes.com

Drabenstott, M. (2001). New policies for a new rural America. *International Regional Science Review* 24 (January):3–15.

Duncan, C.M. (1999). *Worlds Apart: Why Poverty Persists in Rural America*. New Haven, CT: Yale University Press.

European Union (2006). *Fact Sheet: New Perspective for EU Rural Development*. Brussels: European Communities.

Falk, W.W., & L.M. Labao (2003). Who Benefits from Economic Restructuring? Lessons from the Past, Challenges for the Future. pp. 152–165 in D.L. Brown & L.E. Swanson (eds.), *Challenges for Rural America in the 21st Century*. University Park, PA: Penn State University Press.

Ghelfi, L., & D. McGranahan (2004). One in five rural counties depends on farming. *Amber Waves* 2(3), June.

Gieryn, T.F. (2000). A space for place in sociology. *Annual Review of Sociology* 26: 463–496.

Granovetter (1973). The strength of weak ties. *American Journal of Sociology* 78(6): 1360–1380.

Harvey, D. (1996). *Justice, Nature, and the Geography of Difference*. Oxford, UK: Blackwell Publishers.

Harvey, D. (2006). *Spaces of Global Capitalism: Towards a Theory of Uneven Geographical Development*. New York: Verso.

Johnson, S. (2001). Exploring policy options for a new rural America: conference synthesis. pp. 185–193 in *Exploring Policy Options for a New Rural America*. Kansas City, MO: Center for the Study of Rural America, Kansas City, Federal Reserve Bank of Kansas City.

Kaplan, M.S., & O. Geling (1998). Firearm suicide and homicide in the United States: regional variations and patterns of gun ownership. *Social Science and Medicine* 46(9): 1227–1233.

Klimuska, E. (1988). *Lancaster County: The Ex-Garden Spot of America?* Lancaster, PA: Lancaster New Era.

Krugman, P. (1991). *Geography and Trade.* Cambridge, MA: MIT Press.

Leach, W. (1999). *Nation of Exiles: The Destruction of Place in American Life.* New York: Pantheon Books.

Luloff, A.E., & J.C. Bridger (2003). Community Agency and Local Development. pp. 203–213 in D.L. Brown & L.E. Swanson (eds.), *Challenges for Rural America in the 21st Century.* University Park, PA: Penn State University Press.

McGranahan, D.A., & C.L. Beale (2002). Understanding rural population loss. *Rural America* 17(4):2–8.

McKibben. B. (2007). *Deep Economy: The Wealth of Communities and the Durable Future.* New York: Times Books.

Mead, G.H. (1934). *Mind, Self, and Society: From the Standpoint of a Social Behaviorist.* Edited by C.W. Morris. Chicago: University of Chicago Press.

Meyrowitz, J. (1985). *No Sense of Place: The Impact of Electronic Media on Social Behavior.* New York: Oxford University Press.

Molotch, H., W. Freudenburg, & K.E. Paulsen (2000). History repeats itself, but how? City character, urban tradition, and the accomplishment of place. *American Sociological Review* 65 (December): 791–823.

Oldenburg, R. (1999). *The Great Good Place.* New York: Marlowe and Company.

Paulozzi, L.J., L.E. Saltzman, M.P. Thompson, & P. Holmgreen (2002). *Surveillance for Homicide Among Intimate Partners – United States, 1991–1998.* Centers for Disease Control [electronic version], retrieved 12/2/05 from www.cdc.gov/mmwr/preview/mmwrhtml/ss5003.a1.htm

Polyani, K. (1957). *The Great Transformation.* Boston, MA: Beacon Press.

Ray, C. (1999). Endogenous development in the era of reflexive modernity. *Journal of Rural Studies* 15(3):257–267.

United States Department of Agriculture, Economic Research Service (2006). Rural Employment at a Glance.

Whitener, L.A., & T. Parker (2007). Policy Options for a Changing Rural America. *AmberWaves,* May 2007. Retrieved from http://www.ers.usda.gov/AmberWaves/May07SpecialIssue/Features/Policy.htm

Wilkinson, K.P. (1991). *The Community in Rural America.* New York: Greenwood Press.

Wojan, T. (2005). Job losses higher in manufacturing counties. *Amber Waves* 3(1).

Zukin, S. (1991). *Landscapes of Power: From Detroit to Disneyland.* Berkeley: University of California Press.

6

THE POWER OF COMMUNITY

Mark A. Brennan and Glenn D. Israel

Introduction

Despite its central role in community, regional, and national life, the concept of power remains underdeveloped in the community theory literature (Gaventa, 1980; Waste, 1986; Stone, 1986; Fisher and Sonn, 2007; Domhoff, 2007). While community power is formally and informally recognized as important, an exploration of the process by which power emerges, evolves, and is managed within the confines of the community, remains scant in the research and theoretical literature (Gaventa, 1980; Beaver and Cohen, 2004; Fisher and Sonn, 2007). This is in part due to a lack of uniformity in conceptualization, as well as the complex mingling of history, culture, and local capacities which shape power structures. A need therefore exists for a more complete understanding of this important social entity and the complex processes through which it shapes local well-being.

Power, in its most simple definition, reflects the ability to act or influence the ability of others to either act or choose a path of inaction (Gaventa, 1980; Stone, 1986; Beaver and Cohen, 2004; Fisher and Sonn, 2007). However, power is far more complex in its types, dimensions, and applications. In academic and program settings, it is all too often glossed over as being a simple condition resulting from economic, social, or political position. Anecdotally, local power structures are often viewed as insurmountable, entrenched, and a tool used to achieve domination by ruling elites. As well, power has been conceptualized as the consequence of coordinated collective actions of diverse local residents. Regardless of setting, the mechanisms and processes by which power emerges and exists in the community remain largely unexplored.

Contemporary theoretical perspectives pay little attention to the role of power in the emergence of community and community development. When power is explored, it is usually portrayed in a macro context, often in the settings of social

The Power of Community **79**

movements, where a culmination of efforts results in a critical stage where sufficient media, social, economic, and political leverage has been obtained by the powerless. Far less often is the micro level considered. When explored at this level, power is typically tied to the condition that emerges as a result of local empowerment, civic engagement, and/or capacity-building activities (Gaventa, 1980; Beaver and Cohen, 2004; Fisher and Sonn, 2007). However, it is simply assumed or implied that power naturally emerges from these conditions and is successfully exercised. We believe such arguments lack the theoretical foundations and conceptual frameworks necessary to support such assumptions.

It is true that in many instances building local capacity through collective action leads directly to the accumulation of power. Similarly, the power accumulated by citizen mobilization is often seen as providing the ability of local groups to liaise with power-holding elites. On the other hand, community action may emerge but fail to lead to the establishment of power among local residents. It may also be the case that in some settings capacity building might inadvertently, or by manipulation, reinforce existing power structures by aligning new constituencies with local power-holding elites.

The failure of power to consistently emerge from collective mobilization suggests the underlying process is not a universal occurrence, and may only take place under the right conditions. What remains unexplored is the process by which local action manages to exist and not be eliminated, dismissed, or exploited by local power elites. In short, little attention has been given to mechanisms and processes through which local residents successfully develop the capacity to address important local issues as they interact with various power structures.

To facilitate a more complete understanding of community power, we seek to: *(1) explore the ways in which power is conceptualized at the micro level as a component of community development and social change;* and *(2) provide a theoretical framework, based on a field theoretical perspective, for understanding the process by which local citizens amass power, as well as interact with elites that might otherwise limit or facilitate the emergence of local capacity.*

Understanding and Conceptualizing Power

In its broadest context, the exercise of power can be seen as falling into two general camps: pluralism and elitism (Hunter, 1953; Dahl, 1961; Waste, 1986; Domhoff, 1986; Israel and Beaulieu, 1990; Moffett and Freund, 2004). The former is the basis on which our grassroots, democratic, and locally based civic engagement strategies are founded. From this perspective, the collective capacities of diverse local residents form the basis of power and locally driven social change (Waste, 1986; Wilkinson, 1991; Varley and Curtin, 2006; Armstrong, 2006; Reed and McIlveen, 2006; Brennan and Luloff, 2007). Here, power is dispersed across a wide range of often competing local interests. However, such power is diluted because of its fragmented holdings (Waste, 1986; Groarke, 2004; Reed and McIlveen, 2006). Community power, in this context, is tied to efforts aimed at coordinating and harnessing such collective capacity on a consistent and long-term basis (Wilkinson, 1991; Armstrong, 2006; Varley and Curtin, 2006; Brennan, 2007). At the same time, the inherent and underlying assumptions of this viewpoint remain questionable. Indeed, it is often the case that those most in need of civic engagement and participation in the democratic process are just the ones lacking the capacity to do so (usually in terms of educational attainment, financial stability, and limited social networks).

In contrast, elitism is often seen as the basis for the perceived insurmountable local power holdings of local and extralocal dominants (Hunter, 1953; Mills, 1956; Domhoff, 1986; Beaver and Cohen, 2004; Moffett and Freund, 2004; Domhoff, 2007). In such cases, a small number of individuals, based on their social, political, or economic positions, control the community and its decisions. Here, power is distributed hierarchically through the local social structure, with those in visible or hidden positions of authority, prestige, and wealth disproportionately holding power (Mills, 1956; Domhoff, 1986; Beaver and Cohen, 2004; Arcidiacono et al., 2007; Gallardo and Stein, 2007). The ability to obtain and hold power is therefore seen as being outside of the realm of the average citizen. To better understand pluralist and elitist holdings of power, we must first examine its manifestations in the context of conflict and consensus within our communities.

Conflict and Consensus

At its most basic level, community power and decision making are the result of either conflict or consensus situations. These conditions are often portrayed as the "two faces of society" (Dahrendorf, 1959; Bachrach and Baratz, 1970). While both are used as ideal types, they are not necessarily mutually exclusive and can exist at the same time in the same settings. The concepts of conflict and consensus are deeply rooted in social and philosophical thought that attempts to explain how local decisions are made and power structures emerge (Hobbes, 1960; Rousseau, 1978; Ebenstein, 1991). Conflict models see the decision-making process largely from an elitist perspective, represented by constraint, monopolization of power, dominance, and manipulation (Dahrendorf, 1959; Hyman et al., 2001).

Alternatively, the more pluralist consensus models emphasize decision making and resulting social change as the result of shared values, needs, wants, and agreement among community members (Dahrendorf, 1959; Hyman et al., 2001; Armstrong, 2006; Reed and McIlveen, 2006). Generally, those following a populist approach emphasize an integrative model which reflects society as being relatively stable as it meets the common needs of its members. Social interaction is central to this process of consensus and represents the communal efforts of people within a locality (Wilkinson, 1991). However, consensus does not necessarily mean an open acceptance of ideas and decisions. More often, it represents a process where community members reach agreement and compliance with needs and wants that are reflective of the broader community (Wilkinson, 1991; Israel and Beaulieu, 1990; Luloff and Bridger, 2003; Varley and Curtin, 2006; Reed and McIlveen, 2006; Brennan and Luloff, 2007).

In addition to the traditional focus on conflict and consensus, there is an emerging literature on community conflict that argues that power and local decision making are contextual and not necessarily just the result of conflict or consensus (Daniels and Walker, 2001). This perspective argues that effective local decision making emerges from collaborative efforts representing a wide range of local interests. In contrast to consensus, such an approach brings together a wide range of diverse local interests to effectively plan and maximize the use of local resources. Understanding how community power is concentrated and decisions made is essential for understanding the forms power may take and how it is wielded. We turn to this discussion next.

Faces and Dimensions of Power

Five contexts of power relationships are often identified: threat, authority, influence, manipulation, and force (Bachrach and Baratz, 1970). *Threat* power is a rational concept based on the relationship between two or more parties. It is based on compliance with requests or orders by one group as a result of pressure and deprivations by another. This concept is based on reason in that the second party must perceive the threats presented to them and view them as valid considerations. While threat power may work for a short period of time, it tends to arouse resentment and consequently less success, so that long-term implications for sustaining this type of power are limited.

Authority can be similar to threat power, when it is based not on the immediate threat to deprive individuals of something, but on the perceived ability to do so. Authority is found in a belief that those in power maintain legitimacy and a right to that power (Weber, 1957; Coser and Howe, 1977). This authority can take many forms. Some forms rest on a belief in the legitimacy and legality of laws, rules, and the rights of those in power to issue commands. More traditional authority is based on an established belief in the tradition, sanctity, and legitimacy of those exercising authority under them. Similarly, some people are charismatic and their authority centers on people's devotion to the specific and extraordinary characteristics of an individual person, and of the orders given by this person. Finally, authority can rest on an attachment to a set of values or belief systems that is the object of intense commitment.

Influence is a second form of power and involves a belief that a person making a request deserves to, or needs to be, obeyed. Lukes (1974) saw this as the cornerstone of power structures. The ability to influence behavior sets the stage for agenda setting and quiescence (Dahl, 1961; Lukes, 1974; Gaventa, 1980). Obedience and influence may result from who the person is in the community (reputation or respect), or from agreement with the request itself (as a result of discussion and debate). In this setting, one person has influence over others to the extent that the first causes the second to change their course of action.

Manipulation is an invisible power characterized by doing what another wants without being aware of it. In this situation there is a conflict of values in that one person would not take the action without being manipulated. Lukes (1974) and Gaventa (1980) stress the ability of this form of power in shaping agendas and public perceptions of power holders. These abilities allow local elites to dictate local decision making without needing to resort to a final form of power.

Finally, *force* is obvious power. Force involves the application of severe sanctions threatened in a power relationship. In this setting, action is taken against a person's will. The key to the power relationship is whoever chooses the ultimate action.

Building on these contexts, Boulding (1989) distinguishes three forms of power. *Destructive power* refers to the capacity to destroy something or someone. It can sometimes be used constructively, but is most often used to enforce some kind of threat or sanction that has been ignored. It includes killing, injury, and the destruction of property, often by using weapons. *Productive* (or sometimes called *economic*) *power* reflects the ability to obtain something wanted by means of exchange. Following this reasoning, the more an individual has to give in exchange (money, tangible items, labor, knowledge, etc.), the more power they have. Economic power can be acquired temporarily by taking things away from others, but ultimately individuals need to be able to produce more funds or resources to sustain their power. *Knowledge power* (Hyman et al., 2001) represents a special form of productive power and it can play an important role in local action. Given the effects of globalization and the development of a knowledge economy, developing or acquiring this power may become an increasingly important focus of community agency. *Knowledge power* is based on the accumulation of information, skills, and experiences that provide people with a competitive advantage in taking a course of action. *Integrative power* refers to the capacity to get people to act out of respect, care, affinity, or love. The role of integrative power in maintaining a social structure is both, its most important and its least recognized or understood element (Boulding, 1989; Hyman et al., 2001).

With all of these forms of power, the issue of access to various resources and their exploitation becomes central. Those with access to such resources, or those with the capacity to mobilize dispersed resources, accumulate power. With these resources, power is exhibited in destructive, productive, or integrative ways.

Theoretical Perspectives on Power

The concept of power and its role in broad social change has often been at the core of macro-level classic and contemporary theory. Most often cited in this context is the work of Marx, where the holders of power controlled all major aspects of society at the expense of the powerless (Coser and Howe, 1977; Marx, 1994). So absolute was their monopolization of resources that revolution and violent social change were the only likely means of redistributing power among the masses. Gramsci (1971) expands the work of Marx to include the ideas of ideological hegemony as a controlling tool of the elite. Regardless of how powerful and omnipresent they are, ruling elites cannot sustain themselves through force and threats alone. To achieve long-term sustainable power, the popular support of the

The Power of Community **83**

powerless must be obtained to legitimize the regime and maintain stability (Gramsci, 1971; Boggs, 1976; Entwistle, 1979; Scott, 1990). Such support allows power holders and their associates to become integrated into the social structure, so that their presence is seen as a natural condition. This sets the stage for long-term monopolization of power.

C. Wright Mills, in *The Power Elite* (1956), explains power as being monopolized at all levels by coalitions of social and economic elites. Such individuals represent business leaders, government officials, and prestigious families who dictate local life and control access to opportunities by the wider population. Such individuals bond together in an attempt to retain and expand their power holdings. These power holders are also linked by a stratified system in which they bond through common groups, class, organizations, schools, institutions, and social circles. As a result, a more tightly defined structure is evident than would be found in a more diverse pluralist setting. Here, power does not need to be explicitly evident in political or other settings. Instead, it can remain masked and/or hidden at a level where non-decision characterizes local resident life and potentials for social change (Mills, 1956; Domhoff, 1986; Domhoff, 2007; Gallardo and Stein, 2007). Elite power is also characterized by the ability to dictate who runs for political offices, is appointed to decision-making roles, or has a chance to bring issues forward for public discussion (Mills, 1956; Gaventa, 1980; Beaver and Cohen, 2004). Similarly, in the works of Parsons (1977) and other functionalists, power is seen as an integral part of a bureaucracy designed to maintain structure and expected behaviors. Social change, particularly the redistribution of power relations and ruling elites, is unwanted and undesirable.

The above perspectives tend to focus at the macro level. While important, they fail to explore the origins, mechanism, and processes of power at the micro or community level. More contemporary theoretical perspectives, such as interactional theory and social capital perspectives, have acknowledged power at this level, but like their predecessors have often viewed power as a given or the natural outcome of individual efficacy or collective action. While addressing broader processes leading to the emergence of community, attention to the nuances of the power dynamics have been limited. An exception has been the work of Gaventa (1980), which explored the detailed workings of power at the community level.

Power and Powerlessness

Perhaps one of the best and most thorough explorations of community power can be found in Gaventa's *Power and Powerlessness: Quiescence and Rebellion in an Appalachian Valley* (1980). The author argues that community power is far more complex than previous research and theory would suggest. Common explanations, such as poverty, social status, and traditional expectations, are not sufficient explanations for powerlessness. Gaventa suggests power be viewed as a multidimensional process, which results in a variety of outcomes and relationships.

The first dimension of power is characterized by the ability of one group to prevail over another in bargaining over the resolution of key issues. Those with more social, political, and economic resources generally have more bargaining power. In this setting, grievances and challenges raised by the powerless are quickly defeated in traditional political or legal systems.

Building on these conditions, the second dimension is found. This dimension is characterized by a set of values, beliefs, institutions, rituals, and procedures fostered by elites which place them in a position of advantage at the expense of others. This level allows elites to control the actual emergence of issues or their ability to be addressed in any formal setting. Through force, threat, precedent, or formal and informal pressures, the issues of the powerless fail to emerge in the legal or political systems. The exercising of threat, force, and other drastic means is however only sufficient to hold power in the short term (Gramsci, 1971; Boggs, 1976; Entwistle, 1979; Scott, 1990). To facilitate long-term control by ruling elites, power must take on another dimension.

Gaventa's third dimension represents the social construction of meanings that foster a sense of powerlessness among certain groups. It is this level of control which is most unique, and in the long term most commanding. Shaped by social, political, and historical conditions, quiescence emerges when the powerless provide elites with near-mythic abilities and adopt the ideologies dictated by them. In this setting, the powerless are manipulated into reconstructing their worldview in accordance with that of the ruling elites. Force, coercion, or threat is unnecessary, as the powerless have taken on the ideas and beliefs which serve to justify the interests, behaviors, and actions of local elites.

This condition is similar to the ideological hegemony described by Scott (1990) and Gramsci (1971). By establishing an ideological bond between the powerful and the powerless, the actions of elites are legitimized and seen as characteristic of normal life. While the powerless may not be entirely content, they view conditions as normal, not the dominating actions of controlling elites. Scott (1990) further delineates two types of hegemony: thin and thick. The former is indicative of an environment where local residents, while potentially harboring resentments, accept local order and power structures as inevitable. Alternately, thick hegemony reflects an environment where the powerless are manipulated to believe that local conditions are as good as they possibly could get, and therefore just and fair.

Gaventa stresses that these dimensions do not act alone. They are interdependent and reinforce each other on the basis of context and social reactions of community members. According to Gaventa (1980:168):

> Once having prevailed in the decision-making of the organization (first dimension), the leaders develop barriers for the exclusion of certain participants and issues (second dimension), having a further effect upon their consciousness of their own power (third dimension).

While Gaventa provides needed insights into the emergence of power structures, and answers the question of how and why power structures are propagated, his work does not clearly identify the mechanisms for inserting local residents into this

The Power of Community   **85**

process. Neither does he present an explanation of how local-level actions by the powerless are sustained. We suggest an interactional perspective of community helps clarify this process. Wilkinson (1991:24–25) began a discussion of how and why community can confront quiescence:

> The argument that territoriality is class hegemony posing as community, while no doubt true in some cases ... generally underestimates the tendency for quiescence to become conflict (Gaventa, 1980) and the potential for conflict to encourage community development. ... Quiescence changes into conflict when conditions permit a challenge to inequality. The reason this occurs is not because people are forced to give up a treasured state of peaceful subservience but because community – a powerful natural bond – demands that inequality be challenged.

Community is obviously key to challenging quiescence. However, Wilkinson appears to suggest an inevitable process, which the evidence does not always show to be true. We believe the role of interactional capacities or community agency is central to starting the process whereby quiescence is challenged, prevailing doctrines questioned, and local residents empowered. Yet this capacity brings with it the choice to act or not act. An understanding of the interplay between agency and choice is therefore essential. Agency facilitates the emergence of collective capacity and community itself (Wilkinson, 1991; Luloff, 1990; Luloff and Bridger, 2003; Brennan, 2007; Brennan and Luloff, 2007).

A Field Theoretical Approach to Community Power

To understand the emergence of power, we view the community from a field theoretical perspective which emphasizes the roles of local interaction and community agency as the basis for the emergence of community. Community field theory views locality as a place where people live and meet their daily needs together (Wilkinson, 1991; Luloff and Bridger, 2003; Theodori, 2005; Brennan, 2007). In this framework, a local society is seen as a comprehensive network of associations that meet common needs and express common interests. Such associations and the realization of common interests occur around, and are made possible through, social interaction. Interaction is therefore the essential element of community.

All local societies have distinct and diverse social fields or groups where residents act to achieve various self-interests and goals (Wilkinson, 1991). How these individual fields are organized and interact with each other has a great deal to do with how power is distributed within a local society. The community field emerges through the process of coordinating the individual social fields and it reflects purposive community-wide efforts. It cuts across class lines, organized groups, and other entities within a local population by focusing on the general and common needs of all residents. This encompassing field is similar to other individual social fields, but differs in that it pursues the general interests and needs of the entire community (Wilkinson, 1991; Bridger and Luloff, 1999; Luloff and Bridger, 2003; Brennan et al., 2005; Brennan and Luloff, 2007).

The emergence of the community field is affected by the context of local life, but more directly is facilitated by purposive interaction among the diverse residents of a locality. The exercise of power in relation to the emergence of the community field is therefore a fundamental concern. Power can be used to facilitate social interaction, or to suppress it. As Wilkinson (1991: 17) notes, "community implies all types of relations that are natural among people, and if interaction is suppressed, community is limited." To this extent, as interaction is limited, disaffection as a result of fragmentation, anomie, and alienation occur, hindering community from emerging (Luloff and Swanson, 1995; Arcidiacono et al., 2007).

Such a focus on interaction does not imply that structural or system level characteristics are unimportant. Nor does it presuppose a romantic or utopian view of community that is devoid of conflict and self-interest. Indeed, the local economy, sociodemographics, organizations, natural resources, and institutions are vital to the make-up of the community and its residents (Luloff and Bridger, 2003; Brennan et al., 2005; Brennan, 2007). However, they serve only as the backdrop for local participation and reveal little about the motivations and ability of local people to come together to address common needs. Such collective capacity may occur in varying degrees and often in uninspiring, yet essential, forms (Luloff and Swanson, 1995).

As residents and groups interact over issues important to all of them, what has come to be known as community agency, or the capacity for local action and resiliency, emerges (Wilkinson, 1991; Luloff and Bridger, 2003; Brennan and Luloff, 2007). Agency reflects the building of local relationships that increase the adaptive capacity of local people within a common territory. Agency can therefore be seen as the capacity of people to manage, utilize, and enhance those resources available to them in addressing locality-wide issues (Wilkinson, 1991; Bridger and Luloff, 1999; Luloff and Swanson, 1995; Luloff and Bridger, 2003; Brennan, 2007). This is the basis for the development of the community field. As Luloff and Swanson (1995: 2) note:

> The collective capacity of volition and choice, however narrowed by structural conditions, makes the notion of community agency important in understanding community well-being. Just like the individuals that compose them, communities make choices and act on them. But communities are much more than the simple sum of their individuals. How they make these choices, how their perceptions of local issues are constructed, and the ability of the members of the community to find and process information are important factors in the utilization of their economic and social resources.

The key component to this process is the creation and maintenance of linkages and channels of interaction among local social fields that otherwise are directed toward more limited interests (Luloff and Bridger, 2003; Theodori, 2005;

Brennan et al., 2005; Varley and Curtin, 2006; Brennan and Luloff, 2007). Such actions connect social fields and represent the development of the community field. Through interaction, common needs that cut across individual fields and the means to address them are identified. As a result, local people are linked more inclusively and are able to focus on a wider range of community issues. The culmination of this process is the emergence of community. These community interactions, in turn, shape the power capacity of local residents (Wilkinson, 1991; Luloff and Bridger, 2003; Brennan et al., 2005).

The emergence of agency is not always an easy process and is difficult in the face of established opposition from elites. Often, communities are characterized by elites who, formally or secretly, discourage collective mobilization that leads to agency. Under conditions of disaffection and acquiescence, local citizens may believe they are incapable or acting or choose not to act. In this light, Luloff and Swanson (1995: 4) state:

> Central obstacles for community development include overcoming both the under-utilization of local capacities for effective community agency and the institutionalization of undemocratic and elitist local development decision-making processes. We argue that when community agency is limited to the interests of the local elite, regardless how paternalistic, it is inherently restricted.

While the emergence of agency may encounter obstacles, it is far from impossible to achieve. Indeed, exploitation and resulting grievances may serve as the catalyst for local citizens to band together. Collective actions in the form of protests, boycotts, rebellions, challenges to prevailing ideologies, and other activities may emerge. Such actions are relatively uncommon, but emerge when the ability exists for local residents to interact and reach agreements over general needs, and have the potential to mobilize and establish local and extralocal alliances.

Community agency can be seen as a cornerstone of local power, where the ability to mobilize a broad range of local interests is essential to meeting general needs and an equitable utilization of resources. This can be seen in the work of Wilkinson (1991) and others (Luloff and Bridger, 2003; Brennan, 2007; Brennan and Luloff, 2007) where distributive justice is a central element in community well-being. Wilkinson (1991: 73) stresses the importance of this equity:

> Equity in a broader sense than equity-in-exchange refers to human recognition and endorsement of the ultimate *fact* of human equality, a fact underlying even the most uneven systems of distribution of access to such goods as material resources, life chances, and prestige. People are equally human, and recognition of this simple fact, along with the incorporation of this recognition into purposive actions to remove inequalities, would facilitate communication and encourage affirmative, accurate interpersonal responses.

The implications of local capacity building, community agency, and distributive justice are significant. Such conditions set the stage for understanding local responses

88 M. Brennan and G. Israel

to power elites and the emergence of grassroots power. Using this field theoretical perspective, we present a theoretical model of understanding how these conditions shape choices, consequences, and the emergence of community power.

A Theoretical Model for the Emergence of Community Power

The building of local capacity and implementation of collective action strategies can create power (Luloff, 1990; Wilkinson, 1991; Luloff and Swanson, 1995; Brennan, 2007). However, without continued support for the processes of community development and the linkage of social fields, local efforts will be limited in their ability to amass and maintain power (Summers, 1986; Luloff, 1990; Bridger and Luloff, 1999). We suggest power, local capacity, and community action can be better understood within a set of choice and consequence scenarios. Choice can be seen as the decision to pursue action or remain inactive, whereas consequences reflect the positive and negative impacts of both action and inaction. Power exists in all of these scenarios, yet is wielded by different interests in distinctly different ways. It is also the case that different social fields have different opportunities, agendas, and access to resources which might shape choice. Linking social fields is therefore essential. We present four scenarios to explore the conditions which explain local power (Table 6.1). Using these, we can identify the power characteristics, outcomes of the use of power, and who benefits from such use.

TABLE 6.1 The Choice and Consequences of Power

		Choice Setting	
		No Choice	Choice
Consequence	*Negative*	*Characteristics*: Minimal agency or collective capacity to act; quiescence; disaffection among local residents; unconnected social fields; oppression at the hands of the elite; abandonment of hope by locals for overcoming power obstacles.	*Characteristics*: Presence of agency or collective capacity, yet failure to achieve goals. Interacting, but not fully connected, social fields. Development 'in' community where locals interact with elites to enhance segments of the locality but not the entire community.
		Outcomes: Negative life environment with little concern for the masses. Fragmentation of powerless groups.	*Outcomes*: Action seen as a one off occurrence or as successful goal attainment. Action focused on select segments of the community. Failure signals end of local empowerment.
		Benefits: Private.	*Benefits*: Primarily Private and limited Public.
		Example: Exploited labor in a company town; disenfranchised racial or ethnic minorities.	*Example*: Growth Machine and the 'great Buffalo hunt.' Building industrial parks that lay empty.

(Continued)

The Power of Community   **89**

TABLE 6.1 (*Continued*)

		Choice Setting	
		No Choice	Choice
Consequence	Positive	*Characteristics*: Minimal agency or collective capacity to act; quiescence; minimally connected social fields; hidden oppression at the hands of the elite; belief by populace that action is not needed, as the elites will take care of them.	*Characteristics*: Agency, empowerment, and collective capacity. Strongly connected social fields. Development 'of' community. Communities achieve goals, negotiating a place at the decision-making table, mobilizing to facilitate change; fail to achieve goals, yet mobilizing to continue their efforts.
		Outcomes: Good/tolerable life based on the arbitrary positive treatment by elites. *Benefits*: Private and Public. *Example*: 'Town fathers' that take care of the community; the "free rider" problem of apathetic, uninvolved, or acquiescent residents.	*Outcomes*: Episodic action seen as one in the scope of many. Community and development seen in the actions of individuals, not goal attainment. Enhanced social well-being. *Benefits*: Public. *Example*: Community unites to defeat unwanted extralocal development attempts; restoration of significant local historical site and development of cultural center.

No Choice – Negative Consequence – Ritualized Agency

In this first scenario, local citizen action is suppressed, citizens choose not to act, or simply lack this capacity altogether. In this environment, decision making is controlled by local and/or extralocal elites, with minimal or no contribution from local citizens. Similarly, interaction among diverse social fields is limited or, in extreme cases, strictly controlled. Such environments are often characterized by the exploitation of local natural and human resources, leading to an overall negative community quality of life (Hunter, 1953; Gaventa, 1980; Gallardo and Stein, 2007).

Benefits from such a power arrangement go to private interests, and rarely benefit the general public. Such conditions mirror Gaventa's (1980) description of parts of Appalachia and highlight his three dimensions of power. There, extralocal control over resources and economies left communities at the mercy of power-holding elites and their industries. This control, and the choice or inability of local residents to act, is often the result of overt force and threat. In the end, quiescence emerges, where the worldviews of the powerless social fields are transformed to support and comply with local elites. In the short term, power holders are perceived by local residents as being too big, omnipresent, politically connected, and economically advantaged to be overcome. More importantly, in the long term, they may also be seen as the legitimate controllers of local life, economies, and services, who need not be questioned.

Yet, this form of oppressive control is difficult to maintain, leading to power being a fleeting condition in some settings. Such oppression in parts of Appalachia, for example, led to revolt and protest which eventually diminished the strict control of extralocal power holders (Gaventa, 1980). However, this ability to effect such change was often part of a wider social environment. In this example, the natural resource base which fed power structures became more unstable as markets for resources diminished. With this loss, the ability of extralocals to strictly control all aspects of local life also declined. These market conditions coincided with wider social, economic, and political change where regulations, unions, and legal rights (brought on by other coordinated communities under less despotic control) signaled an end to the domination previously seen. Yet, in other communities, quiescence by the powerless was firmly entrenched and the prevailing ideology still remains today.

It may also be the case that a form of suppressed or ritualized agency can be seen. In this context of controlled agendas, limited agency might emerge during proscribed community events. Venues of interaction organized, sponsored, and most importantly sanctioned by elites can set the stage for a minimal local capacity. Through formal community and corporate events such as old home days, 4th of July celebrations, and other events endorsed by elites, the potential for social fields to interact and for agency to emerge are present, albeit in a controlled setting.

In such settings, the question of how disaffection and quiescence can be overcome to achieve a more equitable environment remains. As a beginning point, social fields that otherwise are not interacting and communicating must be encouraged to do so. This is the basis for capacity building, and, more importantly, a beginning for the powerless to break or challenge the ideological bond that exists between the power holders and their subservient population. In this scenario, in particular, structural change and ideological change need to be seen as part of the same concerted effort.

To do this, the powerless must be able to conceive action, mobilize citizens, create awareness, establish partnerships, and foster sustainable action plans that counter the prevailing environment of the powerful (Gaventa, 1980; Wilkinson, 1991; Pigg, 1999). The powerless also need to establish coalitions, partnerships, and alliances with other powerless groups inside, and possibly external to, the community (Pigg, 1999). In this scenario, the environment for significant capacity building is likely insufficient to immediately challenge local elites, but may be sufficient to establish connections and partnerships with similarly disenfranchised extralocal groups, elites, and organizations (Gallardo and Stein, 2007). On the basis of these conditions, the powerless need to develop capacities, issues, and actions if social change is to emerge. They must act when the powerful are weakened, or create conditions which can lead to their being weakened such as the establishment of alliances with extralocal forces. For example, in recent years Appalachia has seen significant local action and extralocal alliances in the face of mountain-top removal and other coal extraction activities. Such alliances and connections to larger environmental protection efforts have empowered and brought together local social fields to challenge power holders in their communities. Through such partnerships, awareness is spread, coalitions established, and actions coordinated to facilitate local and more widespread social change. It may also be the case that the ability of local citizens to obtain knowledge power can help facilitate the emergence of community agency. This knowledge, in a variety of forms (such as legal, skills, information, education), may prove essential in advancing grassroots power and establishing alliances outside the community. Through such structure building, the powerless are empowered to confront the local barriers to power and become part of the decision-making process (Wilkinson, 1991; Luloff and Swanson, 1995; Bridger and Luloff, 1999; Arcidiacono et al., 2007; Gallardo and Stein, 2007).

No Choice – Positive Consequence – Abandoned Agency

In contrast to the despotic picture painted above is a gentler, but nonetheless still controlled, scenario. Here, local life is pleasant, yet power remains private, benefiting elites (Duncan, 1999; Beaver and Cohen, 2004). Social fields remain, at best, minimally connected. The inaction of local citizens is rewarded with social, economic, and other support from powerful elites. Such conditions reflect the firmly entrenched quiescence outlined by Gaventa (1980) and the ideological hegemony presented by Scott (1990). As a result of manipulation and control by elites, the powerless have clearly altered their worldview to openly accept and support the elites without question. Under this benevolent framework, local citizens are provided for, much like a parent sees after a child. Examples of this condition can be found in many communities where the often beloved 'town fathers' hold enormous sway in the decisions affecting local life. Such conditions mask an inactive community, where interactive capacities remain controlled. A tolerable life for citizens comes at the price of their capacity to act. In effect this scenario, while pleasant on the surface, may be direr to local communities than the previous repressive environment.

This citizen response to power is different in theory and practice to the previous scenario, which was based on force, threat, and direct domination. While these tools of domination remain hidden in the background in the event that power holders need them, in this scenario acquiescing to power and complacency comes more in terms of allegiance, love, honor, and respect for those making decisions (Pateman, 1970; Duncan, 1999; Beaver and Cohen, 2004). It is assumed power holders are legitimate and act in the best interests of the populace. Additionally, citizens often believe they are not capable of acting at the same standards of local power elites, and therefore leave action to those they perceive will act on their behalf (Beaver and Cohen, 2004). Pateman (1970) sees this as reflective of authoritative structures in institutions (schools, family, and workplace) where people spend most of their lives. Such environments are often designed to deliberately prevent local people from acting. As a result, these conditions undermine the socialization process, reduce interaction and cooperation, and hinder the involvement of diverse local residents in the collective decision-making process. This acts to concentrate, retain, and reinforce the power of local elites (Luloff and Swanson, 1995).

In this scenario the potential for citizens joining together in collective action most likely is not seen as a threat or concern to power elites, as community mobilization against elites would likely be seen by the powerless themselves as a betrayal. While in a different context from the previous scenario, the failure to act remains an abandonment of citizen capacity for action. The potential for agency may exist, but citizens (while aware of their ability to act) are convinced that there is no utility in doing so. As local residents become convinced elites are acting in their best interests, their ability to act or rebel becomes even more diminished. The long-term result is that the powerless may not be able to overcome the inertia of inaction, even in the face of desperate need, and thus rely on local elites.

In this setting, community agency would have the potential to emerge and contribute to social change. However, a significant challenge to the ideological hegemony that exists is first needed. Gramsci (1971) called for counter-hegemony to be cultivated to challenge the prevailing conditions propagated by ruling elites. Change must be sought not only to the structures of the local community, but, equally important, to the prevailing ideology. To counter existing ideologies the powerless need to be made aware of agenda setting and the visible or hidden ideologies of the powerful. They must also be exposed to other groups which can reinforce the belief that their treatment at the hands of the elite is not normal, but distinctly controlled and different from that of other communities. Before local citizens can act, they need to be able to question and challenge the rights of the elite to rule.

To foster community agency, capacity-building activities that include purposive and focused interaction among social fields are essential. Such interaction and conscious efforts to recruit and involve citizens from all segments of the community would develop connections and ties across social fields, therefore providing a basis for action. It is important that an initial project be selected on the basis of its likelihood for achieving success, because this can become the basis for challenging the ideology that elites can best run the community. In addition, the establishment of explicit processes for hearing all local voices and reconciling differences (but not necessarily reaching consensus) among social fields would lead to a more informed and united community that could challenge prevailing ideologies.

Local citizens' groups can also tap external allies in an effort to change the local power equation within their communities. Such alliances would indicate the limited and inherent capacities of local elites to effectively meet local needs, by highlighting their weaknesses and vulnerabilities. Ultimately, in both "no choice" scenarios, the lack of local interaction among social fields, limited collective capacity, propagation of elite ideologies, and lack of community itself allows an environment to flourish in which existing power structures and elites operate unrestrictedly. In response, networks, interaction, and connections among social fields must first be established and maintained. From these, challenges to prevailing ideologies and power structures can then be made.

Choice – Negative Consequence – Incomplete Agency

In this scenario, a more complete form of agency emerges but fails to achieve desired goals or broader community well-being. Benefits from such a setting are

The Power of Community **93**

designed for the general needs of the community, but remain largely in the private realm. Social fields interact, but fail to exhibit strong channels of communication and purposive interaction. Examples of this scenario include locally based efforts to establish an industrial park coupled to the failure to recruit industry or related businesses, or action that fosters economic growth for some industries and inhibits growth on others. Local capacity may lead to a concerted effort for development, yet this effort may be incomplete, resulting in ineffective actions. In part, this may reflect a narrow focus on specific needs of some community segments (infrastructure and the economy) at the expense of the larger community context (Immergluck, 2005; Israel and Beaulieu, 1990).

While usually presented in a positive light, collective action need not always have this result. The choice to act is not easy or without negative repercussions. Collective action can threaten local power holders and result in obstacles, conflict, and retribution. Similarly, a minimal, unrepresentative, or incomplete organizing of local residents may inadvertently reinforce existing power structures. Ill-prepared groups might be easily manipulated or convinced to align themselves with local power-holding elites. Negative impacts can also be seen in the failure of local mobilizations to achieve goals. Their failure may result in more negative outcomes, such as a loss of confidence among members in their abilities to facilitate change or decreased status associated with being on the losing side. In either situation, without purposive and controlled plans for continued action, local efforts can falter.

From a community development perspective, the building of collective capacity may result in less than positive conditions if the community development process is not maintained. The mobilization and organization of residents, leading to the emergence of agency and community, takes time, effort, and most importantly commitment. Under situations of extreme threat, this process may naturally emerge, such as when communities face severe economic, health, or natural resource threats. All are clear indications of a common general community need, capable of drawing a wide range of citizens into action. Such action is often characterized as a "one-off" situation, where the success or failure of the action signals the end of collective capacity building and efforts to link social fields (Immergluck, 2005). In the end, these responses may do little to contribute to local well-being, long-term capacity building, and/or the emergence of community. Indeed, such limited activities might detract from community building by setting a negative tone in circumstances of defeat and also by highlighting the differences and disagreements that may initially emerge as disparate groups come together to achieve common ground (Varley and O'Cearbhaill, 1999; Immergluck, 2005). In this setting, the collective action process may actually end with these disagreements, fostering disaffection and further fragmenting the powerless (Luloff and Swanson, 1995).

Similarly, community building activities may be too narrowly focused toward select segments of the locality (economy, health care, schools, etc.). This represents what Summers (1986) referred to as development 'in' community, and usually involve a group of homogenous local individuals and groups who liaise with power holders internal and external to the community. This is seen as distinctly different from the development 'of' community, which is characterized by broad-based citizen contributions to decision making and the building of diverse local capacities for long-term sustainable development.

This scenario also reflects the 'growth machine' presented by Molotch (1976), in which competition among power holders over high-value land drives growth, sprawl, and urban development. Such activities, while important, do little to develop broad-based citizen action. Agency can emerge in these settings, but the focus on select social fields may inhibit wider social development. Failure may also result from the lack of resources rather than disagreement.

To advance development, local capacity building might better facilitate access of additional local or extralocal resources. Such mobilization would also help reconcile differences of opinion among diverse local residents, which in turn would lead to the identification of more clearly defined general community needs that all groups could work toward. Without broad-based local capacity building future development efforts may remain unsuccessful, as well as opening the door for manipulation by elites and potentially the emergence of quiescence among those with little power.

Choice – Positive Consequence – Authentic Agency

The fourth scenario, albeit uncommon among contemporary communities, focuses on the positive face of action which is most often presented to highlight the potentials of community action, civic engagement, and grassroots social change. This setting includes the ability of local citizens to access and manage resources, prevent domination by elites, link various social fields or interest groups, and establish a foundation for current and future action (Wilkinson, 1991; Duncan, 1999; Brennan and Luloff, 2007; Brennan, 2007). Benefits of action are clearly focused on the public and are designed to meet the general needs of the community. Social fields interact in a consistent and substantive manner. In this scenario, active communities experience a variety of conditions, including goal achievement, negotiating a place at the decision-making table, mobilizing to facilitate change, and failing to achieve their goals yet mobilizing to continue in their efforts.

Coalitions of residents are broad based and representative of the diversity of communities. Community and its development are seen in the continuous actions of individuals, not goal attainment (Wilkinson, 1991; Duncan, 1999; Luloff and Bridger, 2003; Brennan, 2007). Here, in their purest sense, interaction, collective mobilization of local residents, and local capacity building lead to the emergence of agency and community. This allows for the dispersed power of diverse local residents to be harnessed, overcoming the control of elites (Gaventa, 1980; Varley and Curtin, 2006; Brennan, 2007).

This scenario represents what Summers (1986) describes as the development 'of' community. The bringing together of diverse local groups to develop plans for sustainable long-term action is the basis for the development of community (Brennan et al., 2005; Varley and Curtin, 2006; Brennan, 2007). Efforts to establish

The Power of Community **95**

channels of communication, interaction, and capacity building are essential, and represent an entity greater than the sum of its parts. This collective entity is a force that enables local citizens to obtain power and navigate the nebulous local and extralocal channels of power. Equally importantly, it creates an environment where quiescence and the ill intentions of elites do not emerge to dominate local life.

Conclusion

This article has explored and conceptualized community power. This often nebulous concept is essential to local community life and the relationships that take place within it. Drawing from the work of Gaventa and others, we have examined the complexity of power, its processes, and its context. Building on previous theory and research, we portray local power in a choice/consequence model interpreted through a field theoretical perspective.

In all of the power scenarios discussed, community capacity and agency are central to the empowerment of local citizens. The first step involves identifying the various social fields that make up the community, their roles in decision making, and the linkages that do or should exist between them. Such an assessment provides a description of both the community power structure and the community field. The key to developing the latter is the articulation and creation of linkages among the diverse individual social fields. Through this process the potential exists for common ground to be reached and the dispersed power of local residents to be consolidated. Such activities are a starting point for strengthening the community field and the development of community. Equally importantly, this process is essential in allowing the powerless to remain cognizant of their ability to act, and to the emergence of quiescence.

In the end, understanding power does not serve our ability to monopolize or manipulate its hold on local communities, but more correctly to facilitate social change. In an age of devolution, declining service budgets, globalization, and increasingly fragmented communities, our ability to coordinate resources, agendas, and actions to meet general community needs may in many ways signal survival for our communities. The establishment of channels of communication and interaction among those with and without power should not be seen as a threat to local power or agendas, nor an abandonment of their self-interests, but as a key to their long-term success and well-being.

References

Arcidiacono, C., Procentese, F., & DiNapoli, I. (2007). Youth, community belonging, planning and power. *Journal of Community and Applied Social Psychology,* 17(4), 280–295.

Armstrong, C.L. (2006). Revisiting structural pluralism: A two-dimensional conception of community power. *Mass Communication and Society,* 9(3), 287–300.

Bachrach, P., & Baratz, M.S. (1970). *Power and Poverty: Theory and Practice.* New York: Oxford University Press.

Beaver, W., & Cohen, E. (2004). Power in a rural county. *Sociological Spectrum,* 24(6), 629–650.

Boggs, C. (1976). *Gramsci's Marxism*. London: Pluto Press.

Boulding, K.E. (1989). *Three Faces of Power*. Newbury Park, CA: Sage Publications.

Brennan, M.A. (2007). The development of community in the west of Ireland: A return to Killala twenty years on. *Community Development Journal, 42*(3), 330–374.

Brennan, M.A., & Luloff, A.E. (2007). Exploring rural community agency differences in Ireland and Pennsylvania. *Journal of Rural Studies, 23,* 52–61.

Brennan, M.A., Luloff, A.E., & Finley, J.C. (2005). Building sustainable communities in forested regions. *Society and Natural Resources, 18*(9), 1–11.

Bridger, J., & Luloff, A.E. (1999). Toward an interactional approach to sustainable community development. *Journal of Rural Studies, 15,* 377–387.

Coser, L.A., & Howe, I. (1977). *The new conservatives: a critique from the left*. New York: New American Library.

Dahl, R.A. (1961). *Who governs? Democracy and power in an American city*. Yale studies in political science, 4. New Haven, CT: Yale University Press.

Dahrendorf, R. (1959). *Class and class conflict in industrial society*. Stanford, CA: Stanford University Press.

Daniels, S.E., & Walker, G.B. (2001). *Working through environmental conflict: The collaborative learning approach*. Westport, CT: Praeger.

Domhoff, G. (1986). *The power elite and the state: How policy is made in America*. New York, NY: A. de Gruyter.

Domhoff, G.W. (2007). Commentary: C. Wright Mills, power structure research, and the failures of mainstream political science. *New Political Science, 29*(1), 97–114.

Duncan, C. (1999). *Worlds Apart: Why Poverty Persists in Rural America*. New Haven, CT: Yale University Press.

Ebenstein, William (1991). *Great Political Thinkers*. New York, NY: Holt, Rinehart and Winston.

Entwistle, H. (1979). *Antonio Gramsci: Conservative schooling for radical politics*. London: Routledge.

Fisher, A.T., & Sonn, C.C. (2007). Power in community psychology research and practice. *Journal of Community and Applied Social Psychology, 17*(4), 255–257.

Gallardo, J., & Stein, T. (2007). Participation, power and racial representation: Negotiating nature-based and heritage tourism development in the rural south. *Society and Natural Resources, 20*(7), 597–611.

Gaventa, J. (1980). *Power and Powerlessness: Quiescence and Rebellion in an Appalachian Valley*. Urbana, IL: University of Illinois Press.

Gramsci, A. (1971). *Selections from the Prison Notebooks*. London, UK: Lawrence and Wishart.

Groarke, M. (2004). Using community power against targets beyond the neighborhood. *New Political Science, 26*(2), 171–188.

Hobbes, Thomas (1960). *Leviathan*. Oxford, UK: Basil Blackwell.

Hunter, F. (1953). *Community power structure; a study of decision makers*. Chapel Hill, NC: University of North Carolina Press.

Hyman, D., McKnight, J., & Higdon, F. (2001). *Doing democracy: Conflict and consensus strategies for citizens, organizations, and communities*. New York, NY: Erudition Press.

Immergluck, D. (2005). Building power, losing power: The rise and fall of a prominent community economic development coalition. *Economic Development Quarterly, 19*(3), 211–224.

Israel, G.D., & Beaulieu, L.J. (1990). Community leadership. In A.E. Luloff and Louis A. Swanson (Eds.), *American Rural Communities*. Boulder, CO: Westview Press.

Lukes, S. (1974). *Power: A Radical View*. London, UK: MacMillan.

Luloff, A.E. (1990). Community and social change: How do small communities act? In A.E. Luloff and L.E. Swanson (Eds.), *American Rural Communities*. Boulder, CO: Westview Press.

Luloff, A.E., & Bridger, J. (2003). Community agency and local development. In D. Brown and L. Swanson (Eds.), *Challenges for Rural America in the Twenty-First Century*. University Park, PA: Pennsylvania State University Press.

Luloff, A.E. & Swanson, L. (1995). Community agency and disaffection: Enhancing collective resources. In L. Beaulieu and D. Mulkey (Eds.), *Investing in People: The Human Capital Needs of Rural America*. Boulder, CO: Westview Press.

Marx, K. (1994). *Selected Writings*. Indianapolis, IN: Hackett Publishing.

Mills, C.W. (1956). *The Power Elite*. New York: Oxford University Press.

Moffett, S., & Freund, B. (2004). Elite formation and elite bonding: Social structure and development in Durban. *Urban Forum*, 15(2), 134–161.

Molotch, Harvey (1976). The city as a growth machine. *The American Journal of Sociology*, 82(2), 309–332.

Parsons, T. (1977). *Social Systems and the Evolution of Action Theory*. New York, NY: Free Press.

Pateman, C. (1970). *Participation and Democratic Theory*. Cambridge, UK: Cambridge University Press.

Pigg, K. (1999). Community leadership and community theory: A practical synthesis. *Journal of the Community Development Society*, 30(2), 196–212.

Reed, M., & McIlveen, K. (2006). Towards a pluralistic civic science?: Assessing community forestry. *Society & Natural Resources*, 19, 591–607.

Rousseau, J. (1978). *On the Social Contract*. New York, NY: St Martins Press.

Scott, J. (1990). *Domination and the Arts of Resistance: Hidden Transcripts*. New Haven, CT: Yale University Press.

Stone, C. (1986). Power and social complexity. In D. Waste (Ed.), *Community Power: Directions for Future Research* (pp. 77–113). Thousand Oaks, CA: Sage.

Summers, G. (1986). Rural community development. *Annual Review of Sociology*, 12, 341–371.

Theodori, G. (2005). Community and community development in resource-based areas: Operational definitions rooted in an interactional perspective. *Society and Natural Resources*, 18(7), 661–669.

Varley, T., & Curtin, C. (2006). The politics of empowerment: Power, populism and partnership in rural Ireland. *Economic and Social Review*, 37(3), 423–446.

Varley, T., & O'Cearbhaill, D. (1999). Empowering Communities through Community Action in Rural Ireland: the Case of Muintir na T're. In R. Byron and J. Hutson (Eds.), *Local Enterprise on the North Atlantic Margin: Selected Contributions to the Fourteenth International Seminar on Marginal Regions*. London, UK: Ashgate.

Waste, D. (1986). *Community Power: Directions for Future Research*. Thousand Oaks, CA: Sage.

Weber, M. (1957). *The Theory of Social and Economic Organization*. Glencoe, IL: Free Press.

Wilkinson, Kenneth P. (1991). *The Community in Rural America*. Westport, CT: Greenwood Press.

7

THE TAMAQUA PARADOX

How History Shapes Social Capital and Local Economic Development Efforts[1]

Jeffrey C. Bridger, Paloma Z.C. Frumento, and Theodore R. Alter

Introduction

Over the past several decades, the concept of social capital has become an important component of strategies for building community and fostering economic development. Our purpose in this chapter is to assess the extent to which social capital theory functions to explain economic development activeness, using as a case study the community of Tamaqua, Pennsylvania. We begin with a brief overview of social capital theory, followed by a summary of a 2005 study designed to assess the relationship between social capital and economic development activeness in six rural Pennsylvania communities using a mixed-methods approach which included surveys, key informant interviews, and in-depth community histories. Our primary focus is the historical component, which illustrates how early decisions and actions influence contemporary events relating to economic and community development. This information provides the basis for critical analysis of the applicability of social capital to community and economic development. We argue that social capital theory may be an ineffective framework for development policy in some settings because it does not attend to the historical context that gives rise to alternative forms of rationality, power relations, and subsequent patterns of fractionalization and stratification. We suggest that a narrative approach helps to better understand these processes and their relationship to contemporary decision making. The chapter concludes with a discussion of implications for community development theory and practice.

Social Capital

Although the term 'social capital' appears to have first been coined in the early twentieth century, its recent popularity can be tied to the influential writings of Robert Putnam (1993; 1995; 1996; 2000). Putnam (2000, p. 19) stresses that the term

The Tamaqua Paradox **99**

... refers to connections among individuals – social networks and the norms of reciprocity and trustworthiness that arise from them. In that sense, social capital is closely related to what some have called "civic virtue." The difference is that "social capital" calls attention to the fact that civic virtue is most powerful when embedded in a dense network of reciprocal social relations.

The norms of generalized reciprocity and trustworthiness are the key components of this definition. Generalized reciprocity is characterized by a mutual expectation that a favor or benefit performed now will be repaid in the future. This norm is embodied in the following convention: "I'll do this for you now, without expecting anything immediately in return and perhaps without even knowing you, confident that down the road you or someone else will return the favor" (Putnam, 2000, p. 134). This combination of short-term altruism and long-term self-interest reconciles selfishness and social solidarity because all participants know they will benefit over time. Here, Putnam relies heavily on Coleman's (1990, p. 99) conceptualization of trust: "A rational actor will place trust ... if the ratio of the chance of gain to the chance of loss is greater than the ratio of the amount of potential loss to the amount of potential gain." Bridger and Luloff (2001, p. 467) note that this framework is predicated upon a rational actor model in which people are purposive agents who make deliberate choices to maximize their utility. Their behavior may be constrained by norms and social contexts, but, as Alexander (1992, p. 96) points out, people are ultimately still "discrete, separated, and independent individuals."

When the norm of generalized reciprocity is followed, opportunism can be more easily restrained and the potential for collective action enhanced. In communities where reciprocity is widely practiced, social and economic life are less fractious. And, as Putnam (2000, p. 135) argues, these communities have an economic advantage over less trustful places: "A society that relies on generalized reciprocity is more efficient than a distrustful society, for the same reason that money is more efficient than barter. Honesty and trust lubricate the inevitable frictions of social life."

When people are committed to the norm of generalized reciprocity, a valuable form of trust emerges. This is what Putnam (2000) calls social trust, which he defines as a willingness to give people the benefit of the doubt. Or, to put it in slightly different terms, social trust is captured by an overall belief that people are basically good and can be expected to do the right thing. According to Putnam (2000, pp. 136–137) communities with high levels of social trust produce citizens that are more active and more likely to take an interest in civic affairs:

Other things being equal, people who trust their fellow citizens volunteer more often, contribute more to charity, participate more often in politics and community organizations, serve more readily on juries, give blood more frequently, comply more fully with their tax obligations, are more tolerant of minority views, and display many other forms of civic virtue. ... In short, people who trust others, are all-round good citizens, and those more engaged in community life are both more trusting and more trustworthy.

In his most recent iteration of the concept, Putnam (2000) has introduced a distinction between bonding and bridging social capital. Bonding social capital is a 'sociological superglue' found in very dense, close-knit social networks. Bonding social capital tends to strengthen group solidarity and promotes specific forms of reciprocity. The employment niches that emerge when a particular ethnic group controls a sector of the local labor market are a good example of bonding social capital. Such solidarity might provide substantial benefits to one segment of the population, but it does not necessarily promote the interests of the broader community. In fact, as Putnam and Feldstein (2003) readily acknowledge, a community or society that has only bonding social capital is likely to be fragmented and unable to act collectively.

Bridging social capital, on the other hand, is similar to Granovetter's (1973) concept of weak ties. Instead of creating intimate bonds of solidarity, it builds linkages across social and economic distances. In doing so, bridging social capital provides people and organizations with access to information and resources that would otherwise not be available. And, perhaps most importantly, by creating relationships across class, ethnic, racial, and religious lines, bridging social capital fosters the social trust and norms of generalized reciprocity necessary for effective community action. For this reason, bridging social capital is arguably a more important factor in community and economic development. In its absence, development efforts are uncoordinated and focused on specific groups or neighborhoods (Putnam and Feldstein, 2003).

Study Overview

Putnam's (2000) elaboration and subsequent applications of social capital have become increasingly popular as a strategy for community and economic development. Despite this growing popularity, there is a lack of persuasive evidence documenting how and to what extent it contributes to specific outcomes (DeFilippis, 2001). A key question for community and economic development concerns the conditions that give rise to the norms of social trust and generalized reciprocity, and the implications of this context for development. This was a central focus of our 2005 United States Department of Agriculture (USDA), National Research Initiative study, in which we considered the role played by such factors as power, stratification, economic and labor history in the relationship between social capital and the level of economic development activeness[2] in selected rural Pennsylvania communities. We also consider the role of narrative interpretations of local and regional histories in influencing contemporary decision-making processes.

In order to facilitate a nuanced analysis of our case-study communities, we employed a mixed-methods approach. One set of data was derived from a survey instrument modeled after common national and international question sets

The Tamaqua Paradox **101**

(Bullen and Onyx, 1998; Davis et al., 2008; Edwards, 2004; Green and Fletcher, 2003; Grootaert et al., 2004; Grootaert and van Bastelaer, 2002; Howard et al., 2005; Narayan, 1998; Narayan and Cassidy, 2001; Pew Research Center, 1997; Saguaro Seminar, 2000). Composite measures were developed to assess the following indicators of social capital: individual well-being, individual efficacy, collective efficacy, norms of generalized and specific reciprocity, norms of tolerance and exclusion, norms of participation, generalized social trust, trust in specific known groups, trust in institutions, strength and density of informal networks, strength and density of formal networks, formal network structures, sources of information, and community satisfaction and attachment. Survey results were interpreted and contextualized through a series of key informant interviews and in-depth community histories.

The project focused on six communities in three counties: Schuylkill, Elk, and Tioga. Each reflects conditions that are common across rural Pennsylvania. Schuylkill County, in which Tamaqua is located, forms part of the anthracite region, which was historically dominated almost solely by coal and railroad companies. The development of Elk County, which contains part of the Allegheny National Forest, was linked to timber and related industries. Tioga County, located along the north-central border with New York, boasts a more diverse portfolio of natural resources, including timber, bituminous coal, iron ore, sandstone, and fire clay. Each county transitioned or attempted to transition to a manufacturing-based economy during the twentieth century, and several communities in each are in the process of translating both natural resources and local industrial and social heritage into the basis for a tourism industry. Each has suffered to some degree as the result of the current economic downturn and the outmigration of youth.

From each of these counties, we selected two communities that were similar with respect to structural characteristics (i.e. industrial mix, population, population change, and proximity to urban centers) but dissimilar with respect to levels of economic development activeness. As noted above, social capital theory suggests that surveys should have produced significantly different results between the paired communities; communities where respondents indicated strong norms of generalized reciprocity and high levels of social trust should have been more economically active than their counterparts with low levels of generalized reciprocity and social trust. Instead, differences between the paired communities in each county were statistically significant for only a small number of the composite measures listed above. However, all but one of the composite measures were statistically significant when analysis was widened to analyze differences across all six communities. This finding indicates that other characteristics at the county and regional level, including the social and economic histories and narratives, play an important role in shaping the development of different levels of social capital in rural communities.

In the following sections we will focus on one of these communities, Tamaqua, to illustrate the conceptual shortcomings inherent to social capital theory. Tamaqua is a particularly useful case because it was the only community in which there was a strong divergence between household survey data and the information provided in key informant interviews. In comparison with the other communities included in the study, survey respondents reported the highest overall social division score. This score measured perceptions of social divisions with regard to social class, level of education, race/ethnicity, religious views, political affiliation, and age. Tamaqua reported the highest scores for all categories with the exception of race/ethnicity, for which it came in second. In several instances, Tamaqua was highest by a wide margin. A combined total of 72.5 percent of respondents reported that social class divides people to a moderate or large extent, compared to 58.1 percent in the second-ranking community. A combined total of 73.1 percent of respondents reported that level of education divides people to a moderate or large extent, compared to 56.4 percent in the second-ranking community. The only social category for which less than half of respondents reported moderate or large social division was religion. Similarly, Tamaqua scored relatively low on indicators designed to measure norms of trust. By a small fraction, Tamaqua had the lowest level of average local trust, a measure which included trust in people in the community, trust in neighbors, trust in coworkers, and trust in church members. Tamaqua also ranked low with respect to the perceived impact of local institutions and organizations, trust for these groups of people or organizations, and participation in voluntary organizations. On average, respondents indicated that they participate in approximately two or three voluntary organizations. Finally, Tamaqua scored relatively low with regard to indicators designed to measure the level of diversity within local volunteer organizations and the level of cooperation between diverse groups.

These survey data conflict with information collected through key informant interviews with a variety of local leaders, which focused specifically on recent efforts to foster economic development. Key informants indicated that Tamaqua was characterized by high levels of social trust, norms of generalized reciprocity, participation and cooperation within and across diverse groups. Informants presented evidence that local leaders had opened up their planning and diversification of economic options early, and more than once, in a purposeful and vigorous fashion to volunteers across all strata in order to successfully achieve goals. By virtue of these characteristics and its strong planning mechanisms, they suggested, Tamaqua was in place to take advantage of opportunities to obtain outside funding and training when they became available.

In the remainder of this chapter, we argue that the concept of social capital does not account for the divergence between the high level of development activeness evidenced in statements of key informants and the low levels of both bonding and bridging social capital evidenced in the community survey. This is because it does not attend to the historical trends which may inhibit the development or the function of norms of trust and reciprocity. Nor does it provide a framework for analyzing the power structures that are established, reinforced, or challenged through these historical processes. In order to understand the divergence between key informant and survey data, it is helpful to consider at length the information gathered as part of the community history.

Historical Analysis

Introduction

Data used to construct the community history were drawn from secondary sources such as local and regional histories, newspaper articles, and academic work. In compiling the history, we were concerned not only with 'objective' historical decisions and patterns of social interaction themselves, but also with the trends in interpretation and meaning that emerged from these patterns. We employ the concept of narrative(s) and narrative construction to better analyze residents' understandings of the contemporary community social structure and development possibilities in our discussion.

Early Development

Schuylkill County

Due to a law which prevented the combination of any transportation system with either coal rights or mining operations in the county, early development in Schuylkill county was distinct from other counties in the region, characterized by what Wardell and Johnston (1987, p. 784) call a "more wide-open, individualistic, enterprise system." The authors note that mines were run by small independent operators or tenants who leased the coal rights, less than half of which survived one full year (p. 786).

This system of independent ownership caused high population turnover, particularly during the depressions in the anthracite market. In the depressed year of 1850, an estimated half of the mineworkers left the county (Berthoff, 1965, p. 264). This instability prevented the development of informal social networks that could support formal organization against the incorporation of coal companies. However, it also kept capital in the local economy, which provided for a measure of diversification. Pottsville, the county seat, functioned as the center of banking and financial services for the entire southern rim of the coal region. Local banks provided support for small-scale entrepreneurs such as David G. Yuengling, who established the United States' first family-owned brewery. Insurance and utilities providers were also locally owned.

The volatile mining structure ultimately allowed incorporated coal companies, financed and directed by investors in Philadelphia, New York City, and New England, to consolidate property in the county. In the late 1860s, Philadelphia and Reading Railroad President Franklin Gowen began a campaign for the vertical integration of the entire Schuylkill anthracite coal supply chain. Two major companies, the Philadelphia & Reading Coal & Iron Company (P&RC&I) and the Lehigh Coal & Navigation Company (LC&N), acquired virtually all the land in Schuylkill County. By 1890, leaders in Pottsville had lost control of all but 19 percent of the 48 companies they had controlled prior to 1870 (Davies, 1985, p. 119).

104 J. Bridger, P. Frumento, T. Alter

The consolidation of the Schuylkill mines and railroads under the ownership of extra-local investors allowed for a greater efficiency and increased output. However, it also had significant and lasting negative implications for the class structure of the anthracite region: the uppermost social class did not live in the region and thus had little investment in its overall welfare.

Because resident elites lacked the resources to provide adequate services and social support programs, the resulting "headless society" (Berthoff, 1965, p. 276) forced out-of-work and injured miners to seek help from the ethnic churches and benevolent societies, reinforcing stratification and insularity along ethnic and religious lines. The absentee status of coal operators also made it difficult for workers to challenge policies regarding working conditions or wages. This labor structure impeded early union efforts. According to Yearley (1961, p. 183) mineworkers were "prone to blame the operators directly for their hardships and, as a consequence, to expect immediate redress from them" whereas union leaders, though sharing mineworkers' concerns, "were inclined to look beyond the region to the instability of the anthracite market as the real source of their troubles." These different understandings, in combination with regional differences, made unions vulnerable to internal conflicts as well as external assaults.

Tamaqua

In contrast to county and regional trends, local leaders in Tamaqua continued to control aspects of the economy through the period of consolidation. This can be attributed in part to its location in the Panther Valley, which includes parts of Schuylkill and Carbon counties. According to Dublin and Licht (2005), although the LC&N dominated area economics and politics in the late nineteenth and early twentieth centuries, communities in the Panther Valley could not be characterized as company towns. In the first half of the nineteenth century, Tamaqua developed several manufacturing operations to support the anthracite industry. During the mid-1800s, Tamaqua's five iron and steel firms had the second-highest output among towns in the county (Davies, 1985, p. 118). The two largest were Tamaqua Manufacturing Company and Tamaqua Iron Works, both of which survived well into the twentieth century. In particular, the Tamaqua Manufacturing Company was purchased by the Atlas Powder Company in 1919 and functioned as a military supplier during both world wars. Employment peaked at 1617 in 1947 and declined alongside anthracite (Miller, 1955, p. 346).

By the period of consolidation, manufacturing interests were in fact diversifying. In 1875, local business leaders established the Tamaqua Shoe Factory. Other efforts included the Greenwood Rolling Mill, the Tamaqua Hosiery Company, James Fitzpatrick's shirt factory, and the Potts Powder Company, later purchased by Atlas Powder (Tamaqua S.O.S., Inc, 2008). In addition, passenger trains provided the market for a significant commercial district. Tamaqua became a regional destination for entertainment and social facilities including an opera house, theaters, and a bowling alley.

Ethnic Fractionalization and Labor Organization

Schuylkill County

It is difficult to overstate the role of coal in establishing and maintaining local economic and social structures in the anthracite region. High demand for coal resulted in explosive population growth which began in the mid-1800s and peaked in the mid-1920s. In this monopsonistic labor market, industry leaders were able to construct towns as a composite of fractional interests that would suppress the emergence of coherent community identities. To this end, they pursued recruitment and wage policies that fostered religious and racial diversity to drive down labor prices and prevent organization. This framework for competitive racial interaction has remained largely unchanged as the present-day low cost of living as compared to cities such as Reading and Philadelphia draws new ethnic groups to these towns.

The mining industry attracted immigrant populations in several waves. Miners from the anthracite fields in Wales began to arrive in the 1820s. Immigrants from England, Scotland, and Ireland followed shortly after, along with Germans in the 1840s. Toward the end of the nineteenth century, companies began to seek out immigrants from Eastern and Southern Europe. By 1910 Poles, Lithuanians, Slovaks, Russians, other Slavic groups, and Italians made up a significant percentage of the workforce. To attract new immigrant groups, companies often offered free or low-cost housing for the employees and their families.

However, mining jobs were not equally available across ethnic lines. Each group of immigrants occupied distinct locations in the hierarchies of the coal mine. For most of the nineteenth century, English served as mine owners and bosses, Welsh as skilled miners, and German and Irish as unskilled laborers. This structure created conflict among miners and represented one of the most significant hurdles to organization. Skilled miners were paid piecemeal by the weight of coal produced or, particularly in the Southern field, by their rate of advance into the coal seam, a system which caused conflict between the miners and bosses who evaluated each miner's haul. These miners, in turn, contracted mine laborers and supervised their work. Complaints regarding workplace conditions and wages were most often directed to a specific actor within this structure rather than to companies. In this way, "the industry pitted worker against worker" (Miller and Sharpless, 1998, p. 244).

In the late nineteenth century, companies increasingly recruited Italian and Slavic populations in response to labor organization efforts. These groups were considered to be "cheap men. ... They were willing to work longer hours than the English-speaking miners, do heavier and more dangerous work, and put up with conditions that the English-speaking miners no longer tolerated" (Frank Julian Warne, quoted in Miller and Sharpless, 1998, p. 173). As a result, "[t]hey were often viewed as 'Pauper labor' by established miners" (Davies, 1999, p. 350). 'Native' miners resented Eastern European immigrants not only because they depressed wages, but also because they "posed a status threat to the occupation of the coal miner.

A large presence of these ethnic groups would cause coal mining to become regarded as 'foreigner work,' opening all of its members to derision" (Aurand, 2003, p. 76).

Reflecting these biases, established labor organizations had a complicated relationship with these new immigrants. Many supported initiatives such as miner's certification to protect their trade. In 1889, the state began mandating miner certification for the purpose of accident prevention. Eight years later, it passed an amendment that made English proficiency a part of the certification process. This amendment served to safeguard higher-ranking mine positions for natives. However, weak enforcement rendered certification "unable to retain a mining cast [sic] system based upon ethnic background" (Aurand, 2003, p. 76). Next, the United Mine Workers of America (UMWA) pushed for a tax on mine operators for each adult alien employed. Coal companies responded by paying for this tax out of immigrants' wages. It was eventually turned over as unconstitutional.

Ethnic groups remained insular, forming their own neighborhoods, schools, churches, fraternal and auxiliary organizations, social halls, and even fire companies. Leonard (2005, p. 25) writes: "Schuylkill County was highly diverse ethnically ... [and] densely populated, yet with a significant degree of separation." Ethnically based mutual societies functioned to provide social services the company and local government did not. For example, the state miners' hospitals, founded in the late nineteenth and early twentieth centuries, refused to admit men with incurable diseases, such as black lung (Dublin and Licht, 2005, p. 50).

Although the presence of these ethnic support systems might suggest bonding social capital, ethnic groups, and nationalities did not function as cohesive units. Immigrants brought with them many of the regional, class, and religious prejudices that had existed in the homeland. Identities were often most strongly tied to particular villages; national identities were constructed in the years following immigration to the United States. For example, Kenny (1998, pp. 69–70) notes that Irish immigrants from the Castlecomer region of Kilkenny, one of the few places in Ireland to contain workable deposits of coal, allied with the Welsh in labor disputes: "There were many different sorts of Irish immigrant workers in the anthracite region, and skilled miners from the anglicized southeast evidently had little in common with unskilled laborers from the remote northwest." Berthoff (1965, pp. 266–267) suggests that the most common cause for violence in the area during the late nineteenth and early twentieth centuries was actually intra-ethnic dispute, in part because ethnic leaders were responsible for policing their countrymen.

Nevertheless, the narratively significant acts of violence in regional history are often depicted as (national) ethnic and class conflicts. The most significant example is that of the Molly Maguires, a group "more storied, more researched and more intriguing" than almost any other aspect of local history, which remains a subject of heated debate (Serfass, 1995, p. 49). In the mid- to late-nineteenth century, Irish immigrants in particular encountered "a social dynamic that smacked of the same abuse and discrimination they had known back in Ireland" (Kline and Kline, 2005, p. 22). It was in this social climate that Irish-Catholic laborers organized under the auspices of the Ancient Order of Hibernians (AOH), a national fraternal society which had been founded in New York City in 1836. The AOH was identified by local officials as the foundation for the Molly Maguires, a secret society whose members were found guilty for two major crime waves occurring during the years of 1862 through 1868 and 1874 through 1875 in which sixteen men were assassinated, most of them mine officials. Because few primary sources exist from the Molly Maguires, save their testimonies in a series of trials, the writings of men like Bannan initially played an important role in structuring the dominant narrative understanding of these events.

Despite these conflicts, to a certain extent the danger of coal mining, combined with the monopolistic structure of the coal and railroad companies, encouraged workers to cooperate across boundaries and allowed them to begin to articulate an overarching working-class identity. UMWA President John Mitchell famously told miners: "The coal you dig is not Slavic coal, or Polish coal, or Irish coal. It is coal." Not only did working conditions such as cave-ins, explosions, and black lung, foster cooperation, they also contributed to what Leonard (2005, p. 19) identifies as a sense of "resignation and fatalism" endemic to the entire region.

Changes in voting patterns also provide evidence for the emergence of a shared outlook. According to Kolbe (1975, p. 242), "voting behavior becomes less ethnically identifiable as a more universal value system motivates the bulk of the population." In the 1890s, Schuylkill was a Democratic county as the result of an alliance between German Protestant and Irish Catholic leaders. By 1920, it had become a majority Republican county. In part, this was due to the Reading Company, which used its economic might to influence local politics. Kolbe suggests that the Republican Party also appealed to the "highly generalized, ill defined, but often intensely held local values of individualism and patriotism" which existed across the ethnic and religious spectrum (p. 265).

While the history of accidents and disease, economic decline, and outmigration may have fostered a degree of regional solidarity, this does not signify that ethnic and religious identities were completely eclipsed. For example, Gudelunas (1984, p. 174) provides an alternative interpretation of voting patterns, arguing instead that "the county's legendary ethno-religious voting patterns prevailed despite these dramatic changes." For example, a close look at the township and borough records for the 1960 presidential election provides evidence for polarization between the Irish-Catholic and German-Protestant communities. Gudelunas notes that Catholic candidate John F. Kennedy dominated primarily Irish areas, particularly 'patches' located outside of boroughs, and experienced defeats of more than three to one in heavily German precincts (p. 176). He theorizes that because the county is economically depressed "[u]rbanization pressures are minimal, and therefore, so are pressures to break up and homogenize old ethnic and religious, social and religious ties" (p. 184).

A number of residents and observers in the region have drawn parallels between the historical reception of Eastern and Southern European immigrant groups and contemporary ethnic/racial conflicts. In the past decade, the low cost of living has

108 J. Bridger, P. Frumento, T. Alter

drawn Latino immigrants from Puerto Rico, Central America, and Mexico to towns such as Shenandoah, which was catapulted into the national spotlight in 2008 with the murder of an illegal immigrant from Mexico at the hands of six high-school football players. Shenandoah Valley High School bus driver Joe Sobinsky, of Italian and Polish descent, summarized the social construction of race in the region when he told a Latino student who accused him of racism: "Before you got here I was the brownest" (quoted in Montgomery, 2008, C01). Some people, however, do identify a difference between historical and contemporary ethnic and race relations. According to Tamaqua resident Bob Evans, "Past generations did better with welcoming newcomers than we seem to be doing now with Hispanics. ... banks in this town always had an Irish or Lithuanian teller to attract minority groups, token folks" (quoted in Kline and Kline, 2005, p. 27).

Tamaqua

Social relations in Tamaqua have also been characterized by ethnic tensions. For example, it was the setting of some of the most high-profile Molly Maguire murders, including that of police officer Benjamin Yost. Kline and Kline (2005) report that forms of ethnic discrimination continued throughout the twentieth century. Residents report that as late as the 1970s, the derogatory term 'Hunkie' was used to describe people of Eastern European descent (p. 12). However, at points in time ethnic tensions were overshadowed by cooperation around common economic interests, particularly in strikes and other union efforts.

As was the case with other major mining companies, the LC&N saw fluctuations in the early 1920s as the result of frequent strikes and a significant downturn in market conditions toward the end of the decade. The company's collieries were operating at less than half capacity even before the depths of the Great Depression. The Lehigh Navigation Coal Company (LNC) was created in 1930 to operate the LC&N coal division (Dublin and Licht, 2005, p. 61). LNC officials favored closing the less cost-efficient underground mines and shifting production to strip mining. Tamaqua and other Panther Valley towns had worked together as a subdistrict of the United Mine Workers Association of America (UMWA), District 7. In part through this longstanding formal organization, the communities came to realize a set of shared interests. Panther Valley mineworkers were able to successfully campaign for equalization of work across existing mines, which was the fair distribution of working hours across all the company's holdings, despite opposition from both the LNC and the UMWA.

This campaign was notable because the Panther Valley Equalization Committee marshaled the broad support of not only employed and unemployed mineworkers, but also middle-class merchants and professionals indirectly dependent upon miners' income, including President of the Tamaqua Merchants Association Herman Fenstermacher, who expressed support for the cause in an August 1933 letter to President Roosevelt (Dublin and Licht, 2005, pp. 65–66). Ethnic and religious organizations such as the Lithuanian Catholic Action Convention also appealed to

Roosevelt on behalf of the miners. Dublin and Licht (2005, p. 68) emphasize that the success of the movement owed to the fact that it became "as much a community issue as a union or class issue."

Miller and Sharpless (1998, p. 320) suggest that social activism at the community level during the twentieth century was predicated in particular upon "the existence of militant groups that predated the depression or had a tradition of struggle." In the Panther Valley, labor agitation was most common to Tamaqua. Accordingly, the push for equalization was most enduring in Tamaqua. After the anthracite market bottomed in the winter of 1948–49, LNC officials closed its mines at the end of April 1954 and opened negotiations with the UMWA and local unions. Although five of the six local Panther Valley unions accepted the outcome of negotiations, mineworkers in the Tamaqua Local 1571 picketed collieries across the valley and continued the call for equalization. However, it soon became evident that the coal crisis impacting the region could not be addressed through equalization programs alone. Demand for anthracite was in permanent decline, and, by the 1960s, anthracite mining was all but finished in the community.

Economic Downturn

National Trends

In 1920 anthracite supplied more than 95 percent of the home-heating needs of the Northeastern United States. In contrast, by the early 1950s alternative fuels supplied 56 percent and anthracite only 32 percent of the same market (Miller, 1989, p. 168). Cost differentials do not provide a satisfying explanation for the change; consumers were also alienated by the protracted series of labor conflicts that both impacted coal supply and increasingly exposed the exploitation of workers. In particular, the UMWA strike of 1902 garnered national attention with the outbreak of violence in the region. Due to concern that the coal shortage would lead to more widespread fuel riots, President Theodore Roosevelt came under pressure from politicians across the spectrum to seize the mines under the law of eminent domain. He called a conference between himself, the mine operators, and UMWA President John Mitchell. P&RC&I President George F. Baer famously expressed the position of operators in a letter: "The rights and interests of the laboring man will be protected and cared for – not by the labor agitators, but by the Christian men of property to whom God has given control of the property rights of the country, and upon the successful management of which so much depends." He and the other operators maintained this stance during the conference: they would not commit themselves to abide by an investigative commission's findings, agree to arbitration, or recognize the union.

Negotiations remained at a standstill until the White House leaked the news that the president was considering government takeover of the mines. Pressured by J.P. Morgan, the operators agreed to a commission, with the stipulation that it did not contain any representatives of organized labor. Although the commission did not grant official recognition to the union, it created the Anthracite Board of Conciliation to adjudicate grievances. For this reason, Aurand (2003, p. 85) divides the anthracite industry's pay program into two eras: prior to 1902, a period of unilateral decisions by the operators, and after 1902, the age of collective bargaining.

However, the age of collective bargaining did not allow for greater personal or community agency. As with the earlier consolidation of the coal industry, union leadership increasingly shifted to urban centers outside the region. During the strike of 1902, Mitchell had traveled widely across the anthracite region, and the demands he articulated grew out of his conversations with community leaders and miners. For this reason, mine workers "gave him their personal loyalty, a loyalty stronger than their allegiance to the union he led" (Miller and Sharpless, 1998, p. 286). Even as the strike began to take a toll on unemployed workers, Mitchell received a hero's welcome when he rode into town. Leighton (1939, p. 36) describes a typical reaction: "This pale-faced man belonged to them; they worked for a living at the mines, and this being descended from heaven, this man so close they could touch him, had been a miner also; he was theirs! The cheers, they say, were hysterical."

In contrast, John L. Lewis, who served as UMWA president from 1920 until 1960, ushered in an era in which labor conflict shifted "from the shop floor and the streets to institutional settings (normally, hotel rooms where corporate and union bureaucrats with government mediators negotiated contracts)" (Dublin and Licht, 2005, p. 59). According to Karsh and London (1954, p. 415), this change was typical across industrial labor movements: "as the union succeeds in giving to its members a greater measure of control over their condition of employment, it tends to develop through time an institutionalized bureaucratic structure in which the membership tends to have less control over decision-making process." They argue that Lewis encouraged miners to view the union as a service agency which necessitated centralized control in order to secure benefits for members.

Schuylkill County

The downturn of the coal industry forced the P&RC&I into bankruptcy proceedings from 1937 through 1944. During this period, management remained intact. However, faced with continually declining sales, the company was taken over by outside speculators in the late 1940s and early 1950s. In 1956, the new directors rebranded the company the Philadelphia and Reading Corporation (PRC) and liquidated its coal operations, which were placed under a subsidiary called Reading Anthracite. In its place, the PRC purchased clothing, shoe, optical, toy, and chemical manufacturing firms, none of which were located in the region. Dublin and Licht (2005, p. 99) write: "The collieries of the Pennsylvania anthracite region represented tax shelters for [outside investors] and assets for the taking and selling, not productive facilities." In 1947 manufacturing employment, primarily concentrated in the textile and apparel industries, surpassed mining (Miller, 1955, p. 339).

However, the apparel industry was unable to support the numbers of unemployed miners and mining families in the post-World War II period. Local governments

The Tamaqua Paradox **111**

and county-level organizations, such as the Schuylkill Economic Development Corporation (SEDCO), provided incentives for new industry, but the limited employment such redevelopment efforts brought to the region was low-wage and non-unionized. Small-scale manufacturing operations in the food, fabricated metals, and electric and electronic equipment industries provided the primary means for employment (Miller, 1989, p. 171). Beginning in the 1960s, tertiary industries such as transportation and other public utilities, wholesale and retail trade, finance, insurance and real estate, and services saw the greatest growth. The contemporary economy is supported primarily by manufacturing and the service sector. According to the 2000 Census, 26 percent of the Schuylkill County population aged 16 years or over is employed in manufacturing, 19.5 percent in education, health, and social services, and 12.3 percent in retail trade (McCormick Taylor, 2006, p. 49). Despite the growth of new sectors, unemployment in the anthracite region has never fallen below 10 percent and it has one of the lowest per capita incomes in the entire Northeastern United States (Miller and Sharpless, 1998, p. 323).

As mining jobs disappeared, the region saw significant outmigration, although the decline in population occurred less rapidly than the decline in employment opportunities. The population of towns in the anthracite region as a whole dropped 20 percent between 1930 and 1950, and another 20 percent during the 1950s (Marsh, 1987, p. 345). Ethnic and religious composition remained relatively unaffected by this population shift; however, it had a measurable impact upon other social categories, particularly education level and age. In a study of six anthracite-region high schools between 1946 and 1960, Dublin and Licht (2005, p. 96) found college education to be the strongest predictor of outmigration: "A college degree was a ticket to good employment elsewhere. Parents encouraged their children's education knowing full well that traditional family bonds were endangered."

Those who stayed began to commute to mill and factory positions up to 150 miles away in suburban areas such as Fairless Hills, Pennsylvania, and Linden, Manville, or Elizabeth, New Jersey (Dublin and Licht, 2005, p. 89). Kolbe (1975, p. 242) calls commuting in the anthracite region "prodigious." Marsh (1987, p. 350) writes: "Commuting is a central fact of life in the anthracite region. Some commute away from wife and family for four and a half days a week to work in a city and some who have moved away commute back most weekends to visit friends and relatives." In this regard, the anthracite region is emblematic of broader trends which show an increase in the number of residents of rural areas who fulfill basic needs outside of their communities.

Although employment in the coal industry is virtually nonexistent today, coal continues to carry important symbolic weight, as evidenced by a recent debate regarding heating public facilities. In 2006, Schuylkill County considered a proposal from Honeywell International Inc. to replace coal-fired boilers at the county courthouse and prison with natural gas. The proposal met with controversy among both citizens and lawmakers. Urbina (2008) reports: "For decades, local officials have tried to block natural gas pipelines from crossing Pennsylvania and passed ordinances requiring public buildings to use anthracite, but the recent debate has raised a thorny question about how much is too much to pay to protect local industry and history." Honeywell projected that the new system would save the county $3.2 million over 15 years (Wolfgang, 2008a). In response, Reading Anthracite submitted a counter-proposal. The Pennsylvania Anthracite Council projected that remaining with coal would save Schuylkill $5.5 million over 25 years (Wolfgang, 2008a).

In September 2008 the council reached a compromise after Honeywell International withdrew its proposal, accepting instead a proposal from PPL subsidiary McClure Co. to install new flex boilers that can burn either coal or gas for heat. The county expects to save about $1 million over 15 years by using gas heat during mild months and coal heat during the winter (Wolfgang, 2009). Anthracite interests continue to argue that coal is poised to make a comeback, particularly as gas and oil prices rise. Steinberg (1996) reports: "After slipping for six decades, the production of Pennsylvania anthracite rose to more than 8 million tons last year [1995]." There is a niche market for small anthracite-burning stoves to supplement home heating. In 2008, coal stove manufacturers such as Keystoker Inc., located in Schuylkill Haven, saw record-breaking sales, which some believe indicate "the second coming of the anthracite boom" (Wolfgang, 2008b). The motivation for continued support of the anthracite industry is not only economic benefit, as reflected in Urbina's (2008) above assessment of the heating debate. Urbina quotes a Republican state senator from Schuylkill County, James J. Rhoades: "Heritage should count for something." Residents continue to seek such a second coming, according to Marsh (1987, p. 347), because the historical dominance of coal "has constrained people's repertoire of responses to the world."

This strong attachment to local and regional histories is also manifested in efforts to develop and sustain a tourism economy. As part of these efforts, conflicts for control over meaning are clearly exposed. Joseph Wayne, with the support of the Pennsylvania Labor History Society, campaigned for a posthumous pardon on behalf of his great-grandfather John Kehoe. The pardon was issued by Governor Milton J. Shapp in 1979. However, as Miller and Sharpless (1998, p. 137) argue, "whether the anthracite Irishmen were class heroes or cutthroat vigilantes ... still depends, in the region at least, on which side your ancestors took." In 1998, the Schuylkill County Visitors Bureau drew censure from some in when it staged a reenactment of the hangings of six accused Molly Maguires during the annual Molly Maguire weekend. John Bugbee, the great-great-great grandson of Frank Langdon, a mine official whose murder in 1862 was attributed to the Molly Maguires, worried that "the romanticization of this era could get out of hand" (quoted in Bulik, 1998). Despite such criticism, the Historical Society displays portions of the ropes used to hang the men, trial transcripts, and a revolver used by an adversary of the Mollies.

Tamaqua

Tamaqua has also drawn heavily upon the historical legacy of the coal boom to redevelop the downtown area as a tourist destination. Beginning in 1991, a citizen

The Tamaqua Paradox **113**

organization called Tamaqua Save Our Station (S.O.S.) partnered with the Tamaqua Historical Society, Downtown Tamaqua, the Tamaqua Chamber of Commerce, and State Representative Dave Argell's office for the purpose of restoring the station and its environs. Rededicated in 2004, the station is central to the Tamaqua Historic District, which encompasses more than 900 properties stretching over 50 blocks (Tamaqua S.O.S., 2008). It is also a functional stop along the Reading Blue Mountain and Northern Railroad line, organized from former Conrail tracks (part of which originally belonged to Philadelphia and Reading) in 1990. Kline and Kline (2005, p. 49) describe the contemporary scene: "Abandoned, then slated for demolition after a fire, the Tamaqua train station now offers art shows, locally made chocolates, a bridal and home furnishing stores, and an outstanding new restaurant reminiscent of the borough's heyday."

In addition, some former anthracite communities such as Tamaqua are seeking alternative uses for former mines and related infrastructure. As a means for generating income, many have used abandoned strip and underground mines as landfills for out-of-town and out-of-state waste. In 2004, the state Department of Environmental Protection (DEP) approved the practice of filling abandoned mines with a mixture of coal ash and muck dredged from river bottoms as a means of preventing accidents and stopping the discharge of acidic water (Avril, 2004). The LC&N, which had a permit to dump coal ash into the Springdale Pit in Tamaqua, applied to begin this new practice and reached an agreement with the Tamaqua Borough Council to pay the borough $800,000 annually, pending individual approval from the DEP (Dublin and Licht, 2005, p. 174). Avril (2005) writes: "The concept is hailed not only as an environmental two-for-one, but as a tool for economic development."

Although the borough council initially approved the agreement, subsequent election cycles saw the replacement of several members of the council. In 2006, the council became the fifth local government in the country to abolish the rights of corporations and establish the rights of ecosystems. The local government worked in tandem with community groups, including the one-thousand-member Schuylkill County citizen organization Army for a Clean Environment and the Community Environmental Legal Defense Fund, to draft the ordinance (Price, 2006).

Discussion

Like many other communities in the anthracite region, Tamaqua is characterized by two broad countervailing trends with regard to the impact of coal on the development of community. The first is the fractionalization promoted by coal companies through hiring practices and the division of labor in the mines. The second is the solidarity demonstrated by coal miners at two levels: (1) within ethnic and religious groups through fraternal societies and churches, and (2) at the community level through formal labor organizations and a common work culture. In Tamaqua, especially, this solidarity was enhanced by the early growth of a local business class and the emergence of strong connections between the networks of collieries in the surrounding area, as seen in the equalization movement, for example.

Thus, fractionalization and solidarity coexisted. On one hand, fractionalization prevented the establishment of norms of social trust and generalized reciprocity, which form the basis of social capital. On the other hand, collaboration around economic and other shared interests sometimes did override these tensions. These two distinct yet intertwined patterns of interaction help to explain the divergent results of our survey and key informant interviews. These findings are not well explained by social capital theory, which would suggest that – in the absence of social trust and norms of generalized reciprocity – collaboration and collective action would be highly unlikely.

Narrative analysis provides a more useful framework for explaining this paradox. Over time, the trends described above gave rise to two competing narrative understandings of community history that persist into the present day and have implications for decision-making processes. Community narratives can best be described as selective representations of the past that feed into and are partially driven by contemporary circumstances (Bridger, 1996). Survey results reflect a narrative of decline that emphasizes the negative legacy of coal through continuing class and ethnic tensions, disaffection, and a strongly felt lack of collective efficacy in addressing economic issues. More optimistic key informant interviews, on the other hand, reflect a revitalization narrative, which draws upon the early and recurring collaboration across social groups for the purpose of forwarding shared economic interests as an important foundation for contemporary development efforts.

It is important to note here that these different narrative understandings are both equally legitimate representations of Tamaqua's past. Although residents share a common history and vocabulary, they emphasize and emplot the same set of events in different ways. Indeed, as White (1980, pp. 17-18) argues, there can be no objective narrative because plot "endows events, whether real or imaginary, with a significance that they do not possess as a mere sequence." The use of narrative fuses form and interpretation together. Events are envisioned as part of a linear or horizontal process that leads to or culminates in some end: "Common opinion has it that the plot of a narrative imposes a meaning on the events that comprise its story level by revealing at the end a structure that was immanent in the events *all along* [emphasis original]" (p. 23). The explanatory power of narrative makes it a critical resource for establishing and maintaining social power. In most communities, narratives are contested; there is rarely only one community history to draw upon in arguing for courses of action in the present. Bridger (1996, p. 370) suggests that narrative creation is "… a dynamic process in which differentially empowered interest groups selectively reinterpret the past and project desired futures in light of changing local conditions and events."

Because narrative understandings provide context and direction for contemporary decisions, they have important implications for courses of action and, more broadly, trajectories for communities. For instance, conflicts over narrative control are evident not only in discourse, but in development and redevelopment efforts themselves. As Molotch et al. (2000) argue, there is a dialectical relationship between social (including narrative) and physical structures. To some degree, physical structures representing 'memory trace material' allow for continuity in social structures even with the movement of populations. Contemporary development, such as the restored train station, celebrates the period of consolidation during which the town saw its greatest social and economic growth. However, it is notable that the period considered to be Tamaqua's 'heyday' was also the period in which local business leaders were largely replaced by absentee corporate operators. It was also the period marked by some of the most violent labor conflict in the anthracite region's history, including the Molly Maguire murders. Local reaction to another physical artifact of the anthracite industry, the significant environmental damage which plagues the region, illustrates a backlash against the continuation of this power structure. In the opposition to dumping coal ash into the Springdale Pit, for instance, the community was mobilized against a potential development project that reflected the historical domination by outside entities.

These actions relating to the representation of the coal industry underscore the important role that non-economic forms of rationality play in community development efforts. The various debates and their narrative underpinnings highlight values, such as pride in local history, that have strong emotional resonance and can influence decisions. This appeal to values has important implications for the application of social capital to community development policy, because, as we pointed out above, the concept relies so heavily on a very narrow view of rationality. Miller (1992, p. 29) summarizes this position when aggregated to the community level: 'community is composed of strategically rational individuals who participate in collective action because they wish to avoid sanctions or receive incentives from the community … bringing community, culture, and social norms in through the back door.'

Miller (1992) argues that other forms of rationality, particularly Habermas's (1984) 'communicative rationality,' better account for the role of cultural traditions, social integration, and normative structures such as values and institutions. Fischer (2000, p. 132) similarly describes a 'cultural rationality' which 'is geared to – or at least gives equal weight to – personal and familiar experiences rather than depersonalized technical calculations.' Fischer (2009, p. 192) argues that citizens and politicians alike interpret arguments and make decisions through the lens of various narrative structures about "how the society works, how it should work, and what sorts of measures are needed to make it work that way." In other words, people are not simply rational actors who develop norms of trust and reciprocity on the basis of some sort of technical calculation about the benefits or sanctions associated with particular forms of behavior. As Christoforou (2011, p. 693) points out, norms and networks are always located in a broader social and political context that impacts their relationship with decision-making processes, "where the principles of expected utility, individual preference and market exchange become one of many that determine human behavior." To the extent that this is an accurate representation of collective action, an emphasis on building social capital is an ineffective strategy for development in some communities.

In the context of Tamaqua, although economic rationality may have dominated historical organizing efforts, particularly in the form of the labor union, contemporary organizing suggests greater emphasis on alternative forms of rationality, such as communicative and cultural. This explains why some development projects, such as the restoration of the Tamaqua Station and Depot Square Park, are successful and others, such as the dumping of coal ash into the Springdale Pit, have been subject to backlash. From an economic point of view, the rational decision may have been to dump ash into the Springdale Pit. However, as suggested above, more than economic rationality was at work.

Conclusion

In Tamaqua, social divisions reflect a set of historical processes which have depressed participation of some socioeconomic and ethnic groups in development initiatives. The powerful role that coal monopolies played in structuring community life, particularly in promoting ethnic and class fractionalization, inhibited the development of bridging and bonding social capital. Even though both forms of social capital were lacking, a shared interest in place provided the basis for collaboration around issues of community and economic development. A narrative lens can be a useful tool for revealing these sorts of tensions and understanding how contemporary decision making and actions actually occur. This is because such an approach takes into account competing understandings of local history and visions for the future, and provides for a more complex view of rationality and motivation. We have found that a mixed-methods approach is particularly useful for elucidating these narratives. Taken alone, each dataset used in the study paints a partial picture. The household social capital survey captures historically embedded ethnic and social tensions. Key informant interviews highlight collaboration and action around economic issues, and, more broadly, a particular perception of community identity. The historical data provides a basis for exploring and explaining this Tamaqua paradox.

From a practical perspective, our findings suggest that community and economic development professionals must take into account the historical processes which would make the development of norms of social trust and generalized reciprocity particularly untenable. Because the creation of social capital is time and labor intensive, it is necessary for residents, local leaders, policy-makers, extension educators, and other community development specialists to have an understanding of the conditions under which it is most likely to facilitate development. Places that are marked by power imbalances and historical relations of domination are not good candidates for a social capital approach. It may be a more appropriate strategy in places where there is a foundation for building social trust and norms of generalized reciprocity. In short, context matters. For this reason, we argue that a more historical, synthetic, and holistic understanding of community history and change is an important part of the process of theorizing and practicing community development.

Notes

1   This research was supported by the USDA's National Research Initiative Competitive Grants Program.

2 It is important to stress that we focused on the relationship between social capital and economic development activeness rather than the relationship between social capital and successful economic development as measured by job and income growth. Wilkinson (1991, p. 94) summarizes the logic behind this decision when he argues: "To require success would be to ignore the complex forces other than purpose that contribute to community change." Building local capacity to address important issues depends on residents taking action, whether those actions achieve specific goals or not.

References

Alexander, J.C. (1992). Shaky foundations: The presuppositions and internal contradictions of James Coleman's 'Foundations of social theory'. *Theory and Society*, 21(2), 203–217.

Aurand, H.W. (2003). *Coalcracker culture: Work and values in Pennsylvania anthracite, 1835–1935.* Selinsgrove, PA: Susquehanna University Press.

Avril, T. (2004, March 3). PA says river muck is OK for mines. *The Philadelphia Inquirer*, p. B3.

Avril, T. (2005, October 17). Dredging and filling. *The Philadelphia Inquirer*, p. A1.

Berthoff, R. (1965, July). The social order of the anthracite region, 1825–1902. *The Pennsylvania Magazine of History and Biography*, 89(3), 261–291.

Bridger, J.C. (1996). Community imagery and the built environment. *The Sociological Quarterly*, 37(3), 353–374.

Bridger, J.C., & Luloff, A.E. (2001). Building the sustainable community: Is social capital the answer? *Sociological Inquiry*, 71(4), 458–472.

Bulik, M. (1988, July 4). Dark days of mayhem finally emerge in the light. *The New York Times*, p. A9.

Bullen, P., & Onyx, J. (1998). Social capital questionnaire. In *Measuring social capital in five communities in NSW: A practitioners guide* (pp. 88–92). New South Wales: Management Alternatives. Retrieved from http://www.mapl.com.au/pdf/scquest.pdf

Christoforou, A. (2011). Social capital: A manifestation of neoclassical prominence or a path to a more pluralistic economics? *Journal of Economic Issues*, 45(3), 685–702.

Coleman, J. (1990). *Foundations of social theory.* Cambridge, MA: The Belknap Press of Harvard University Press.

Davies, E.J., II (1985). *The anthracite aristocracy: Leadership and social change in the hard coal regions of Northeastern Pennsylvania, 1800–1930.* DeKalb, IL: Northern Illinois University Press.

Davies, J. (1999). Authority, community, and conflict: rioting and aftermath in a late-nineteenth century Pennsylvania coal town. *Pennsylvania History*, 66(3), 339–363.

Davis, J.A., Smith, T.W., & Marsden, P.V. (2008). *General Social Surveys, 1972–2006: Cumulative codebook.* Retrieved from University of Chicago Web National Opinion Research Center Web site: http://publicdata.norc.org:41000/gss/Documents/Codebook/FINAL%20 2006%20CODEBOOK.pdf

DeFilippis, J. (2001). The myth of social capital in community development. *Housing Policy Debate*, 12(4), 781–806.

Dublin, T., & Licht, W. (2005). *The face of decline: The Pennsylvania anthracite region in the twentieth century.* Ithaca, NY: Cornell University Press.

Edwards, R.W. (2004). *Measuring social capital: an Australian framework and indicators* (Information Paper No. 1378.0). Australian Bureau of Statistics.

Fischer, F. (2000). Citizens, experts, and the environment: The politics of local knowledge. Durham, NC: Duke University Press.

Fischer, F. (2009). *Democracy & expertise: Reorienting policy inquiry.* Oxford: Oxford University Press.

Green, H., & Fletcher, L. (2003). *Social capital harmonised question set: A guide to questions for use in the measurement of social capital.* United Kingdom: Office for National Statistics.

Grootaert, C., & van Bastelaer, T. (Eds.) (2002). Annex 1: Instruments of the Social Capital Assessment Tool. In *Understanding and measuring social capital: a multidisciplinary tool for practitioners* (pp. 152–216). Washington, DC: The World Bank.

Grootaert, C., Narayan, D., Jones, V.N., & Woolcock, M. (2004). *Measuring social capital: An integrated questionnaire* (World Bank Working Paper No. 18). Washington, DC: The World Bank.

Granovetter, M. (1973). The strength of weak ties. *American Journal of Sociology*, 78(6), 1360–1380.

Gudelunas, W.A. (1984). The ethno-religious factor reaches fruition: The politics of hard coal, 1945–1972. In D.L. Salay (Ed.), *Hard coal, hard times: Ethnicity and labor in the anthracite region* (pp. 169–188). Scranton, PA: The Anthracite Museum Press.

Habermas, J. (1984). *The theory of communicative action: Reason and the rationalization of society* (T. McCarthy, Trans.). Boston, MA: Beacon Press. (Original work published 1981.)

Howard, M.M., Gibson, J.L., & Stolle, D. (2005). *The U.S. Citizenship, Involvement, Democracy Survey*. Retrieved from Georgetown University Center for Democracy and Civil Society Web site: http://www8.georgetown.edu/centers/cdacs/cid/CIDEnglish.pdf

Karsh, B., & London, J. (1954). The coal miners: A study of union control. *The Quarterly Journal of Economics*, 68(3), 415–436.

Kenny, K. (1998). *Making sense of the Molly Maguires*. New York: Oxford University Press.

Kline, M., & Kline, C.N. (2005). *Come to the old country: A handbook for preserving and sharing Schuylkill County's cultural heritage*. C.R. Kegerise (Ed.). Pottstown, PA: Schuylkill River National & State Heritage Area.

Kolbe, R.L. (1975). Culture, political parties and voting behavior: Schuylkill County. *Polity*, 8(2), 241–268.

Leighton, G.R. (1939). Shenandoah, Pennsylvania: The rise and fall of an anthracite town. In *Five cities: The story of their youth and old age* (pp. 9–48). New York, NY: Harper & Brothers Publishers.

Leonard, J.W., III (2005). *Anthracite roots: Generations of coal mining in Schuylkill County, Pennsylvania*. Charleston, SC: History Press.

McCormick, T. (2006). *Schuylkill County comprehensive plan*. Retrieved September 3, 2008, from Schuylkill County Planning & Zoning Web site: http://www.co.schuylkill.pa.us/////opt50.pdf

Marsh, B. (1987). Continuity and decline in the anthracite towns of Pennsylvania. *Annals of the Association of American Geographers*, 77(3), 337–352.

Miller, B. (1992). Collective action and rational choice: Place, community, and the limits to individual self-interest. *Economic Geography*, 68(1), 22–42.

Miller, D.L., & Sharpless, R.E. (1998). *The kingdom of coal: Work, enterprise, and ethnic communities in the mine fields*. Easton, PA: Canal History and Technology Press.

Miller, E.W. (1955). The Southern Anthracite Region: a problem area. *Economic Geography*, 31(4), 331–350.

Miller, E.W. (1989). The anthracite region of Northeastern Pennsylvania: An economy in transition. *Journal of Geography*, 88(5), 167–171.

Molotch, H., Freudenberg, W., & Paulsen, K.E. (2000). History repeats itself, but how? City character, urban tradition, and the accomplishment of place. *American Sociological Review*, 65(6), 791–823.

Montgomery, D. (2008, September 2). Melting point. *The Washington Post*, p. C1. Retrieved September 9, 2008, from http://www.washingtonpost.com/dyn//////.html

Narayan, D. (1998). *Global Social Capital Survey*. Retrieved from The World Bank web site: http://siteresources.worldbank.org/INTSOCIALCAPITAL/Resources/400219-1150464137254/ugquest.pdf

Narayan, D., & Cassidy, M.F. (2001). A dimensional approach to measuring social capital: development and validation of a social capital inventory. *Current Sociology*, 49(2), 59–102.

Pew Research Center for The People & The Press (1997, April 18). Greater Philadelphia Social Trust Survey. In *Trust and citizen engagement in metropolitan Philadelphia: A case study* (pp. 88–114). Retrieved November 3, 2008, from http://people-press.org/http://people-press.org/files/legacy-pdf/110.pdf

Price, B. (2006, September 20). Tamaqua law is first in nation to recognize rights of nature. In *Press Releases*. Retrieved September 18, 2008, from The Community Environmental Legal Defense Fund Web site: http://www.celdf.org/////.aspx

Putnam, R.D. (1993). *Making democracy work: Civic traditions in modern Italy*. Princeton, NJ: Princeton University Press.

Putnam, R.D. (1995). Bowling alone: America's declining social capital. *Journal of Democracy*, 6(1), 65–78.

Putnam, R.D. (1996). The strange disappearance of civic America. *The American Prospect*, 7(24), 34–38.

Putnam, R.D. (2000). Bowling alone: The collapse and revival of American community. New York, NY: Simon and Schuster.

Putnam, R.D., & Feldstein, L.M. (2003). *Better together: Restoring the American community*. New York, NY: Simon and Schuster.

Saguaro Seminar: Civic Engagement in America (2000, August 4). *The Social Capital Community Benchmark Survey*. Retrieved September 23, 2008, from John F. Kennedy School of Government at Harvard University Web site: http://www.hks.harvard.edu/saguaro/communitysurvey/docs/survey_instrument.pdf

Serfass, D.R. (1995). *Iron steps: Illustrated history of Tamaqua, Pennsylvania*. Tamaqua, PA: Author.

Steinberg, J. (1996, March 3). Ideas & trends: Coal tries for a comeback. *The New York Times*. Retrieved June 29, 2009, from http://www.nytimes.com/1996/03/03/weekinreview/ideas-trends-coal-tries-for-a-comeback.html?pagewanted=all&src=pm

Tamaqua S.O.S., Inc. (2008). Tamaqua National Historic District. In *Tamaqua Railroad Station*. Retrieved September 5, 2008, from http://www.tamaquastation.com/.aspx?pageid=263

Urbina, I. (2008, June 10). King coal country debates a sacrilege, gas heat. *The New York Times*, p. A1. Retrieved June 29, 2009, from http://www.nytimes.com/2008/06/10/us/10coal.html

Wardell, M., & Johnston, R.L. (1987). Class struggle and industrial transformation: The U.S. anthracite industry, 1820–1902. *Theory and Society*, 16(6), 781–808.

White, H. (1980). The value of narrativity in the representation of reality. *Critical Inquiry*, 7(1), 5–27.

Wilkinson, K.P. (1991). *The community in rural America*. New York, NY: Greenwood Press.

Wolfgang, B. (2008a, June 24). Council to county: Keeping coal may save $5M. *The Pottsville Republican-Herald*.

Wolfgang, B. (2008b, September 7). Coal: the past, the future. *The Pottsville Republican-Herald*.

Wolfgang, B. (2009, June 1). County launches heating upgrades: Officials expect $1M savings over 15 years. *The Pottsville Republican-Herald*.

Yearley, C.K., Jr (1961). *Enterprise and anthracite: Economics and democracy in Schuylkill County, 1820–1875*. Baltimore, MD: The Johns Hopkins Press.

Section three

COMMUNITY, LOCAL DECISION MAKING, DEMOCRATIC PARTICIPATION, AND SOCIAL CHANGE

8

POPULISM, POWER, AND RURAL COMMUNITY DEVELOPMENT

Tony Varley and Chris Curtin

Introduction

What might 'theory' possibly mean in community development? One approach to this question would be to start from the perspective of the activists themselves and the general values they see as informing the manner community development should rightfully be organised in the modern world. There is potentially a wide spectrum of general values to choose from here, but fairness, equality, solidarity, participation, and sustainability are ones that frequently surface in community development discourses. Against a backdrop in which such values are often revered as normative ideals, we will explore the possibility that much rural community development can be construed as a 'populist' or underdog reaction to a realisation that the way power is distributed and structured unequally between the urban and rural worlds tends to militate against the achievement of fairness and equality in particular. Such a realisation can give rise to perceived forms of rural popular powerlessness that can open up possibilities for community development. In this chapter, our task will be to develop this insight by assessing the adequacy of a 'populist' or 'underdog' approach to rural community development.

To begin, we will introduce a set of four oppositions between perceived forms of relative popular powerlessness and structural power that have featured already in the academic literature on populism and that are relevant to rural conditions (Canovan, 1981, pp. 4–8). The possibilities of using community development to counteract perceived forms of rural powerlessness will then be addressed. Here the 'power to' and 'power over' distinction, well known to students of power, will be introduced to begin to conceptualise actor-centred popular and state challenges to perceived forms of structural power and inequality in the countryside.

Of course, to say that certain collective and state action can potentially counteract perceived forms of rural powerlessness tells us little about the character and scope of this collective and state action. Two ideal-typical scenarios – the radical and the pragmatic – will therefore be outlined as an aid to theorising the character and scope of populist and underdog community development and 'participative' forms of pro-community state intervention. As these two ideal-typical scenarios consciously exaggerate and simplify complex empirical realities, the pictures they provide us with may be empirically possible, but they cannot be regarded as either empirical descriptions or explanations in any strict sense. Their prime purpose is rather to provide interpretive benchmarks that can facilitate our reading and comparison of real-world cases. Ever since Max Weber's pioneering methodological discussions, modelling via ideal types, or scenario modelling, has been found to be a potentially useful tool in the comparative historical and social sciences (Burger, 1987, pp. 154–179).

There is another sense besides in which our ideal-typical scenarios introduce a dimension of 'theory' to our discussion. Broadly speaking, our radical ideal-typical scenario veers more towards a recognisably 'conflict' interpretation while, in contrast, our pragmatic scenario presents a relatively more 'integrationist' interpretation. Reflecting this divergence of interpretation, our ideal-typical scenarios can be said to reflect the 'conflict'/'consensus' divide that runs like a fault line through contemporary social theory (Alexander, 1987, pp. 8–9).

Our contention will be that the approach to rural community development that focuses on the generation of popular or state power so as to counteract the operation of structural power – or, for short, the underdog power approach – has a number of strengths in its favour. First, it highlights the gulf that can open up between the normative ideals of fairness and equality in community development and the perceived unfair and unequal realities that often characterise the rural condition. Second, it ties, via the four oppositions between power and powerlessness, perceptions of unfairness and inequality with both the operation of powerful structural forces and the construction of underdog identities. Third, it highlights two different conceptions of power, one based on various forms of structural 'power over' and the other based in the potential counteracting 'power to' of collective action and state intervention. Fourth, it suggests that an important distinction in the contemporary power literature – that which distinguishes the 'power over' and the 'power to' – can usefully be deployed in conceptualising agent-centred community-based collective action and participative pro-community state interventions that strive to generate the local power required to counteract instances of popular powerlessness by challenging instances of structural power. And fifth, in focusing throughout on the perspective of those who project themselves as relatively powerless or those who claim to speak on their behalf, the underdog power approach takes the construction of underdog identities as a central element of the politics of rural community development.

On the debit side, we will contend that populism, in spite of the very substantial academic literature the phenomenon has attracted, is not without its shortcomings. The question in considering these limitations – as they relate to populism as both an aid to interpretation and as a descriptive term in the sphere of community

Populism, Power, and Development **125**

development – will be to determine whether they are sufficiently serious to negate whatever usefulness populism might possess. Our contention will be that while populism can be a valuable aid to interpretation, its value as a descriptive term has been fatally compromised. For this reason we would ultimately prefer to drop 'populism' and 'populist' as the descriptive identifier of the underdog power approach to rural community development and pro-community state intervention we are arguing for here.

Four Oppositions between Powerlessness and Power

Four specific oppositions between forms of perceived rural popular powerlessness and urban-based structural power, each one resonating with a general populist opposition that pits relatively powerless groups of people in society against powerful establishment forces, will now be introduced. These oppositions associate relative powerlessness with rural areas in general, small-scale economic activity, beleaguered local communities and with perceived inadequacies in the political representation of local community interests. Not alone do these four oppositions point to how the bases and experience of rural popular powerlessness may vary across these four overlapping constituencies, but they also hint at the range of dominating structural forces perceived to be at work in producing perceived forms of popular powerlessness.

The idea that rural areas find themselves increasingly powerless and subordinate in modernising societies – a long-established theme in social and political commentary (Canovan, 1981, p. 8) as well as the basis of our first opposition – is one that both predates and outlasts the flowering of North American rural populism in the late nineteenth century. An early articulation of the relative rural powerlessness thesis is to be found in the remark of Marx and Engels that the countryside would find itself increasingly subjected "to the rule of the towns" as the global capitalist order unfolded (Marx and Engels, 1997, p. 7). "What a growing part of agriculture all over the world had in common," Eric Hobsbawm (1997, p. 206) similarly observes of the 1848–1875 period, "was subjection to the industrial world economy." If anything, relative rural powerlessness became ever more pronounced as farmers' assigned role as cheap food providers developed, the size of the farming population contracted sharply with labour-saving mechanisation, urban employment opportunities opened up for millions of rural migrants, and organised farming interests were progressively co-opted by a state whose overriding concern was the safeguarding and promotion of urban economic interests. On a global basis, urban domination of the countryside was set to increase in the twentieth century and to condemn many rural inhabitants to a future of uneven and imbalanced development that would have migration, dislocation and marginalisation among its legacy of negative consequences (Roberts, 1995).

Can conflicts between rural and urban interests give rise to political conflict? In tracing the lines of modern European political development, Lipset and Rokkan (1967) identify the rural–urban cleavage as one of four major historical cleavages. In their view, relations between "landed and urban interests," formed around commodity markets, produced conflicts that could but "did not invariably prove party-forming" (Lipset and Rokkan, 1967, p. 21). While conflicts between landed and urban interests may now have faded, it has been suggested that "the cleavage may now be acquiring a new, 'postindustrial' relevance" as middle-class urban flight shrinks the tax base of cities, farmer subsidies fall with the liberalisation of agricultural trade, and conflicts erupt around countryside management issues (as with the bitter dispute provoked when the United Kingdom banned foxhunting in 2003 and 2004) (Gallagher et al., 2006, p. 268).

Since the nineteenth century, rural populists (and their intellectuals) – appearing in a variety of guises, and identifying with and taking the side of those underdog interests perceived to be losing out in the new urban-centred industrial world – have been critics of urban domination (Kitching, 1989; Lipton, 1977). The challenge for rural populists historically has been to find a *modern* alternative to the dominant urban-based model of modernity that has large-scale capitalist industrialisation at its centre. Central to many historical populist political projects has been the dream of delivering sustainable futures to rural populations suffering under severely imbalanced and adverse socio-economic conditions.

'Small man' populism, the product of our second opposition, has long been associated with movements of agrarian interests (peasants and small-scale family farmers especially) and small business interests who find themselves losing out and in danger of marginalisation and disappearance in the modern world (Canovan, 1981; Kitching, 1989; Mudde, 2002). Typically, rural small man populists attribute the declining and relatively powerless position of the constituencies they claim to represent to the threats they associate with the structural power of dominant centralising and concentrating urban-centred large-scale forces and developmental tendencies, and with the individuals that come to personify the presence and operation of such forces and tendencies.

The decline of small man economic interests in the countryside has often been associated with a complex of crisis conditions. Behind specifically *economic* crisis conditions we find the interplay of a number of factors, in particular the actions of distant exploitative "middlemen and moneylenders" (Paige, 1975, p. 47), and the operation of scale tendencies that leave small-scale agriculture and business regularly battling for survival. Fuelling *social* crisis in the countryside is declining morale among a steadily diminishing number of tightly squeezed small-scale economic actors, and the rural exodus that has been part and parcel of a dominant industrial/ post-industrial and urbanised society.

When the state (or segments of it) is prepared to intervene on behalf of small man interests on the land it may seek to regulate market forces so as to protect farmers or small-scale business interests from exploitative middlemen or 'unfair' competition. More positively, state intervention may attempt to stimulate small-scale agriculture and business with a view to making it more productive and economically and socially viable. Pro-small man manufacturing state intervention – particularly prominent in inter-war eastern and central Europe – was distinctive in

Populism, Power, and Development **127**

proposing an industrialising policy that would favour a spatially dispersed form of industrialisation (Canovan, 1981, p. 126; Kitching, 1989, pp. 57–59).

How does the powerlessness/structural power opposition work in the case of beleaguered rural communities? Behind 'communitarian' populism we find a commitment to 'community life' and to the welfare and preservation of local communities and other associated community-based interests. "Many populist writers," Midgley (1995, p. 90) remarks:

> place emphasis on the community as a locus for people's activities. They believe that communities form the basis of society and that the enhancement of community life offers the best opportunity for promoting people's happiness, a sense of belonging and identity.

A leading communitarian populist fear, one that is echoed in the academic literature that dwells on the decline of community (Etzioni, 1995; Putnam, 2000), is that the modern world becomes progressively more hostile to community. The challenges of resisting the forces that produce decline is all the more immense in disadvantaged rural communities with but weak economies to sustain them.

But what specifically makes these forces so inimical to community? As with our rural and small man populists, communitarian populists can see the interests they seek to defend as being threatened by the way structural power becomes ever more centralised and concentrated politically and economically in the modern world. A typical charge is that modern societies have become:

> excessively centralised and remote from their citizens. "Communities" have been in decline and, as a result, ordinary people have not been stimulated to engage in a form of public life which appears to affect them only in an indirect manner. (Parry et al., 1992, p. 13)

Frequently our rural small man and communitarian strands of oppositional populism blend together. When this occurs, a strong underlying preference for smallness of scale can be discovered behind the desire for community; and small man populist commitments, in their turn, are likely to embrace the local community. Thus the sorts of equalitarian and communitarian worlds that Kitching's (1989, p. 22) populists and neo-populists imagine are populated by:

> approximately equal 'small men' and small enterprises, competing against each other to be sure, but in a way which is moderated and restrained by community and co-operative links, both formal and informal.

What does the central opposition articulated by 'representational' populism consist of? Within this strand of populism (which again may be closely related to the rural small man and communitarian oppositional strands), it is the opposition between the relative powerlessness of the people and the power of established (and typically city-based) *political* elites that stands out. Here populist thinking turns on the way certain groups see themselves being left relatively powerless by the way their interests are neglected, or perhaps entirely ignored, within liberal democracies by those whose duty is to provide 'the people' with adequate representation (Canovan, 1981, p. 9; Wiles, 1969, p. 167).

Alienated "from the centres of power" (Wiles, 1969, p. 167), representational populists tend to consider established political elites not merely as out of touch with the people but lying beyond "popular control" (Canovan, 1981, p. 27). Instead of adequately representing popular interests, the political and economic establishment tends to be seen as incompetent, possibly corrupt, and as contributing significantly to the relative powerlessness and further decline of popular interests, especially by pursuing damaging state policies.[1] Rural representational populists are at one with their small man and communitarian counterparts in tending to see the structural tendency to centralise and concentrate political and economic power in the city as vital to the generation of popular powerlessness in the countryside.

When a sympathetic and responsive state (or segments of it) becomes alert to rural crises of representation a political and official rhetoric of widening 'participation,' or even of aspiring to equality of participation, is to be expected. In the official conception of participation, notions of economic and social inclusion and exclusion are also likely to feature significantly. State exponents of this 'participative' strand of representational populism are apt to give voice to a radical-sounding rhetoric of returning power to the people by expanding the opportunities for popular participation and active citizenship through revamping local government or, in the arena of local development, through instituting new partnership-based governance initiatives and institutions.

When this participative strand of representational populism assumes a strongly communitarian complexion it typically proceeds by inviting the participation of the disadvantaged 'local community,' or of socially excluded community-based local interests, in a process of finding and implementing solutions to local development problems within new partnership-based institutional arrangements. Frequently such an invitation carries the promise that community interests can expect to be 'empowered' as a product of partnership-based local governance and development being rolled out.

Negotiating Powerlessness

There is, of course, more to populism than the use of oppositions to make sense of the relative powerlessness that rural interests routinely experience in the modern world. What rural populist movements and state interventions centrally aim to achieve is real social, economic, and political change. To begin then to interpret the politics of negotiating perceived forms of rural powerlessness via collective and state action, we will now introduce the distinction between 'power over' and 'power to' familiar to students of power (Goverde et al., 2000, pp. 37–38; Morriss, 2002, pp. xiii–xiv). The populist desire to expose sources of what are often obscure or

Populism, Power, and Development **129**

concealed forms of 'power over' domination resonates with that contemporary strand of the power literature that seeks to reveal power's hidden persona. Steven Lukes's (2005) second dimension of power attempts to capture the ability of the powerful to set agendas and so determine what issues are considered legitimate topics for debate and decision. His third dimension of power – which is even less observable than the power exercised in agenda setting and issue manipulation – revolves around the ability of the powerful to exert hegemonic power that can secure "the [willing] compliance of those they dominate" (p. 12). The most consequential effect of hegemonic power is that the relatively powerless find it difficult, if not impossible, to become alive to their *real* interests (p. 10).

The concerns of the collective and state actors of interest to us may not always be the unmasking of the sorts of power that are of prime concern to Lukes, but in a sense their basic desire is quite comparable. In their case, too, revealing the locus and character of dominating (and often hidden or obscure) 'power over' forces – so that they can be contested and challenged – becomes a preoccupation. A critical step in negotiating powerlessness therefore involves assisting the relatively powerless to become alive to their real interests with a view to bringing about some change for the better.

The idea of relying on collective action to counteract structural 'power over' forces (whether covert or overt) is central to that strand of the power literature that emphasises the 'power to' capacities collective actors can tap into and build upon. The collective character of 'power to' capacities finds a well-known exposition in Hannah Arendt's (1970, p. 44) conception of power as:

> the human ability not just to act but to act in concert. Power is never the property of an individual; it belongs to a group and remains in existence only so long as the group keeps together.

What such a conception implies is that the ability of the relatively powerless to form stable groups, capable of engaging in effective collective action, becomes in itself a central first step in generating the 'power to' counteract forms of 'power over' domination.

When we bring the 'power to' and the 'power over' dimensions together, we can therefore construe rural underdog collective action as beginning or continuing a process of generating the 'power to' capacities required to bring 'power over' structural forces under a measure of effective control. In their turn, participative state interventions can be viewed as drawing on the state's 'power to' capacities to create conditions in which relationships of domination can be negotiated to the advantage of those constituencies perceived to be left relatively powerless by the play of dominating 'power over' forces (some of which may have their origins in past state actions or inactions).

This discussion of the 'power to' and 'power over' aspects of power is meant to underline the centrality of generating counteracting power via collective action and participative pro-community state intervention; and, to the extent that this generation of counteracting power can bring about some measure of structural change, the centrality of the negotiable character of our four oppositions between powerlessness and power. What the 'power to' and 'power over' distinction does not address, of course, is the variety of forms assumed by rural underdog collective action and pro-underdog participative state interventions. Nor does it shed any light on the crucial issue of *how far* collective and state actors may be prepared to go in attempting to negotiate perceived oppositions between power and powerlessness effectively. To theorise these issues pertaining to organisation, tactics and scope, we will now bring our radical and pragmatic ideal-typical populist scenarios into the discussion.

Radical and Pragmatic Ideal-Typical Scenarios

Our ideal-typical radical and pragmatic collective and state actors will be made to differ fundamentally in their standards of effective collective and state action and in the conditions they take to be necessary for turning collective and participative pro-community state intervention into effective forms of counteracting power. These differences find expression in diverging conceptions of 'the people' and 'the community,' of aims and objectives as well as of organisational and tactical choices. Despite the differences that divide them, the analysis of our ideal-typical radical and pragmatic collective and state populists starts out in each case with an appreciation of the realities of relative rural powerlessness and a suggestion that urban-based centralising and concentrating political, economic, and social power can leave rural interests at a serious disadvantage in the modern world.

Influenced by 'small man' and communitarian commitments to the normative ideals of fairness and equality and the desire to find alternatives to a future of long-term and cumulative structural rural decline, the radical populist conception of effective collective action begins with two basic contentions: the suggestion that the gap between urban structural power and rural powerlessness widens progressively with the passage of time; and a principled rejection of the inevitability of widening urban domination and rural subordination. Nor is this radical analysis content to stop at mere analysis and critique. Its fundamental aim is to uncover the dynamics of structural decline with a view to reshaping the rural economy and society in ways that give primacy to struggling small man economic interests and to the most disadvantaged local communities. Besides attributing popular powerlessness to the dominance of external structural forces, the radical populist gaze falls as well upon the way local power structures can mediate the operation of structural forces (Gaventa, 1980, pp. 259–260).

Three considerations underpin the pragmatic populist conception of effective collective action. There is first a pragmatic acceptance of the overwhelming dominance of urban power in modern society as an unalterable (if lamentable) fact of modern life. While the gap between urban power and rural powerlessness is viewed as substantial, it is also seen as waxing and waning in cyclical or irregular patterns that reflect the play of a wide set of contingencies. In consequence, the pragmatic analysis is disposed to think in mildly reformist and restorative terms of

Populism, Power, and Development **131**

achieving incremental or marginal improvements in the context of the tacit acceptance of an inevitably unequal and unfair balance between rural and urban interests. In their analysis of how to restore the *status quo ante* and to pursue minor reforms, pragmatists pride themselves in addition on a realism that accepts the need for a balance between big and small-scale economic activity and for a rural and regional policy that does not dwell exclusively on the most disadvantaged places.

In their conception of the relatively powerless people, our radical populists [agents] look to small and struggling economic interests rather than to all rural economic interests and to the most disadvantaged rural communities rather than to rural communities in general. On this basis 'poor', 'marginal', 'peripheral' and 'disadvantaged' places are swept into the radical net. Of course, to take 'whole communities' (albeit the most disadvantaged ones) as relatively powerless risks obscuring the presence of relatively advantaged individuals in disadvantaged places and so ending up with a somewhat inclusive conception of the people and of the community. Accepting that such risk may sometimes leave our ideal-typical radical populists partly straddling the inclusive–exclusive divide, it is at the same time patently not the interests of the relatively better off that our radical populists are keen to safeguard and advance. Their conscious concern is to defend the interests of those who constantly lose out and are systematically left behind in relatively disadvantaged rural communities.

While our radical populists insist that some rural places and interests have to be seen as relatively more powerless vis-à-vis other rural places and interests, our pragmatic populists contrastingly choose to emphasise how the countryside as a whole relative to the city is relatively powerless. And in contrast to the overwhelmingly exclusive conceptions of the people and of community that radical populists accept, the position our ideal-typical pragmatic populist collective actors assume is unmistakably inclusive in its reach. The characteristic pragmatic populist desire, reflecting the view that the countryside as a whole finds itself relatively powerless vis-à-vis the city in the contemporary world, is thus to speak for *all* local economic and social interests and for *all* rural communities.

Radical populist thinking on the organisational conditions perceived to be necessary for effective collective action draws on deeply implanted egalitarian and communitarian values to argue for an intense democratisation that entails *active* and ongoing rank-and-file participation. By contrast, effective organisation, in pragmatic populist eyes, is visibly skewed in favour of the more powerful notables of local society and the directive leadership style these are wont to practise. While the constituencies they wish to reach out to differ significantly, both our radicals and pragmatists are drawn to co-operatives, local development associations and interest associations as forms of organisation (Esman and Uphoff, 1984, pp. 61–68). Equally, radicals and pragmatists are prepared to resort to campaigning alliances and movements as circumstances permit.

What can be said about radical and pragmatic tactical considerations? Here we would see radical populist collective actors having little choice (reflecting their desire for transformative change of a sort they assume the state will be reluctant to concede) but to have recourse to oppositional or adversarial tactics in their dealings with the state. The tactical approach favoured by populist pragmatic collective actors offers quite a contrast. Accustomed to working within 'the system', well-networked rural notables are seen as ultimately prepared to work closely with the state so as to maintain or restore a more favourable power balance between the urban and rural worlds and to pursue the minor reforms they desire. For all these tactical differences, our radicals and pragmatists alike realise the importance of being able to mobilise what resources are to hand (including the underdog identity they construct for themselves and their constituencies) and to skilfully exploit what crisis conditions are to hand (whether viewed as cumulative and persisting or sporadic and fleeting) to their own advantage.

What ideal-typical features characterise radical and pragmatic state intervention in rural communities? The radical ideal-typical scenario begins with the possibility that segments of the state (in contrast to the analysis of radical collective actors) may come under the control of politicians or functionaries who profess sympathy with radical populist ideals. Such a stance leads them to favour the disadvantaged countryside, struggling small man economic interests and the most vulnerable rural communities and community-based interests in the policies they choose; and, more specifically, to consciously channel job creation measures and partnership-type participative development schemes towards the most vulnerable rural groups and places. On such a basis radical policy aspirations hope to redistribute a significant measure of economic, political, and social structural power (in the decision-making sense) to the most disadvantaged rural interests.

The political and policy stance of our ideal-typical pragmatic populist state agents is decidedly less ambitious. While they too may habitually project the countryside and small-scale enterprise as relatively embattled and disadvantaged, they also insist on seeing large- and small-scale economic interests as tending to complement each other. The state intervention they accordingly prefer aims to maintain or restore some acceptable balance between large- and small-scale economic interests. Participative development schemes are seen as a means of defusing short-term crisis conditions and of pursuing some of the minor changes required to achieve some marginal re-balancing of power relations both within the countryside and between the countryside and the city. In addition, the pragmatic policy commitment to stimulate regional and rural economic activity and community development seeks to 'bet on winners' by selectively favouring those places that can be deemed most suitable from an efficiency standpoint.

Recognising that the relationship between the city and the country is unequal and will continue to be so, our ideal-typical pragmatic populists are more optimistic in seeing well-organised rural interests as being capable of exploiting the opportunities generated by urban dependence on the countryside to their own advantage. The future looks bright in this regard to the extent that the city, in an increasingly post-productivist countryside, becomes the source of a host of new income-generating possibilities associated with tourism, long-distance commuting and second-home ownership (Marsden, 2003).

Populism's Strengths and Weaknesses

It is now time to assess populism's usefulness as an aid to interpretation and as a descriptive term in the sphere of community development. The positive case for populism as an aid to interpretation rests on a number of general foundations: the prominence of rural themes in the academic literature on populism, the historical appearance of self-styled populist movements of rural defence, and the tendency for state elites to take the side of rural underdog interests on occasion.

Of greatest importance to us is the centrality of four distinguishable oppositions between powerlessness and power to rural populist thinking about development and its prospects. Upon these oppositions we have built an underdog power approach to the study of rural collective action and certain state interventions. The analysis of power relationships that this underdog populist approach contains is distinctive for three main reasons. First, it thinks in terms of oppositions between powerlessness and power as a means of making sense of rural predicaments. Second, these oppositions become a key aspect of collective agency insofar as they help inspire a range of collective and state actions aimed at producing change that will either diminish or eliminate structural unfairness and inequality. And third, the underdog power approach focuses its attention throughout on the perspective of those who project themselves as relatively powerless or those who claim to speak on their behalf.

The inadequacies of populism can be identified as 'interpretive' and 'descriptive' in character. There is a wide consensus that a major difficulty with populism as an interpretive category is its extreme diffuseness. The term populism has been applied to phenomena as varied as liberal democratic and autocratic states and leaderships, left- and right-leaning ideologies (Stoker, 2006, pp. 134–136), participatory and elitist leadership styles, a broad set of public policies and a collection of diverse (but often rural) social movements (Canovan, 1981, Ch. 1; Worsley, 1969).

Another interpretive difficulty flows from populism's alleged intolerance and tendency to scapegoat. There is in fact a long history of intellectuals taking exception to political populists' tendency to vilify and scapegoat their opponents (Canovan, 1981, pp. 47–48; Lowndes, 2005). A related intellectual objection to political populism is based on its tendency to see the world in over-simplistic terms that inevitably lead to faulty analyses and conclusions. Sometimes technocratic and elitist preferences, suspicious of popular wisdom, can be detected behind this objection to populism. As Stoker (2006, p. 132) summarises:

> The perils posed by modern populism come from its tendency to demonize opponents and the political environment in general, and from its failure to appreciate the complexities of democratic practice and the communities in which we live. Populism too often collapses into the politics of blame and simplistic solutions.[2]

While accepting that populism may sometimes be intolerant and heavily one-sided in its analysis, we would contend that the charge that populism is too diffuse to be a coherent aid to interpretation does not pose a critical problem for us. In elaborating our ideal-typical scenarios we have sought to turn populism's diffuseness to our own advantage. Contrasting elitist and participatory democratic populist tendencies, for instance, have been central to our exploration of the radical-pragmatic range of organisational possibilities.

In comparison with the difficulties posed by populism's diffusiveness, the difficulties with populism as a descriptive term are not so easily accommodated. Here we can distinguish between 'emic' terms used by the actors themselves and 'etic' terms introduced by observers intent on providing an objective or scientific account of what is afoot. While the earliest North American rural activists may have been self-styled populists, this tends to be no longer the case. For instance, the contemporary US 'ecopopulists' that Szasz (1994) introduces us to do not describe themselves as such. Likewise, Panizza (2005, p. 1) draws our attention to the way that populism, even if inherently a 'contested concept,' "... has become an analytical attribution rather than a term with which most political actors would willingly identify." Why this is so bears witness to populism's increasingly negative reputation as a descriptive marker of identity at the 'emic' level.

In the contemporary world the profoundly negative reputation populism has gained for itself in many quarters has become more general and has come to identify the phenomenon above all else. Especially in the arena of party politics both 'populist' and 'populism' are widely used today as pejorative and abusive terms. A relatively mild instance of this is when one politician calls a rival 'populist' with a view to diminishing her or him in the eyes of the voting public (McGuigan, 1992, pp. 1–2). More extreme versions of dark-side populism are also prominently in evidence. If anything, political populism's recent revival in Europe has reinforced the long-held academic view of populism as a phenomenon whose identity has been fatally flawed by its association with a right-wing politics of extreme reaction and intolerance (Hayward, 1996, p. 20; Mouffe, 2005, pp. 68–69; Taggart, 2000, Ch. 7).

The contemporary rise to prominence of 'dark side' political populism looks set to continue to have a negative bearing on how contemporary rural collective and state actors are likely to be disposed to using 'populism' and 'populist' to describe themselves and their activities. For those who subscribe to a view of social science that takes seriously the emic viewpoints and sensibilities of the actors we presume to study, this poses a major, and for us ultimately a fatal, difficulty with populism as a useful descriptive term.

Conclusion

Our case for anchoring our rural underdog power approach in populism began by introducing a set of four oppositions between powerlessness and power – each one resonating with a more general populist opposition that pits underdog powerlessness against establishment power – that can be related to rural conditions and that have featured prominently in the academic literature on populism (Canovan, 1981, pp. 4–8). While the 'powerlessness' we have been discussing takes four distinguishable

Populism, Power, and Development   **135**

forms, the 'power' side of our four oppositions has always a double identity, referring to various forms of structural power on the one hand and to the potential counteracting power of collective action and state intervention on the other. We have introduced the distinction between the 'power to' and the 'power over' to highlight the possibilities of generating popular power and counteracting forms of structural power via collective and participative state action. To explore the different directions that rural underdog community development might conceivably take, we have also outlined radical and pragmatic ideal-typical scenarios. These scenarios are intended to stand as benchmarks by reference to which real-world instances of community politics and participative state interventions can be interpreted and compared. Of course, how well these real-world realities converge with or diverge from our interpretive benchmarks has ultimately to be decided empirically.

Five specific strengths of the underdog power approach to rural community development are worthy of note. First, it takes as central the gulf between fairness and equality as normative ideals in community development and the perceived realities of unfairness and inequality that frequently typify the rural condition. Second, perceptions of unfairness and inequality are linked – via the four oppositions between power and powerlessness – both with the presence of powerful structural forces and with the construction of underdog identities. Third, two different conceptions of power, one based on forms of structural 'power over' domination and the other on the potential counteracting 'power to' capacities that collective action and state intervention can generate, are introduced. Fourth, an important distinction in the contemporary power literature – that which distinguishes between the 'power over' and the 'power to' – is used to assist in conceptualising agent-centred community-based collective action and participative pro-community state interventions that seek to counteract instances of popular powerlessness by building the 'power to' capacities required to challenge instances of structural power. And fifth, by focusing throughout on the perspective of those who project themselves as relatively powerless or those who claim to speak on their behalf, the underdog power approach takes the construction of underdog identities as central to the study of the politics of rural community development.

But how well is our underdog power approach to community-based collective action and participative state intervention served by linking it to populism as an aid to interpretation and as a descriptive term? Populism's extreme diffuseness, its alleged intolerance and tendency to over-simplify complex realities have been identified as serious difficulties. We would accept that populism can sometimes be intolerant and be highly one-sided in its analysis. The charge of diffuseness, however, does not present us with insurmountable problems at the interpretive level.

While our four oppositions are offered as the primary reason why populism as an aid to interpretation offers many useful insights, populism as a descriptive term is overloaded with negative baggage. Indeed, the paradox of populism in the present context arises from the manner it retains considerable strength as an aid to interpretation while being hopelessly compromised as a descriptive term. Nor, given the increasingly negative reputation 'populism' and 'populist' have acquired in everyday life at the emic level, can matters be expected to improve in this regard in the near to medium future. In light of this we would choose ultimately to describe the approach to rural community development we are advocating here as simply the rural underdog power approach.

Notes

1 Wiles (1969, p. 167) is not alone in observing that this sort of populism is "prone to conspiracy theories."
2 Not everyone would agree with such an assessment. For instance, Nugent (1963) takes tolerance to be a hallmark of populism; and Sanders (2002, p. 46), writing likewise of North American populism, has suggested that "... most of the national legislative fruits of the Progressive Era had their unmistakeable origins in the [populist] agrarian movements of the 1870s, 1880s, and 1890s."

References

Alexander, J.C. (1987). *Sociological theory since 1945*. London: Hutchinson.

Arendt, H. (1970). *On violence*. London: Allen Lane.

Burger, T. (1987). *Max Weber's theory of concept formation: History, laws and ideal type*. Durham: Duke University Press.

Canovan, M. (1981). *Populis*. London: Junction Books.

Canovan, M. (2002) - please provide details.

Esman, M.J., & Uphoff, N.T. (1984). *Local organisations: Intermediaries in rural development*. Ithaca: Cornell University Press.

Etzioni, A. (1995). *The spirit of community: Rights, responsibilities and the communitarian agenda*. London: Fontana Press.

Gallagher, M., Laver, M., & Mair, P. (2006). *Representative government in modern Europe* (4th ed.). Boston, MA: McGraw Hill.

Gaventa, J. (1980). *Power and powerlessness: Quiescence and rebellion in an Appalachian Valley*. Oxford: Clarendon Press.

Goverde, H., Cerny, P.G., Haugaard, M., & Lentner, H. (Eds.) (2000). *Power in contemporary politics: Theories, practices, globalizations*. London: Sage.

Hayward, J. (1996). The populist challenge to elitist democracy in Europe. In J. Hayward (Ed.), *Elitism, populism and European politics*. Oxford: Clarendon Press.

Hobsbawm, E. (1997). *The age of capital 1848–1875*. London: Abacus.

Kitching, G. (1989). *Development and underdevelopment in historical perspective: Populism, nationalism and industrialization*. London: Routledge.

Lipset, S.M., & Rokkan, S. (1967). Cleavage structures, party systems, and voter alignments: An introduction. In S.M. Lipset & S. Rokkan (Eds.), *Party systems and voter alignments: Cross-national perspective*. New York, NY: The Free Press.

Lipton, M. (1977). *Why poor people stay poor: A study of urban bias in world development*. London: Temple Smith.

Lowndes, J. (2005). From founding violence to political hegemony: The conservative populism of George Wallace. In F. Panizza (Ed.), *Populism and the mirror of democracy*. London: Verso.

Lukes, S. (2005). *Power: A radical view* (2nd ed.). Houndmills, Basingstoke: Palgrave Macmillan.

Marsden, T. (2003). *The condition of rural sustainability*. Assen: Van Gorcum.

Marx, K., & Engels, F. (1997). *The Communist Manifesto*. Oxford: Oxford University Press.

Populism, Power, and Development **137**

McGuigan, J. (1992). *Cultural populism.* London: Routledge.

Midgley, J. (1995). *Social development: The developmental perspective in social welfare.* London: Sage.

Morriss, P. (2002). *Power: A philosophical analysis* (2nd ed.). Manchester: Manchester University Press.

Mouffe, C. (2005). The "end of politics" and the challenge of right-wing populism. In F. Panizza (Ed.), *Populism and the mirror of democracy.* London: Verso.

Mudde, C. (2002). In the name of the peasantry, the proletariat, and the people: Populisms in Eastern Europe. In Y. Mény & Y. Surel (Eds.), *Democracies and the populist challenge.* Houndmills, Basingstoke: Palgrave.

Nugent, W.T.K. (1963). *The tolerant populists: Kansas populism and nativism.* Chicago, IL: University of Chicago Press.

Paige, J.M. (1975). *Agrarian revolution: Social movements and export agriculture in the underdeveloped world.* New York, NY: The Free Press.

Panizza, F. (2005). Introduction: Populism and the mirror of democracy. In F. Panizza (Ed.), *Populism and the mirror of democracy.* London: Verso.

Parry, G., Moser, G., & Day, N. (1992). *Political participation and democracy in Britain.* Cambridge: Cambridge University Press.

Putnam, R.D. (2000). *Bowling alone: The collapse and revival of American community.* New York, NY: Simon & Schuster.

Roberts, B.R. (1995). *The making of citizens: Cities of peasants revisited.* London: Arnold.

Sanders, E. (2002). Agrarian politics and parties after 1896. In G.E. Gilmore (Ed.), *Who were the progressives?* New York, NY: Palgrave.

Stoker, G. (2006). *Why politics matters: Making democracy work.* Houndmills, Basingstoke: Palgrave Macmillan.

Szasz, A. (1994). *Ecopopulism: Toxic waste and the movement for environmental justice.* Minneapolis, MN: University of Minnesota Press.

Taggart, P. (2000). *Populism.* Buckingham: Open University Press.

Wiles, P. (1969). A syndrome, not a doctrine: Some elementary theses on populism. In I. Ionescu & E. Gellner (Eds.), *Populism: Its meaning and national characteristics.* London: Weidenfeld and Nicolson.

Worsley, P. (1969). The concept of populism. In I. Ionescu & E. Gellner (Eds.), *Populism: Its meaning and national characteristics.* London: Weidenfeld and Nicolson.

9

WHAT KIND OF DEMOCRACY INFORMS COMMUNITY DEVELOPMENT?

David Mathews

Thanks to many of the authors in this book, I have become more aware of the rich body of literature on community development and the lively debates among scholars in this field on a considerable array of issues.[1] The focus of the Kettering Foundation's studies, however, is on just one central issue. It is the issue at the heart of citizens' concerns about their role in a world they see as increasingly uncertain and dangerous, and a world structured around large institutions that people no longer consider effective in solving their problems or responsive to their concerns. This issue is summed up in a question communities ask: how can *we* come together, despite our differences and disagreements, to solve the problems that endanger all of us? What people mean by community is the place where they live, work, and raise their families, the place where there are (or aren't) jobs, the place where natural disasters sweep over them, the place where they get their water and breathe the air. People have always lived in many communities – religious, fraternal, and social – that aren't bound by place. Yet none of us lives in a Petri dish divorced from place, physical, and human.

This question people ask about working together to solve problems is a quintessentially democratic one. And it informs the foundation's understanding of democracy. We see democracy as a political system where citizens generate the power to rule themselves by joining forces to solve common problems. They work both through local civic organizations and through large institutions like those of government and education.

This chapter asks what such a concept of democracy means for professionals and practitioners in community development. But since the foundation isn't in this field and hasn't mastered its literature, we are limited. I can only raise the question and describe what Kettering has learned about the work citizens do when they join forces. My hope is that practitioners and scholars in community development will explain how their work can relate to (and perhaps reinforce) the work citizens do to rule themselves.

A Thought Experiment

I suggest a mental exercise or thought experiment along these lines: this chapter will report on what the Kettering Foundation is learning from its studies of how democracy can work as it should.[2] Then, to complete the experiment, professionals in community development (scholars and practitioners) would identify the implications of what the foundation reports for their work. Doubtless, this exercise will generate views of how democracy should work that are different from those of the foundation, which is appropriate because a debate about what democracy should mean is one of the characteristics of democracy.

A Hypothesis to Test

Kettering has had opportunities to meet professionals in a wide variety of fields who are grappling with their relation to democracy, including those in journalism, health care, education, philanthropy, and public administration. The ways professionals go about their work usually meet the objectives and standards in their field. That's as it should be. Yet what professionals do isn't always well aligned with the way people go about their work as citizens. Professionals may overlook or even disrupt the work of citizens without intending to — much in the same way that civil engineers once filled in wetlands and dug channels through barrier islands in the name of progress. The foundation's hypothesis is that a better alignment would both benefit professionals and serve the cause of democratic self-rule.

By a better alignment I mean a complementary relationship between the work of professionals and the work of citizens. I am not talking, however, about just a pleasant or even just a mutually supportive relationship; I mean a relationship that meets the test of democracy, which is one that results in citizens having a stronger hand in shaping their future. Just how important this democratic criterion is was brought home to the foundation by what we learned from communities devastated by Hurricane Katrina in 2005.[3]

One of the communities hardest hit was Bayou La Batre, which is located in Alabama, near the Mississippi line. This haven for commercial fishing is around 300 years old and was once part of Spanish West Florida, which remained outside the United States until well after the American Revolution. The residents include descendants of the original French and Spanish settlers (families like the Bosarges), and settlers largely of Scotch, Irish, and Welsh backgrounds who came down from the "North," that is, Tennessee, Georgia, and the Carolinas. They were joined by West Africans, many of whom did not come voluntarily. Later on, the community became home to immigrants from Southeast Asia.[4] This was no homogeneous community; differences of opinion on nearly every subject were common.

After Katrina, the area was in ruins: buildings destroyed and boats pushed inland into the fields. A group of citizens standing in the midst of all the rubble posed a very simple yet difficult question: in effect, they wanted to know, is there anybody who can talk to *us* about how *we* can come together to rebuild this community?

140 D. Mathews

And that was the question that influenced the foundation's concept of democracy. We were reminded of John Dewey's observation that the "neighborly community" is the home of democracy. Perhaps that is so because, as Henrik Ibsen reminded us, "a community is like a ship; everyone ought to be prepared to take the helm."[5]

The question raised by Katrina has a history. The people in Bayou La Batre knew from three centuries of experience that Katrina wouldn't be the last hurricane. They knew that their survival would depend on their coming together despite their differences because, for the first 72 hours, emergency personnel wouldn't be able to get to them. Roads would be washed away; electricity would be out; there would be no water. Neighbors would be dependent on neighbors.[6]

Even after the initial shock of Katrina had passed, the long-term future of the community was an issue. Many were afraid that if they didn't come together, not only would they be vulnerable to the next storm, but also to developers who would turn the area into another Disneyland. Many liked Disneyland, and some would have welcomed the jobs that could come with development, yet most wanted to keep living in a fishing village.

Unfortunately, the people in this community reported that they had a great deal of difficulty finding anyone who could talk to them about how *they* could come together. Outsiders offered food and shelter. Foundations had grants, the government provided loans, and higher education gave training along with technical assistance. Residents appreciated all of that. But it wasn't what they were asking for.

Their question isn't confined to communities in hurricane-prone areas. Communities can be destroyed by all kinds of disasters, particularly by economic ones these days. Coming together as a community is a universal challenge. In a democracy, it includes developing the civic capacity needed to become resilient to any kind of disaster.

Democracy Writ Large

Such a universal and basic question leads to a concept of democratic politics that includes more than what politicians do. For some, democracy is a form of government based on majority rule. It can also be a political system that promotes justice and equity or a way of life that encourages respect and freedom of association. In its research, Kettering uses something close to the ancient Greek concept of democracy, which locates sovereignty and legitimate power, or control, in the people or what the Pilgrims called a "civic body politic." Citizens use this power to rule themselves and shape their future.

A certain logic follows from this premise. Sovereign monarchs exercise power by acting. So the sovereign citizenry, it follows, is a collective political actor, a producer, not a beneficiary or constituency. It isn't a dependent body to be acted for or upon.

A sovereign citizenry acts together to make things that serve the good of all. Making things together without coercion, that is freely, is self-organizing.

And self-rule requires self-organizing. (How could it be self-rule if it didn't?) Self-rule by self-organizing with people who aren't kin to or alike one another is much older than the Greek's version of democracy. It probably dates back to the time when inclusive communities evolved beyond tribal villages. Without a single chief with authority over all, people had to find ways to organize community life themselves.[7] That was self-organizing.

The things people produce by working with others – often called *public goods* – bring about change, which is what having power or control means. Public goods are made through public or civic work; that is, work done by citizens joining forces.[8] Historically, the things citizens have made have included schools, hospitals, even the country itself. Today, the products of citizens' collective efforts – their civic work – range from campaigns that get drunk drivers off the road to neighborhood watches that make communities safer.

Nobel Prize-winner Elinor Ostrom has demonstrated that the things citizens make can reinforce what institutions and their professionals produce. In her research on this *coproduction* she writes:

> The term "client" is used more and more frequently to refer to those who should be viewed as essential co-producers of their own education, safety, health, and communities. A client is the name for a passive role. Being a co-producer makes one an active partner.

Citing her husband, Vincent Ostrom, she argues that:

> Institutions of self-governance depend upon the development of a science and art of association where citizens rely upon various forms of voluntary association to make the formal institutions of government serve the interests that citizens share with one another in human communities.[9]

The Work of Citizens as Democratic Practices

The way citizens go about the civic work of producing public goods might be called *democratic practices*. Practices are different from purely instrumental *techniques*, a distinction made by the ancient Greeks. This difference is subtle yet crucial, particularly given today's multitude of techniques for facilitating meetings and going about planning. Nothing is wrong with techniques; they just aren't the same as practices since they don't have moral value. For example, hammering is a carpenter's technique; its only benefit is driving a nail or shaping metal, although a degree of skill is involved. Practices are different; they express the virtues associated with democracy – good judgment, cooperation, social responsibility. Democratic practices can be cultivated, but they aren't a set of skills to be taught. They are sources of the moral energy that generates the political will and the commitments needed to drive civic work.

142 D. Mathews

To date, Kettering research has identified six practices used in the work citizens do with citizens. These practices are elements in a theory of democracy that has everyday applications in the life of a community. The practices are democratic in that they increase the control that people have over their future. I'll describe them very briefly here and then elaborate later.

For professionals, the challenge is to align their work with democratic practices. So before going into detail, I'll sketch out the differences between what occurs in civic work and the routines usually followed by professionals. Neither is better than the other, and their differences are appropriate. In fact, professional routines can be confused with democratic practices because their objectives are similar. That is, all politics, civic or professional, involves identifying and solving problems. Decisions have to be made all along the way, and after a course of action has been determined, resources must be located and deployed. Then citizens and professionals alike must assess the results. The greatest misalignment of professional routines and democratic practices occurs when professionals see that citizens are trying to accomplish the same tasks as they are but don't recognize the differences in *how* the tasks are done.

Naming

The first democratic practice involves identifying or describing a problem and selecting the terms to be used. It begins when something has happened (the local economy has collapsed) and people talk about how they and their families are affected. Citizens see problems in terms of what is most valuable to them, and when they name problems to capture what they hold dear, the naming takes on a democratic coloration. Professional names, on the other hand, tend to reflect professional expertise.

The way a problem is named and who gets to name it controls public participation. Rather than assuming people have to be brought out of private life through some type of inducement, the assumption behind the emphasis on naming is that people already have things they hold dear in public life. For instance, most people know, deep down, that security is collective. That was abundantly clear to people after Katrina because they depended on their neighbors to clear the rubble. Once the name of a problem resonates with what they value, people recognize that they are already engaged. This is why the name given to a problem is so crucial.[10]

Framing

The second practice has to do with what citizens think should be done about a problem, which follows from what they think the problem is. People propose various options for dealing with a problem, depending on what is most valuable to them. Each option has advantages and disadvantages. When all the major options are laid out, with their pros and cons fairly presented, it creates a democratic framework for decision making. Recognizing that every option has advantages as well as disadvantages also exposes the tensions that have to be worked through. Professionals create frameworks for decision making as well, but their options are typically based on technical feasibility and the weight of scientific evidence.

Deliberative Decision Making

The third practice is deciding which option is best. Obviously, decisions are being made in many ways all of the time. Deciding becomes a democratic practice when people make decisions by weighing options against all that they value; they deliberate together. Professionals also make decisions, sometimes using their own type of deliberation. Professionals are not indifferent to the appeal of the things all citizens value, yet they're more likely to weigh hard evidence rather than intangibles.

Most deliberative decision making occurs in small groups of people who may have similar demographic profiles, though not similar opinions. While lacking the demographic representativeness of focus groups, deliberative forums are more likely to be similar to the groups people confer with when making decisions. These forums do not lack for disagreements, and the conversations are authentic. That is, they capture the way people actually make up their minds.[11]

Identifying and Committing Resources

The fourth practice involves identifying the resources needed to solve a problem and getting commitments to use them. Civic resources are assets found in the experiences and talents of people.[12] Typically, they are less tangible than professional resources and can't be commandeered. They have to be committed in the mutual promises people make to one another.

Organizing Complementary Acting

Ideally, the actions decided on in public deliberations (usually many) complement one another. When they do, the power of what citizens do increases because of mutual reinforcement; the whole of their efforts becomes greater than the sum of the parts.[13] Professional action tends to be uniform and based on a single plan. Civic action isn't; it is as varied as the number of civic actors and more orchestrated than organized, more strategically opportunistic than directed by a plan.

Public Learning

Public learning isn't a separate practice but rather something that can occur throughout the work of citizens. It's the most important practice of all because it provides the momentum to keep the work moving ahead on the most difficult of problems, those that defy professional expertise and persist despite institutional efforts to eradicate them. Professionals tend to learn by comparing results to fixed goals; a citizenry is more likely to learn by reassessing what it thought was most valuable as well as the results of its collective efforts.

144 D. Mathews

What about Couch Potato Citizens?

Why don't professionals always see these distinctive democratic practices? One reason is that the people they encounter don't practice the practices. Here are some of the complaints we've heard from professionals in many fields:

1. People are apathetic; they don't respond when asked to become involved. Corporate interests tend to dominate the community.
2. Citizens don't trust one another and are more likely to disagree (particularly by race and class) than work together. They may even be afraid of one another. And they don't trust the systems professionals work in either.
3. If citizens do become interested in an issue, they are usually just emotionally involved and make ill-advised decisions. For example, people may only want jobs and not think about the consequences of growth.
4. There really isn't much people can do; they don't have the resources.
5. Even if people promise to do something together, many won't show up, and there is no way to enforce what they promised.
6. People are too disorganized to be effective; everyone wants to go his or her own way.
7. Even when a civic project gets started, it often stops; the momentum is easily lost.
8. There isn't any way to tell if civic projects have been effective; citizens seldom evaluate, at least not objectively. Building democratic capacity takes years and doesn't produce the hard numbers that funders demand.

Professionals aren't imagining these problems; they are real and to some degree unavoidable. Still, while not surefire antidotes, democratic practices can be counter-forces. For instance, as noted earlier, naming problems in terms of the things citizens care deeply about engages them. Framings that bring out tensions help citizens work through disagreements. Deliberative decision making increases the chances that the public's judgment will be sound, and it counters polarization. This type of decision making also enriches people's understanding of a problem, which helps them recognize untapped resources. Commitments to use these resources can be enforced by the covenants people make with one another when legal contracts are inappropriate. Deliberative decision making, while not ending in total agreement, can result in a common sense of purpose and direction that allows civic initiatives to complement one another with a minimum of coordination. And learning throughout civic work not only maintains civic momentum but also fosters evaluations that go deeper than conventional assessments of results.

Suggsville: Democratic Practices in Everyday Life

Skeptics often say that democratic practices may be antidotes to a lack of civic engagement, to combating polarizing disagreements, and to the other deficiencies seen in the citizenry, yet they doubt that the practices can develop and emerge in everyday life and not just in books and articles.

Opportunities to encourage democratic practices and to better align professional work with civic work do, in fact, occur every day. The key is to recognize the opportunities. Seizing these opportunities and aligning the two types of work doesn't require professionals to do more or different work. They can often take advantage of the potential in opportune moments by working in different ways.

To show where opportunities to develop democratic practices occur every day, the foundation has drawn on its observations in scores of communities to create a composite town, an avatar, which we call Suggsville.[14] The Suggsville composite is based on places where conditions were less than ideal in order to emphasize the difficulties citizens encounter in doing their work.

Naming Problems to Capture What is Most Valuable to Citizens

Suggsville was rural and poor. Once a prosperous farming community, the town began to decline during the 1970s as the agricultural economy floundered. By the 1990s, the unemployment rate soared above 40 percent. Property values plummeted. With little else to replace the income from idle farms, a drug trade flourished. A majority of Suggsville's children were born to single teenagers. The schools were plagued with low test scores and high dropout rates. Not surprisingly, disease rates were greater than for most communities. Obesity was becoming epidemic, and alcoholism was pervasive. Everyone who could leave the town had done so, especially college-educated young adults. Making matters worse, the community was sharply divided: rich and poor, black and white.

After church services and in the one grocery store that survived, Suggsvillians discussed what was happening with friends and neighbors. Different groups made small talk and mulled over the town's difficulties. No decisions were made or actions taken. Then a group of professionals from a nearby university, which had been consulting, suggested that Suggsvillians meet together, assess their situation, and decide what they might do. Initially, the university's proposal for a town meeting drew the predictable handful. People sat in racially homogeneous clusters – until someone rearranged the chairs into a circle and citizens began to mingle. After participants got off their favorite soapboxes, told their own stories, and looked for others to blame, they settled down to identifying the problems that concerned everyone. Economic security was at the top of the list, but it wasn't the only concern. Crime was another.

The Suggsville conversation was an opportunity to develop a democratic practice. People could name their problems in terms that resonated with the things they valued.[15]

Finding out what people consider valuable isn't difficult; just ask how a problem affects them and their family or what is at stake. However, naming a problem in terms of what people hold dear (in public terms) isn't simply describing it in everyday language. When people talk about what's at stake, they bring up concerns that are deeply important to most everyone – to be free from danger, secure from economic privation, free to pursue their own interests, and to be treated fairly by others. These collective motives are counterparts to the individual needs that Abraham Maslow found common to all human beings. They are more fundamental than the interests that grow out of our particular circumstances (which may change). And they are different from values.[16]

Some individual needs are quite tangible (food, for instance); others (being loved) are intangible. The same is true in collective matters. One of the communities Kettering heard from was facing corruption in high places and egregious crimes on the streets. Citizens there asked themselves what they valued most. Virtually all said that, more than anything, they wanted to live in a place that made them proud. Pride is an intangible aspiration rarely mentioned in planning documents or lists of goals. Still, the need to be proud of a city is a powerful political imperative.

This distinction between concrete planning goals and the intangibles people hold dear is illustrated in Wendell Berry's story of an economist who told farmers that it was cheaper to rent land than to buy it, which was factually correct at the time. A farmer responded, however, by telling the economist that his forebearers didn't come to America to be renters.[17] Something the farmers valued in addition to profits was at stake.

The names that professionals give issues, while technically accurate, often exclude the more subjective values that people associate with issues. The unfortunate result is that people don't necessarily feel any connection to issues that professionals see as important. Professionals may interpret this lack of connection as indifference on the part of the public.

Professional names can also suggest that there is little citizens can do about a problem except to support professionals and the institutions where they work. Consequently, people are disinclined to get involved because they don't see how they could make a difference. For instance, invitations from an economic development organization that encourage citizens to participate in solving a problem may sound hollow because of the way the problem has been named.

Professionals in all fields worry about apathetic citizens. Yet naming problems in public terms facilitates the deepest kind of civic engagement because the names people use dispose them to own their problems. And owning problems is a potent source of energy for civic work.

Framing Issues to Identify All the Options

As the town meetings continued, Suggsvillians laid out a number of concerns reflecting the things they valued. People didn't choose one name and discard all the others. The economy was just the first name for the town's problem, and it resonated with concerns about security. Then people identified other problems such as family instability and an increase in drug abuse. These, too, touched on different notions of security, which citizens also held dear.

Not incidentally, as people added names for problems, they tended to implicate themselves in solving them. They could do something about the alcoholism that was threatening both families and the social order. And they could do something about the children who suffered when adults took little responsibility for their well-being.

Given concerns about the economy, one of the first proposals was to recruit a manufacturing company. No one rejected the suggestion; it stayed on the table, but some participants in the conversations had a practical objection – every other town was competing for new industries, and some development authorities recommended a grow-your-own business strategy. Not convinced that this was a good recommendation, a few who felt strongly about recruiting new industry left the group and went to the state office of economic development for assistance. Nonetheless, the majority of the participants continued to discuss what they might do to support local businesses. Several mentioned a restaurant that had opened recently; it seemed to have the potential to stimulate a modest revival downtown. Unfortunately, that potential wasn't being realized because unemployed men (and youngsters who liked to hang out with them) were congregating on the street in front of the restaurant – and drinking. Customers shied away.

Notice what was happening in the Suggsville meetings. At this point, the group was putting on the table possible courses of action to revive the economy. Almost everyone assumed that the problem was, indeed, the economy, but that was changing as other concerns suggested other courses of action. No one was ready to delve into the pros and cons of the various proposals beyond noting they all had advantages and disadvantages. Hearing everyone's vision of Suggsville's future was an opportunity to create a comprehensive and democratic framework for the decisions that needed to be made about how to make the visions realities.

Issues are constantly being framed in communities by the media and officeholders. Sometimes an issue is framed around a single plan of action. The framework tells citizens to take it or leave it. Another common framework pits two possible solutions against each other and encourages a debate between advocates. Neither of these frameworks promotes the kind of deliberation that leads to civic work. Public decision making is better served by a framework that includes all the major options (usually three or four) and also identifies tensions among the things people consider valuable, which are embedded in the options. As already noted, recognizing these tensions is key to dealing with disagreements.

As people wrestle with what their community should do, they find themselves pulled and tugged in different directions. They want to do something that reinforces

148 D. Mathews

what they value without losing or compromising something equally important. Citizens face tensions like these in their personal and public lives. Even things that are universally valued, like freedom and security, can still conflict. Under certain circumstances, providing more security will impinge on something else that is valued, personal freedom. People will differ over how far they will go to sacrifice their freedom in order to increase their security.

Why emphasize tensions and run the risk of provoking disputes when the political environment already suffers from partisan rancor and incivility? After all, tensions invariably arouse strong feelings, and nothing will make the emotions disappear. However, if the framing begins by recognizing what citizens value, people may realize that their differences are over the means to the same ends. (We all value security and freedom but differ on how to balance the two.) Just this recognition has the potential to change the tone of the disagreements.

Recognizing tensions among us also makes us more aware of tensions within us. And when we realize that we are pulled in different directions personally, we tend to be less absolute in our opinions and more open to the views of others, even those with whom we disagree. This openness allows us to see problems from different perspectives. The result is that we have a more complete view of the problems confronting us. This enlarged sense is crucial to effective problem solving.

As people work through tensions by facing up to tradeoffs, they can reach a point where the community is able to move ahead in dealing with a problem.[18] A sense of which actions are or aren't likely to be supported is enough, since complete agreement is rare.

If framing is key to dealing with disagreements, how does it occur in real time? The everyday question, "If you are that concerned, what do you think should be done?" can start the process. As happened in Suggsville, people usually respond by talking about both their concerns and the actions they favor. Typically, the concerns are implicit in the suggestions for action.

People's concerns, and there are usually many, will generate a variety of specific proposals for action. For instance, if Suggsville were hit hard by a rash of burglaries, most people would be concerned about their physical safety, which is surely a basic political motive. Some would want the police visible on the streets. Others might favor a neighborhood watch. Even though each of these actions is different, they center around one basic concern – safety. In that sense, they are all part of one option, which might be characterized as protection through surveillance. An option is made up of actions that have the same purpose or move in the same direction.

A framework that recognizes all of the relevant concerns and lays out the main options for addressing them, along with the various actions and actors that would have to be involved, sets the stage for a fair trial. For a trial to be truly fair, each option has to be presented with its best foot forward, as well as with attention to its drawbacks. Fairness is particularly important when professionals encounter polarizing issues such as disposing of hazardous materials or closing schools.

Democracy and Community Development   **149**

Deliberating Publicly to Make Sound Decisions

> At the next Suggsville town meeting, attendance was larger, and people started talking about what could be done to save the restaurant. The police chief argued that the problem was loitering, and he recommended stricter enforcement of ordinances. The chief was aware that there were downsides to strict law enforcement, but thought they were less serious than the loitering. Others weren't so sure. Strict enforcement, even if it worked to clear the streets, could give the community the appearance of a police state. This was a tension to be worked through. Still others worried about problems they thought contributed to the loitering. One woman suggested that loitering was symptomatic of widespread alcoholism.
>
> As citizens put their concerns on the table, they struggled with what was most important to the welfare of the community. People valued a great many things. The Suggsville that they hoped to create would be family friendly and safe for kids. It would have good schools, as well as a good economy. Yet everything that would have to be done to reach those objectives had potential downsides, as was the case with stricter law enforcement. Tensions were unavoidable. People were ready to weigh the potential consequences of different options because they had to decide what was really most valuable to the community.

Step outside Suggsville again and look at the opportunity for turning a discussion into a democratic practice, public deliberation. In the meetings, the door was open to raise questions like: if we did what you suggest – and it worked – but also had negative consequences, would you still stand by your proposal?

Deliberating helps the citizenry move from initial reactions and hastily formed opinions to more shared and reflective judgment. Of course, we can never know whether our decisions have been wise until we see the results. Nonetheless, decisions are more likely to be sound if the course of action we choose is consistent with what we believe is most important to our well-being. Perhaps that is why the ancient Greeks called deliberation the talk we use to teach ourselves before we act.[19] (Of course, public judgments may prove faulty in time; the voice of the people is not infallible.)

Citizens deliberate to work through the tensions within and among options. This work – choice work – occurs in stages, never all at once, and these stages would seem to have important implications for practitioners.[20] Knowing where citizens are – and aren't – in their thinking is crucial in engaging them.

Initially, citizens may not be sure there is an issue they should be concerned about. Nothing dear to them seems at stake. A bit later, they may become aware of a problem that touches on something they value, yet simply gripe about it. The "issue" will be who is to blame. At this stage, people may not see the tensions or the necessity for citizens to act. If the tensions do become apparent, people usually struggle as they weigh the advantages and disadvantages of various options. Eventually, citizens may work through an issue and settle on a range of actions that move in a common direction.

Consider what these stages suggest for civic engagement strategies. When citizens aren't sure there is a problem they should be concerned about, professionals may be well advised to start where people start, even though experts may have moved on in their thinking. Citizens aren't ready to consider solutions at this point. The issue that has to be addressed is: what is the issue?

When people do, indeed, recognize there is a serious issue yet look for a scapegoat, revisiting the nature of the problem seems, again, more likely to be successful than promoting a solution. Even when citizens move past blaming, they may still be unsure of what their options are and what tradeoffs they have to make. If so, they are very susceptible to being polarized, particularly if politicians engage in a hard-sell strategy. However, when people reach the point of struggling with tradeoffs, they are likely to be open to information that is relevant to their concerns.

When it comes to the stages of deliberation, the implications for community development seem fairly obvious. For instance, while information provided by experts is important, this can't substitute for the deliberating people must do in order to make decisions. The reason that expert information isn't enough lies in a significant difference between the way citizens go about informing their decisions and the way professionals inform theirs.

In the first place, the kinds of decisions each make are different; professionals have to decide what is factual and feasible. Citizens in a democracy have the final say in what *should be*. Professionals decide what they should do by consulting evidence produced through rigorous scientific analysis. On the other hand, when citizens decide what *should be*, they are dealing with moral or normative matters that require sound judgment. (There are no experts on moral issues.) Citizens inform their judgment by weighing options about what should be done to solve a problem against all that they value or hold dear. The knowledge they use in deciding comes from comparing experiences in the cauldron of deliberation. This is socially constructed knowledge that relies on the human faculty for judgment. Facts are essential in making sound decisions, yet, alone, aren't sufficient.[21]

When citizens finally settle on a general direction to move forward, it doesn't give professionals a set of orders to carry out, but professionals should have a clearer sense of what is and isn't supportable. In some cases, professionals will think that the best course of action is outside the politically permissible. In these cases, public deliberations can tell professionals how the citizenry went about making up its mind, so professionals can engage this thinking where they believe it errs.

Although deliberating is difficult, it doesn't require any special skills; it's a natural act. Citizens deliberate with family and friends on personal matters all the time. People are attracted to deliberative decision making because their experiences and concerns count as much as professional expertise and data. (Pubic deliberation couldn't be for experts only and still be a democratic practice.)

The deliberative decision making that the foundation has seen in communities produces the kind of "contingent consent" and "bounded uncertainty" that can be found even among people who are mutually suspicious. This and other democratic practices can eventually become ingrained in political norms, but the regard for others and the civility that the practices foster are, in the foundation's experience, more the product of the practices rather than the preconditions.[22]

Identifying and Committing Resources

> In Suggsville, as people worked through tensions, they turned to implementation. For instance, some worried about what was happening to children and thought there were too many youngsters with too little adult supervision. Several community members responded with offers of things they were willing to do if others would join them: organize baseball and softball leagues, provide after-school classes, expand youth services in the churches, form a band. The observation that alcoholism was also part of the town's difficulties prompted one of the participants in the meetings to propose that a chapter of Alcoholics Anonymous be established. Where would it meet? Someone offered a vacant building free of charge. As projects developed and citizens called on other citizens to join them, new recruits began coming to the meetings. Rather than deciding on a single solution, people mounted an array of initiatives that were loosely coordinated because they were all consistent with the sense of direction that was emerging from the deliberations.

The naming, framing, and deliberating in Suggsville would be of little consequence unless actions followed. Decisions have to be implemented, and that requires identifying and committing resources. Even though citizens have resources that can reinforce institutions and benefit communities, they often go unrecognized and unused. Opportunities to identify these resources occur in deliberating as citizens enlarge their understanding of a problem. When people see a problem more completely, resources that seemed irrelevant take on new significance. The same is true of the people and organizations that control those resources. Suggsvillians who knew how to coach youngsters in baseball weren't an asset until community revitalization was seen as more than a strictly economic problem. Unfortunately, institutional and professional routines can overlook the resources that citizens have because they aren't like institutional resources. Civic resources are often intangible or are based on personal experiences and skills.

Actually, recognizing resources can be prompted early on in framing issues by including citizens in the list of potential actors. Institutions – governments, schools, hospitals, and major nongovernmental organizations – are obvious actors; yet, while necessary, they are seldom enough to deal with a community's most persistent problems. These problems come from many sources, and the citizenry throughout a community must act on them.

The difficulty in many cases is that local institutions don't take advantage of the work citizens do with citizens. After citizens have deliberated over an issue and made decisions about what they think should be done, politics-as-usual takes over. When it comes to implementation, citizens are pushed to the sidelines. Institutions may acknowledge what people have decided, yet fall back on familiar routines like planning. Some assume that once people have spoken, it's time for professionals to follow up with institutional resources. And institutional plans don't normally include provisions for civic work.

One reason planning overlooks the work that citizens do with citizens is that institutions aren't sure they can count on people to produce. Institutions have money and legal authority; they can rely on enforceable contracts. The democratic public can't command people or deploy equipment, and it seldom has legal authority. So why do people do things like organizing patrols on crime-ridden streets when there is no financial inducement or legal obligation? After all, battling street crime isn't just time consuming; it's dangerous. Most people will often do what they have pledged to do – in public – because their fellow citizens expect it of them. These commitments are reciprocal; one group promises another, we will do thus-and-so if you will do thus-and-so. These mutual promises are the covenants mentioned earlier.

Public covenants may sound idealistic, yet they work. They have their own kind of leverage.[23] It is social or peer group leverage. A community leader explained the generally high attendance at the Suggsville meetings this way: "If you don't show up, somebody will say something to you about it." As in Suggsville, it is not uncommon for deliberations to be followed by mutual promises, either at forums or at subsequent meetings.

Organizing Complementary Acting

> As Suggsville's revival progressed, several people returned to the argument that while encouraging local businesses was fine, it would never provide enough jobs to revive the economy. The town still had to attract outside investment, they insisted. Someone quickly pointed out that the center of town, especially the park, was so unsightly that no one of sound mind would consider Suggsville an attractive site for a new business. Even though some saw little connection between the condition of the park and recruiting industry, no one denied that the town needed a facelift. Suggsville's three-member sanitation crew, however, had all it could do to keep up with garbage collection. Did people feel strongly enough about the cleanup to accept the consequences? That is, would they show up to clean the park? In the past, response to similar calls had varied from substantial to minimal. This time, after one of the

community forums, a group of people committed themselves to gathering at the park the following Saturday with rakes, mowers, and trash bags.

During most of the meetings, the recently elected mayor sat quietly, keeping an eye on what was happening. The forums began during his predecessor's administration, and the town's new leader felt no obligation to the participants. In fact, he was a bit suspicious of what they were doing. Members of the town council believed the public meetings would result in just another pressure group, or thought that citizens should identify needs and then step aside so that local agencies could take over. No one made any demands on the town's government, although some citizens thought it strange that the mayor hadn't offered to help with the cleanup. But, before Saturday arrived, people were surprised to find that the mayor had sent workers to the park with trucks and other heavy equipment to do what the tools brought from home couldn't.

Just as the public has its own distinctive way of moving from decision to action, it also has its own distinctive way of acting and organizing action. Government agencies act on behalf of the public, and people act individually by volunteering for all sorts of civic projects. Both are beneficial, yet neither is the public acting, which is made up of many collective efforts that have a common purpose. Opportunities for citizens to act together occur as people decide on the directions their efforts will take and the results they hope to achieve. This is what happened in Suggsville.

Various civic initiatives that reinforce or support each other create complementary acting, which is the fifth of the practices. Complementary acting is more than cooperation among civic groups, and it is not only multifaceted but also mutually reinforcing. Consequently, this way of acting can be coherent without being bureaucratically coordinated. That means the cost of getting things done can be lower than institutional costs. Even though complementary acting requires a degree of coordination (everyone should show up to clean up the park on the same day), it isn't administratively regulated and doesn't have administrative expenses.

The payoff from complementary acting goes beyond the concrete products of civic work. Researchers have found that the work people do together (such as cleaning up the park) is valued, not just because the park looks nicer but because it demonstrates that people joining forces can make a difference.[24] Working together also builds political trust. When people work together, they get a more realistic sense of what they can expect from one another. This political trust isn't quite the same as personal trust and shouldn't be confused with it. Political trust can develop among people who aren't family or friends. All that is necessary is for citizens to recognize they need one another to solve their community's problems.

To repeat: rather than substituting for institutional action, complementary public acting supplements it, a fact long recognized in research on urban reform. For instance, Clarence Stone reports that citizens in poorer neighborhoods formed alliances that

154 D. Mathews

accomplished far more than any institutions alone could.[25] Professionals have little difficulty in encouraging this type of acting when they value and make a place for it.

Learning as a Community

> Over the next two years, the ad hoc group in Suggsville organized into a more formal civic association. New industry didn't come to town, although the restaurant held its own. Drug traffic continued to be a problem, but people's vigilance, together with more surveillance by the police department, reduced the trade. The crowd loitering on the streets dwindled away. Alcoholism remained an issue, but more people attended the A.A. meetings. A new summer recreation program became popular with young people, and teenage pregnancies decreased a bit, as did school dropouts.
>
> In time, the ad hoc Suggsville improvement group became an official civic association. The association had the usual internal disputes that detracted from community problem solving. Still, when a controversy was brewing in the community or an emerging issue needed to be addressed, people turned to the association for help. As might be expected, some of the projects didn't work. Fortunately, in most cases, association members adjusted their sights and launched more initiatives. Perhaps this momentum had something to do with the way the association involved the community in evaluating projects. The association regularly convened meetings in which citizens could reflect on what they had learned, regardless of whether the projects succeeded. Success wasn't as important as the lessons that could be used in future projects.

The sixth practice is community or public learning. This is the kind of reflection Amartya Sen seems to have in mind when he writes of democracy as more than a mechanical condition.[26] As is true of all the other practices, public learning is a variation on a normal routine (evaluating), yet quite distinctive. Although unlike traditional evaluations, public learning can supplement the outcome-based assessments that are often used by funders. In public learning, the citizenry or community itself learns, and the learning is reflected in changed behavior. In other words, the unit of learning is the community, and the measure of learning is community change.

There are obviously a great many opportunities for a citizenry to learn after a community has acted on a problem. Everyone wants to know if the effort has succeeded. The press declares the results to be beneficial, harmful, or inconsequential. One-on-one conversations bubble up at the supermarket. Outside evaluators make "objective" assessments. The citizenry, however, may not learn a great deal from the media's conclusions, chance conversations, or professional evaluations.

One reason the citizenry doesn't learn is that conventional evaluations interfere unintentionally. In order for citizens to learn, people have to focus on themselves as

Democracy and Community Development **155**

a community. The evidence to be evaluated can't just be what projects have achieved; it has to include how well citizens have worked together.

Public learning is also different from conventional evaluation in that outcomes aren't measured against fixed, predetermined goals. When a democratic citizenry learns, both the objectives of civic efforts and their results have to be on the table for inspection, not the results alone. As people learn, they may realize that what they first thought was most valuable turned out not to be as important as it seemed.

Opportunities for public learning aren't confined, however, to final evaluations; they can occur in all the practices. To name an issue in public terms is to learn what others value. To frame an issue is to learn about all of the options for action – as well as the tensions that need to be worked through. To decide deliberatively is to learn which actions are consistent or inconsistent with what is held most valuable. To identify resources is to learn what the problems are in the fullest sense, what resources are relevant, and where potential allies might be found. To organize complementary action is to learn which initiatives can reinforce one another.

In many ways, public learning is renaming, reframing, and deciding again – after the fact. It is deliberation in reverse. The questions are much the same: Should we have done what we did? Was it really consistent with what we now think is most important?

A learning community is like the ideal student who reads everything assigned and then goes to the library or surfs the internet to find out more. These students don't copy a model or use a formula. Imitation is limitation. Learning communities study what others have done, but they adapt what they see to their own circumstances.

Learning communities know how to fail successfully. Community projects that aim for success tend to end when goals have been met. This can occur even if problems remain. On the other hand, projects that don't succeed disappoint people, and they, too, stop. So success and failure can have the same result: people quit in either case. When communities are learning, they tend to push ahead because they look beyond success and failure. As Rudyard Kipling wrote, they "treat those two imposters just the same." In learning communities, if the work goes well, they try to improve on it. If they fail, they learn from their mistakes.

Six in One

> Attendance at the Suggsville association meetings continued to rise and fall depending on which problems were being addressed. Some citizens dropped out because the association refused to get drawn into local election campaigns or to endorse special causes. Few worried about these fluctuations because they considered getting people to come to the association meeting to be less important than building ties with other civic groups and rural neighborhood coalitions as well as with institutions such as the county sheriff's office, economic development office, and health department. Creating networks

> around projects seemed more important than getting up to scale on any one project.
>
> Suggsville wouldn't make anyone's list of model communities today; still, the town has increased the capacity of its citizens to influence their future. Asked what years of civic initiatives produced, one Suggsvillian said, "When people banded together to make this a better place to live, it became a better place to live."[27]

The secret of democratic practices is that they aren't stand-alone techniques; they fit inside one another like the wooden *matrëshka* nesting dolls from Russia. When people lay out their options for acting on a problem, they continue to mull over the name that best captures what is really at issue. Even as they move toward making a decision, they continue to revise both the framework and the name of the problem. As they deliberate, people anticipate the actions that will need to be taken and the commitments they may have to make. They recall lessons learned from past efforts. Citizens may make commitments to act while they are deliberating. The six practices are essential elements in the larger politics of people ruling themselves.

The practices, taken together, are a response to the question raised on the Gulf Coast and in every community facing troubling circumstances. When people were asking, "Who can talk to us?" they weren't necessarily asking for the name of a person or organization with answers. They were asking where they could find a conversation that would help them find their own answers. One place that conversation can occur is around the democratic practices, which are ways of learning, not just doing.

Practical Applications?

As I said initially, this chapter ends short of where it should be; that is, without a full explanation of the practical implications of a democracy based on the work of citizens for community development. Others interested in the resilience of community would appreciate hearing more from professionals in community development about how they are aligning or could work to align their routines with democratic practices. Already professionals in other fields such as public health and journalism are trying to align their work with democratic practices. And we've heard some of the questions they struggle with. For example, when designing their strategies, professionals usually wonder where to begin: With deliberation? Or before that, with naming problems? Does it matter? Some experiments have started with professionals working with citizens to name issues in public terms while others have begun by encouraging deliberative decision making in public forums.

There is really no one right place to begin. However, beginning in a democratic fashion is essential if the objective is to strengthen democratic self-rule. Jay Rosen,

Democracy and Community Development **157**

a journalist who has worked with the foundation, put the matter succinctly: the way anyone enters politics has to be consistent with the politics they want to encourage. It's counterproductive to inaugurate a project of choice work with a citizenry that hasn't chosen to participate. Where experiments in alignment start doesn't seem to be as important as treating the practices as parts of a larger whole, a democratic way of governing.

We also heard questions about timing. For instance, it is unrealistic to try to stop a community in the midst of solving a problem and ask people to start over by renaming the issue at hand. Professionals are better advised to "build on what grows," as one community leader put it. Look for opportunities to introduce democratic questions into the regular routines of naming, framing, and so on: Does anyone see another side to this problem? Are there other options we should consider? Almost everyone thinks we should do this, but are there any negative consequences we ought to examine? Rather than trying to teach deliberative decision making as a skill, it may be more effective to just start deliberating.

The foundation has been particularly interested in experiments done by professionals to engage citizens who are engaging other citizens.[28] That is, they engage citizens as they employ democratic practices. Examples include professionals who frame issues *with* citizens rather than *for* them and listen to the citizenry deliberating as they formulate policies for their institutions. These experiments are promising because they treat the public as more than a fixed or static body (an audience, a constituency, an electorate). There is a sense in which the public is not static at all but rather a dynamic force, more like electricity than a light bulb. The practices are citizens in motion, which is like an electrical current. To follow through on this analogy, professionals can plug into electricity. When they do, it gives new meaning to civic engagement.

At first glance, aligning professional routines with democratic practices doesn't seem all that difficult. Professionals can take into account the names people give problems, and they can create frameworks for decision making that include the intangibles that citizens value. Professionals can learn from public deliberation and recognize the resources that communities can bring to the table. They can also make use of the coproduction of goods that come from civic work. And they can modify their evaluations so as not to interfere with public learning.

The difficulty for professionals is often doing this within the accepted routines of their work. When professionals have introduced deliberation into their public meetings, they have sometimes run into resistance for coloring outside the lines. And just involving citizens in projects has sparked criticism. Scholar-practitioner David Pelletier was charged with "mucking around down at the community level," rather than gathering data to give to policymakers.[29]

As in Pelletier's case, academics may have a particularly difficult time aligning their work with democratic practices because, as I noted earlier, the way citizens go about knowing is at odds with the way many academics go about creating knowledge. The academy's lack of respect for the way citizens generate knowledge from their experiences is ironic because there is a rich academic literature on the way citizens

158 D. Mathews

inform their decisions, which goes back to the works of Isocrates, Thucydides, and Aristotle.[30] Philosophers have long recognized the importance of the moral reasoning that makes use of the human faculty for judgment, which neuroscientists have now been able to locate physically in the brain.

Among the academics concerned with community development, professors such as Theodore Alter, Frank Fear, and Scott Peters are the trailblazers in challenging higher education's disdain for civic work and the scholarship that grows out of this work.[31] Ted Alter at Pennsylvania State University makes a strong case for broadening the definition of research to include public scholarship. Scott Peters at Cornell University has identified academics doing such studies and told their stories. And Frank Fear at Michigan State University has pushed the boundaries of the university engagement movement by challenging academe's concept of the role of citizens. The list of public scholars goes on.[32]

Perhaps the biggest challenge of all for the academy is that concepts of democracy like the one in this chapter assume the academy (and other professionalized institutions) are part of a larger public life and accountable to it. Public life is where democratic practices are practiced and the academy affects those practices – intentionally or not. The academy is not a detached observer outside the world of citizens.

Bringing concepts of democracy to bear on community development and trying to foster a better alignment between the work of professionals and citizens will undoubtedly create more of the kind of problems the foundation has heard about. Yet the field of community development is in a position to take advantage of the growing recognition that communities do, indeed, matter as places where citizens can gain a stronger hand in shaping their future.

In Bayou La Batre and far beyond, citizens have an agenda based on a question that can't be answered by technical expertise or the best professional service. People want to hear from anyone who has something useful to say about how they, different as they are, can come together, not for the sake of being together, but to join forces to build, to create. Much of what they want to create – by working with others and through institutions – is for the benefit of their communities. Surely these aspirations are a mandate for professionals in community development. I can think of no better place to fashion an understanding of the democracy needed for the 21st century than in a profession with community at its core.

Notes

1   While by no means an authority on the subject, the foundation has had some exposure to the community development literature, thanks to friends like Hustedde (2009), author of "Seven Theories for Seven Community Developers." The democratic implications of community and economic development can be found in such works as Briggs (1998), Checkoway (2001), Johnson (2001), and Warren (2001). Additionally, we've noticed that some of this literature is explicitly about democracy, e.g. Shaw & Martin (2000).

2   The foundation's understanding of democracy is fairly close to the one held by Paul Woodruff (2005) in his book *First Democracy: The Challenge of an Ancient Idea*. Additionally, we've drawn from a response to that work crafted by Sartori (1987). Although self-rule appears to be older than Greek democracy and not confined to one country, the

foundation's research staff has found helpful sources, such as the contemporary works of Hansen (1991), Meier (1990), and Ober (1989).

3 Gaillard et al. (2008).

4 Local institutions included a physician's office where Dr Regina Benjamin, who later became Surgeon General of the United States, practiced.

5 Dewey (1882).

6 The need for professionals to appreciate what citizens can and must do on their own is discussed by Schoch-Spana et al. (2007).

7 See Scarre (2009); Possehl (1998).

8 The foundation developed its concept of *civic work* by drawing from Boyte and Kari (1996).

9 Ostrom (1993).

10 There is literature on public participation that emphasizes creating constituencies, inclusiveness, and equality. See Chrislip (1995), Schlozman et al. (1999), and Shortall (2008).

11 See the reports on National Issues Forums deliberations from 1983 to the present. These are on file at the Kettering Foundation and available online at http://www.nifi.org/reports/.

12 McKnight and Kretzmann (1993) show that people, even in the most impoverished communities, can generate their own power. These two scholars have documented what can happen when the collective abilities of people and not just their needs are recognized.

13 I have learned that interactional theory defines the community field in much the same way, that is, a whole larger than the sum of its parts (Bridger et al., 2011).

14 The Suggsville story is drawn from more than 50 communities observed over 30 years. These include Tupelo, Mississippi, as described by Grisham (1999), and "Smalltown," Alabama, as described by Sumners et al. (2005). Also, see Kettering Foundation (2002).

15 The practices presented here are based on insights about how democracy *should* work. Being normative, these insights aren't like the findings of social scientists. On the other hand, the practices based on the insights are real. That is, all have occurred at various times in many different places. The way the practices are described by Kettering reflects the foundation's conceptualization of experience.

16 The foundation's concept of "things held valuable" was stimulated by Rokeach and Ball-Rokeach (1989). While it is common to think of politics as turning on differences in objective interests, we have found that people are also motivated by deeper concerns.

17 Berry (1986).

18 Framing issues in this fashion has had a 30-year track record of countering polarization. This has been demonstrated in the use of the National Issues Forums books in thousands of public forums. These forums are sponsored by a nonpartisan, nationwide network that includes an array of civic, educational, religious, and professional groups. They promote nonpartisan public deliberation in communities around the country. To learn more, visit www.nifi.org.

19 In the "Funeral Oration of Pericles," Pericles describes the talk (*logo*) used before people act in order to teach themselves (*prodidacthenai*) how to act (Plutarch and Bernadotte, 1910).

20 The concept of stages in deliberation comes from Yankelovich (1991).

21 Note that public deliberation is more than coldly rational calculations. Things that people hold dear are at stake and that generates strong emotions. The deliberations that the foundation has seen are much like the decision making that recent studies of the human brain describe. For an overview, see Lehrer (2009).

   Also note that the difference between professional or academic knowledge and the knowledge citizens use has been reported in the literature of sociology and community psychology. This distinction is found in articles by Bridger (1996), Rappaport (1995), and Welcomer (2010).

22 This is the same conclusion that Schmitter and Karl (1991) came to in their review of political theory.

23 More information on covenants is in Elazar and Kincaid (1979).

160 D. Mathews

24 This research was done by the Harwood Institute for Public Innovation and was reported to the foundation on June 22, 2011.
25 Stone (1998).
26 Sen (1999).
27 A similar comment was actually made by a citizen from the Naugatuck Valley community in Connecticut (Brecher, 1990).
28 A number of professionals in community development have used deliberative forums to engage citizens who are engaging citizens, including Ronald Hustedde, who I mentioned earlier; Lionel (Bo) Beaulieu at Mississippi State University; Sandra Hodge at the University of Missouri; Jan Hartough at Michigan State; and Renee Daugherty and Sue Williams at Oklahoma State.
29 Peters, 2005.
30 Aristotle (1953); Isocrates (2000).
31 Harry Boyte, founder and codirector of the Center for Democracy and Citizenship, Augsburg College, has also been a leader in this movement and has already been cited for developing the concept of public work. Bo Beaulieu at Mississippi State also belongs on this list, as do others too numerous to name here.
32 Alter (2005); Fear et al. (2006); Fear (2010); Peters et al. (2010).

References

Alter, T.R. (2005). Achieving the promise of public scholarship. In S.J. Peters, N.R. Jordan, M. Adamek, & T.R. Alter (Eds.), *Engaging campus and community: The practice of public scholarship in the state and land-grant university system* (pp. 461–487). Dayton, OH: Kettering Foundation Press.

Aristotle (1953). The ethics of Aristotle: The Nicomachean ethics (J.A.K. Thomson, Trans.). London: Penguin Books.

Berry, W. (1986). *The unsettling of America: Culture and agriculture.* San Francisco, CA: Sierra Club Books.

Boyte, H., & Kari, N.N. (1996). *Building America: The democratic promise of public work.* Philadelphia, PA: Temple University Press.

Brecher, J. (1990). If all the people are banded together: The Nantucket Valley project. In J. Brecher, & T. Costello (Eds.), *Building bridges: the emerging grassroots coalition of labor and community* (p. 93). New York, NY: Monthly Review Press.

Bridger, J.C. (1996). Community imagery and the built environment. *The Sociological Quarterly, 37*(3), 353–374.

Bridger, J.C., Brennan, M.A., & Luloff, A.E. (2011). The interactional approach to community. In J.W. Robinson Jr & G.P. Green (Eds.), *Introduction to community development: Theory, practice and service-learning* (pp. 85–100). Thousand Oaks, CA: Sage.

Briggs, de Souza, X. (1998). Doing democracy up-close: Culture, power, and communication in community building. *Journal of Planning Education and Research, 18*(1), 1–13.

Checkoway, B. (2001). Community change for diverse democracy. *Community Development Journal, 44*(1), 5–21.

Chrislip, D. (1995). Pulling together: Creating a constituency for change. *National Civic Review, 84*(1), 21–29.

Dewey, J. (1927). *The public and its problems.* Athens, OH: Swallow Press.

Elazar, D.J., & Kincaid, J. (1979). Covenant and policy. *New Conversations, 4,* 4–8.

Fear, F. (2010). Coming to engagement: critical reflection and transformation. In H. Fitzgerald, C. Burack, & S.D. Seifer (Eds.), *Handbook of engaged scholarship, volume 2: Community–campus partnerships, contemporary landscapes, future directions.* East Lansing, MI: Michigan State University Press.

Fear, F., Rosaen, C.L., Bawden, R.J., & Foster-Fishman, P.G. (2006). *Coming to critical engagement: An autoethnographic exploration*. Lanham, MD: University Press of America.

Gallard, F., Hagler, S., & Denniston, P. (2008). *In the path of the storms: Bayou La Batre, Coden and the Alabama coast*. Auburn, AL: Pebble Hill Books.

Grisham, V.L. (1999). *The evolution of a community*. Dayton, OH: Kettering Foundation Press.

Hansen, M.H. (1991). *The Athenian democracy in the age of Demosthenes*. Oxford: Blackwell.

Hustedde, R. (2009). Seven theories for seven community developers. In R. Phillips, & R.H. Pittman (Eds.), *An introduction to community development*. New York, NY: Routledge.

Isocrates (2000). *Antidosis* (Vol. 2) (G. Norlin, Trans.). New York, NY: Putnam's Sons. (Original work published 1929).

Johnson, C. (2001). Local democracy, democratic decentralization and rural development: Theories, challenges, and options for policy. *Development Policy Review*, 19(4), 521–532.

Kettering Foundation (2002). *For communities to work*. Dayton, OH: Kettering Foundation.

Lehrer, J. (2009). *How we decide*. Boston, MA: Houghton Mifflin Harcourt.

McKnight, J., & Kretzmann, J. (1993). *Building communities from the inside out: A path toward finding and mobilizing a community's assets*. Chicago, IL: ACTA Publications.

Meier, C. (1990). *The Greek discovery of politics*. Cambridge, MA: Harvard University Press.

Ober, J. (1989). *Mass and elite democratic Athens: Rhetoric, ideology, and the power of the people*. Princeton, NJ: Princeton University Press.

Ostrom, E. (1993). Covenanting, co-producing, and the good society. *PEGS Newsletter*, 3(2), 8.

Peters, S. (2005). Findings. In S.J. Peters, N. R. Jordan, M. Adamek, & T. R. Alter (Eds.), *Engaging campus and community: The practice of public scholarship in the state and land-grant university system* (p. 408). Dayton, OH: Kettering Foundation Press.

Peters, S., Alter, T.R., & Schwartzbach, N. (2010). *Democracy and higher education: Traditions and stories of civic engagement*. East Lansing, MI: Michigan State University Press.

Plutarch & Bernadotte, P. (1910). *Cimon and Pericles with the funeral oration of Pericles*. London: Charles Scribner's Sons.

Possehl, G.L. (1998). Sociocultural Complexity without the state: The Indus civilization. In G.M. Feinman, & J. Marcus (Eds.), *The archaic states* (pp. 261–191). Santa Fe, NM: School of American Research Press.

Rappaport, J. (1995). Empowerment meets narrative: Listening to stories and creating settings. *American Journal of Community Psychology*, 23(5), 795–807.

Rokeach, M., & Ball-Rokeach, S.J. (1989). Stability and change in American value priorities, 1968–1981. *American Psychologist*, 44, 775–784.

Sartori (1987) – Please give details.

Scarre, C. (Ed.). (2009). *The human past: World prehistory and the development of human societies* (2nd ed.). London: Thames and Hudson.

Schlozman, K., Verba, S., & Brady, H.E. (1999). Civic participation and the equality problem. In T. Skocpol & M.P. Fiorina (Eds.), *Civic engagement in American democracy* (pp. 427–459). Washington, DC: Brookings Institution Press.

Schmitter, P.C., & Karl, T.L. (1991). What democracy is … and is not. *Journal of Democracy*, 2(3), 75–88.

Schoch-Spana, M., Franco, C., Nuzzo, J.B., & Usenza, C. (2007). Community engagement: Leadership tool for catastrophic health events. *Biosecurity and Bioterrorism: Biodefense Strategy, Practice, and Science*, 5(1), 8–25.

Sen, A. (1999). Democracy as a universal value. *Journal of Democracy*, 10(3), 3–17.

Shaw, M., & Martin, I. (2000). Community work, citizenship, and democracy: Re-making the connections. *Community Development Journal*, 35(4), 401–413.

Shortall, S. (2008). Are rural development programs socially inclusive? Social inclusion, civic engagement, participation, and social capital: Exploring the differences. *Journal of Rural Studies*, 24(4), 450–457.

Stone, C.N. (1998). Linking civic capacity and human capital formation. In M.J. Gittell (Ed.), *Strategies for school equity: Creating productive schools in a just society* (pp. 163–176). New Haven, CT: Yale University Press.

Sumners, J.A., Slaton, C., & Arthur, J. (2005). *Building community: The Uniontown story*. Dayton, OH: Kettering Foundation.

Warren, M.R. (2001). *Dry bones rattling: Community building to revitalize American democracy*. Princeton, NJ: Princeton University Press.

Welcomer, S. (2010). Reinventing vs. restoring sustainability in the Maine woods: Narratives of progress and decline. *Organization Environment*, 23(1), 55–75.

Woodruff, P. (2005). *First democracy: The challenge of an ancient idea*. New York, NY: Oxford University Press.

Yankelovich, D. (1991). *Coming to public judgment: Making democracy work in a complex world*. Syracuse, NY: Syracuse University Press.

10

THE BASICS

What's Essential about Theory for Community Development Practice?

Ronald J. Hustedde and Jacek Ganowicz

Introduction

There are at least three major limitations of theory for community developers. First, it can be argued that the profession is undergirded with theories from so many disciplines that it is difficult for practitioners to sort through them all. The situation is compounded by disciplines that seldom cross academic boundaries. Community development-oriented anthropologists, community psychologists, sociologists, social welfare professionals, community economists, and others have their own disciplinary approaches and publications. Even interdisciplinary groups such as the Community Development Society and its publications tend to be dominated by those with a domestic rather than an *international* perspective. This fragmentation makes it difficult to sort through what is important for community development research or practice.

Second, the balkanization of theory is compounded by theoreticians whose language is cumbersome and fraught with jargon that scares away most practitioners. For example, one of the leading theorists of the day, Jurgen Habermas, has a lot to offer community developers about free and open communicative action. However, his books and articles take so much time to decipher that few practitioners have the time or patience to do so. Further, theoreticians strive to explain the world but do not necessarily apply their theories to day-to-day practices of community development. Unfortunately, this situation leads some practitioners to conclude that theory is irrelevant.

Third, the culture of the community development profession consists of many practitioners who often want to dispense with theory and "get down to earth." They want studies to shed light on issues such as urban slum life, growth versus the environment, globalization, or a range of other issues that need immediate attention. Hence, there is more interest in empirical research or practical initiatives than in theory itself. The field is supported by classical community development texts, which focus on the philosophical underpinnings of various community development strategies such as Rothman's three approaches (conflict, technical and locality based) (Rothman and Gant, 1987), or the process of doing community development (Biddle and Biddle, 1965; Christenson and Robinson, 1989). If one looks at most community development publications since that time, one might say that the field is theoretically poor because many community development texts tend to focus on process or content rather than theory.[1]

The purpose of this paper is to ask what is essential about theory and to identify several theories that are essential for community development research and practice. Bhattacharyya's (1995) definition of community development as solidarity and agency is offered as a starting point to select theories that are most relevant for the field. We argue that the most important issues for community development theory concern structure, power, and shared meaning. These are expressed in functionalism, conflict, and symbolic interaction theory. No single theoretical approach is sufficient on its own because it is argued that societies, communities, and social change are complex.

Why Theory?

Theories are explanations that can help us understand people's behavior. Theories can provide a framework to community developers to help them comprehend and explain events. A good theory can be stated in abstract terms and can help develop strategies and tools for effective practice. If community developers want others to conduct relevant research, or if they want to be involved in participatory action research, it is important that they have theoretical groundings. Theory is our major guide to understanding the complexity of community life and social and economic change (Collins, 1988; Ritzer, 1996).

The starting point is to offer a definition of community development that is both distinctive and universal and can be applied to all types of societies from the post-industrial to the pre-industrial. Bhattacharyya (1995) met these conditions when he defined community development as the process of creating or increasing solidarity and agency. He says solidarity is about building a deeply shared identity and a code for conduct. Community developers sort through conflicting visions and definitions of a problem among ethnically and ideologically plural populations to help groups and communities build a sense of solidarity. Bhattacharyya argues that community development is also agency, which means the capacity of a people to order their world. According to Giddens, agency is "the capacity to intervene in the world, or to refrain from intervention, with the effect of influencing a process or the state of affairs" (Giddens, 1984, p. 14). There are complex forces that work against agency. However, community development has the intention to build capacity, and that is what makes it different from other helping professions. Community developers build the capacity of a people when they encourage or teach others to create their own dreams, to learn new skills and knowledge. Agency or capacity building occurs when practitioners assist or initiate community reflection on the lessons they have learned through their actions. Agency is about building the capacity to understand, to create and act, and to reflect.

Following this definition of community development, three major concerns involve solidarity and agency building: (1) *structure*; (2) *power*; and (3) *shared meaning*. Figure 10.1 suggests these concerns are interrelated and influence the direction and impact of community development practice.

Structure refers to the social practices or to organizations and groups that have a role to play in solidarity and capacity building and their relationship to one another. Some of these social practices and organizations may have a limited role and there may be a need to build new organizations or expand the mission of existing organizations for solidarity and agency to occur.

Power refers to relationships with those who control resources such as land, labor, capital, and knowledge, or those who have greater access to those resources than others. If community development is about building the capacity for social and economic change, the concept of power is essential.

Shared meaning refers to social meaning, especially symbols, that people give to a place, physical things, behavior, events, or action. In essence, solidarity needs to be built within a cultural context. Individuals and groups give different meanings to objects, deeds, and matters. For example, one community might see the construction of an industrial plant as a godsend that will bring prosperity to the town, while another community might see a similar construction as the destruction of their quality of life. Community developers need to pay attention to these meanings if they wish to build a sense of solidarity in a particular community or between communities.

In essence, structure, power, and shared meaning are integral aspects for solidarity and capacity building. These three aspects of the community development triangle (Figure 10.1) form the basis for essential community development theory. Horton (1992) shared similar concerns about African-American approaches to community development. He emphasized historic power differences and the influence of culture and black community institutions in his black community development model. Chaskin et al. (2001) focus on neighborhood and other structures and networks in

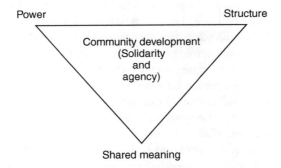

FIGURE 10.1 Three Key Concerns in the Community Development Field

their work on capacity building. However, the authors also include concepts about power and building a sense of community or shared meaning in their interdisciplinary approach. The concepts of empowerment and strengthening community capacity are frequently interwined in the community development literature (Perkins, 1995; Jeffries, 2000). Beliefs and values evolve in community through daily experiences that lead to pragmatic conclusions about the community's own social reality or shared meaning (Ejigiri, 1996).

What Is Essential Community Development Theory for Practitioners and Researchers?

The three key community development issues – structure, power, and shared meaning – have each been a starting point for three key orientations in modern social theory: *functionalism, conflict theory,* and *symbolic interactionism*. The former two originated in the European tradition of macro-structural thinking preoccupied with large-scale social phenomena, such as social classes, societal system, culture, norms, i.e., macro objectivity and macro subjectivity, whereas symbolic interactionism, with its roots in the Chicago school of social pragmatism, is considered a micro approach, focusing on individuals and small group behavior, psychological characteristics, and properties of interaction.

Conflict theory, going back to the towering figure of Karl Marx, addresses the macro concerns of power. Functionalism, originally laid out in its contours by Auguste Comte, Herbert Spencer, and Emile Durkheim, centers on the macro structural concerns of social cooperation and solidarity. The symbolic interactionists, and the related approaches, follow the opposite tack from both the macro approaches, taking the individuals and the micro behavior as their starting point.

We will look at each of these three theoretical perspectives and how they can be applied to community development practice.

Concerns about Structure: Functionalism

First, let us look at structure, which is about organizations and group capacity to bring about or stop change. In essence, structure is related to the Giddens concept of agency or capacity building. The theoretical concept concerned with structure is known as *structural functionalism*. It is also called *systems theory, equilibrium theory,* or simply *functionalism*. According to this theoretical framework, societies contain certain interdependent structures, each of which performs certain functions for the maintenance of society. Structures refer to organizations and institutions such as health care, educational entities, businesses and non-profit groups, or informal groups. Functions refer to their purpose, mission, and what they do in society. These structures form the basis of a social system. Talcott Parsons (1951, 1960) and Robert K. Merton (1968) are the theorists most often associated with this theory. According to Merton (1968), social systems have manifest and latent functions. Manifest functions are intentional and recognized. In contrast, latent functions may be

Theory and Community Development Practice **167**

unintentional and not recognized. For example, it could be argued that the manifest function of urban planning is to ensure well-organized and efficiently functioning cities, whereas the latent function is to allocate advantages to certain interests such as those involved with the growth machine or real-estate developers.

Functionalists such as Parsons argue that structures often contribute to their own maintenance, not particularly to a greater societal good. Concern for order and stability also led functionalists to focus on social change and its sources. They view conflict and stability as two sides of the same coin. If the community developer wants to build community capacity, he or she will have to pay attention to the organizational capacity for stimulating or inhibiting change. Structural functionalism helps one to understand how the *status quo* is maintained. Some critics claim its fallacy is that it does not offer much insight about change, social dynamics, and existing structures (Turner, 1998; Ritzer, 1996; Collins, 1988).

How Can Structural Functionalism Guide Community Development Practice?

Structural functionalism is a useful tool for practitioners. Let us look at a case study of an inner city neighborhood that is struggling to create micro-enterprise businesses that will benefit local people. If one applied structural functionalism to community development practice, one would help the community analyze what organizations are committed to training, nurturing, and financing micro-enterprise development and what their latent or hidden functions might be. A functionalist-oriented practitioner is more likely to notice dysfunctions in organizations. If the existing organizations are not meeting local needs in this area, the functionalist would build the capacity of the community by creating a new organization that focuses on small-scale entrepreneurs or adapting an existing organization to meet the same concerns. A functionalist would also want to build links with broader social systems such as external organizations that could help the community's micro-entrepreneurs to flourish. In essence, a functionalist would see structures as important components of capacity building. While structural functionalism is an important tool for community development, it is limited because it does not fully explore the issue of power that can be found in other theories.

Concerns about Power and Conflict Theory

Power is the second key issue for community development. Power is about who controls or has access to resources (land, labor, capital, and knowledge). If community development is about building capacity, then concerns about power are pivotal. Insights about power tend to be found in political science or political sociology. Theorists that are more contemporary have added to the richness of the literature. Foucault (1985), in his later writings, argued that where there is power, there is resistance. He examines the struggles against the power of men over women, administration over the ways people live, and of psychiatry over the mentally ill. He sees power as a feature of all human relations (Foucault, 1965, 1975, 1979, 1980, 1985; Nash, 2000). It has a fluidity in the sense that power can be reversed and there are different degrees of power. Foucault's focus extends beyond conventional politics at the stale level to the organizations and institutions of civil society and to interpersonal relations.

Wallerstein (1984) applied Marxist theory to understand the logic behind the expansion of capitalism to a globalized system, which needs to continually expand its boundaries. "Political states" such as Japan, the UK, and the USA are the core-developed states based on higher-level skills and capitalization. These states dominate the peripheral areas, with weak states economically dependent on the "core." The low-technology states form a buffer zone to prevent outright conflict between the core and the periphery. Some have applied Wallerstein's world system theory to regional economics, with places like Appalachia serving as a "periphery" to global market forces. Mills (1959), one of the earliest American conflict theorists, examined some of the key themes in post World War II American politics and argued that a small handful of individuals from major corporations, federal government and the military were influencing major decisions. He believed this triumvirate shared similar interests and often acted in unison. Mill's research on power and authority still influences theories about power and politics today.

However, Mills also had critics such as Dahl (1971), who believed that power was more diffused among contending interest groups. Galbraith (1971)asserted that technical bureaucrats behind the scenes had more power than those in official positions. Neo-Marxists argued that Mills and Dahl focused too much on the role of individual actors. They believed that institutions permit the exploitation of one class by another and that the institution of the state intervenes to correct the flaws of capitalism and to protect the status quo, which is in their interests.

In essence, conflict theory suggests that conflict is an integral part of social life. There are conflicts between economic classes, ethnic groups, young and old, male against female, or one race versus another. There are conflicts between developed "core" countries and those that are less developed. It is argued these conflicts result because power, wealth, and prestige are not available to everyone. Some groups are excluded from dominant discourse. It is assumed that those who hold or control desirable goods and services or who dominate culture will protect their own interests at the expense of others.

Conflict theorists such as Coser (1956), and Dahrendorf (1959), have looked at the integrative aspects of conflict and its value as a force that contributes to order and stability. Conflict can be constructive when it forces people with common interests to make gains to benefit them all. Racial inequalities or other social problems might never be resolved at all unless there is conflict to disturb the *status quo.* Simmel discusses how conflict can be resolved in a variety of ways, including disappearance of the conflict, victory for one of the parties, compromise, conciliation, and irreconcilability. (Schellenberg, 1996).

This theoretical framework about power of one party over another and the potential for conflict is not intended to be exhaustive – but it points to some of the major concerns that can guide community development practice.

How Can Conflict Theory Serve as a Guide for Community Development Practice?

Community organizers tend to embrace more readily conflict theory as a pivotal component of their organizing work. However, we argue that community developers also need conflict theory if their goal is to build capacity. Power differences are a reality of community life and need to be considered as development occurs. Let us take the case of an Appalachian community that is near a major state forest. The Department of Transportation (DOT) wants to build a highway through the state forest. They claim it will lead to more jobs and economic development. A group of local citizens have questioned this assumption. They believe the highway could pull businesses away from the prosperous downtown area to the edge of town, and will lead to sprawling development that will detract from the quality of life. They also believe, the proposed highway will lead to the destruction of a popular fishing hole and could harm the integrity of the forest. The DOT has refused to converse with the community; they claim the proposed highway's economic benefits are irrefutable. Conflict theory can serve as a reference point for moving the community's interests further. At first glance, it appeared the DOT was in charge of making the major decisions about the highway. However, the community developer incorporated conflict theory into practice. Community residents were encouraged to analyze the community's political, technical, economic, and social power as well as the power of the DOT. Through its analysis, the group was expanded to include downtown business people, hunters, environmental, and religious groups. In this particular case, the community decided it needed power that is more technical. They were able to secure the services of university researchers (economists, foresters, sociologists, and planners) who had the credentials to write an alternative report about the impact of the proposed highway. This report was widely circulated to the media and prominent state legislators from the community. Gradually, external support (power) emerged and the DOT decided to postpone the project.

In a similar situation, the use of conflict theory took another twist. The opponents of a DOT-proposed road sought the role of a mediator/facilitator to help them negotiate with the DOT and other stakeholders. They believed a third-party neutral could create a safe climate for discussion, and that during such discussions power differences could be minimized. In this particular case, their use of conflict theory paid off because the dispute was settled to everyone's satisfaction.

In summary, community developers need conflict theory because it provides insights about why there are differences and competition among groups and organizations within the community. These theories can help us understand why some peoples are silent or have internalized the values of elites, even to their own disadvantage. Practitioners and researchers can use Simmel's understanding of conflict to see how people resolve their differences, or they can borrow from Marx and neo-Marxists to see why people believe there are sharp differences that relate to class economic interests, gender, race, culture, and other concerns.

170 R. Hustedde and J. Ganowicz

Conflict theory can help communities understand competing interests among groups or whether power is concentrated in the hands of a few or more broadly distributed. One can also explore how communities can use conflict to upset the equilibrium through protests, economic boycotts, peaceful resistance, or other ranges of possibilities, especially if competing groups or institutions refuse to budge or negotiate.

While conflict theory is an essential tool for capacity building, it should be noted that critics claim it is limited because it ignores the less controversial and more orderly parts of our society (Turner, 1998; Ritzer, 1996; Collins, 1988). It does not help us understand the role of symbols in building solidarity. This leads us to another theoretical framework about shared meaning.

Concerns about Shared Meaning: Symbolic Interactionism

Shared meaning is the third key concern about community development shown in Figure 10.1. If community development is about building or strengthening solidarity, then practitioners must be concerned about the meaning that people give to places, people, and events. Symbolic interactionism is about symbols. Herbert Blumer (1969) gave this name to the theory because it emphasizes that human interaction is symbolic rather than a mechanical pattern of stimulus and interaction. For symbolic interactionists, the meaning of a situation is not fixed but is constructed by participants as they anticipate the responses of others. Mead (1982) explored the importance of symbols, especially language, in shaping the meaning of the one who makes the gesture as well as the one who receives it.

Goffman (1959) argued that individuals "give" and "give off" signs that provide information to others on how to respond. There may be a "front" such as social status, clothing, gestures, or a physical setting. Individuals may conceal elements of themselves that contradict general social values and present themselves to exemplify accredited values. Such encounters can be viewed as a form of drama in which the "audience" and "team players" interact.

In his last work, Goffman (1986) examined how individuals frame or interpret events. It involves group or individual rules about what is to be "pictured in the frame" and what should be excluded. For example, a community developer's framework about a community event might exclude ideas such as "citizens are apathetic." It will probably include our shared "rules" such as "participation is important." The emphasis is on the active, interpretive, and constructive capacities of individuals in the creation of a social reality. It assumes that social life is possible because people communicate through symbols. For example, when the traffic light is red, it means stop, or when the thumb is up, it means everything is fine. Flora et al. (2000) investigated how two opposing community narratives moved through the stages of frustration, confrontation, negotiation, and reconciliation. Their case study could be viewed as the employment of symbolic interactionism. Among the symbols that humans use, language seems to be the most important because it allows people to communicate and construct their version of reality. Symbolic interactionism

Theory and Community Development Practice **171**

contends that people interpret the world through symbols, and they stand back and think of themselves as objects.

For example, a group of Native Americans view a mountain as a sacred place for prayer and healing, and they react negatively when someone tries to develop it or alter their access to the mountain. Developers, foresters, tourism leaders, and others are likely to have other meanings about the mountain.

Different individuals or groups attach a different meaning to a particular event, and these interpretations are likely to be viewed by others as a form of deviance, which may be accepted, rejected, or fought over. Social interactionists contend that one way we build meaning is by observing what other people do, and by imitating them and following their guidance.

How Can Symbolic Interactionism Serve as a Tool for Community Development Practice?

We believe symbolic interactionism is essential for community development because it provides insight about how people develop a sense of shared meaning, an essential ingredient for solidarity.

When a community developer helps a community to develop a shared vision about its future, he or she is helping to build a sense of unity. A community-owned vision comes about through interaction of people and is told through symbols: pictures, words, or music. A symbolic interactionist would be keen on bringing people together to develop a shared understanding about something.

For example, let us take a case where some citizens have expressed an interest in preserving the farmland adjacent to the city and they have asked a community developer for assistance. If one employed a symbolic interactionist perspective, one would ask them what the presence of farmland means to them. One would link them with farmers and others to see if there is a different or competing meaning; participants would be asked how they developed their meaning about farmland. A symbolic interactionist doesn't ignore the concept of power. Participants would be asked questions such as whose concept of farmland dominates public policy. Through the employment of symbolic interaction theory, a sense of solidarity can gradually be established in a community.

A symbolic interactionist would spot groups that deviate from the dominant meaning about something and would engage them with the others in order to move the community towards solidarity. Symbolic interactionists also use symbols to build capacity. For example, a community may choose to preserve a historic structure because they believe it is beautiful, or they may say it is an important part of a labor, class, racial or gender struggle, or some other interest. A community developer can augment their meaning with data about the historical and architectural meaning that external agents see in the structure. Community capacity can be built in other ways, such as providing information about tax credits for historic structures or how to locate grants for preservation. Increasingly, community development researchers and practitioners are asked to help citizens reflect and understand the meaning of their work. We can use the symbolic interactionist concepts to aid us in collective evaluations. Essentially, it all boils down to what it means and who gives it meaning.

Symbolic interactionists probe into the factors that help us understand what we say and do. They look at the origins of symbolic meanings and how meanings persist. Symbolic interactionists are interested in the circumstances in which people question, challenge, criticize, or reconstruct meanings.

Critics argue that symbolic interactionists do not have an established systematic framework for predicting *what* meanings will be generated or for determining *how* meanings persist or for understanding how meanings change. For example, let us say a group of Mexican workers and a poultry processing firm move into a poor rural community that has been historically dominated by Anglo-Saxon Protestants. The event may trigger cooperation, good will, ambivalence, anger, fear, or defensiveness. The cast of characters involved in this event may be endless. What really happened, and whose interpretation best captures the reality of the situation? Symbolic interactionists have limited methodologies for answering such questions. In spite of these limitations, we hope we have made a strong case to explain why symbolic interactionism is an essential theory for community development practice.

Moving beyond Classical Theory towards Giddens's Structuration Theory

We have argued that the classical macro theories of structural functionalism and conflict theory are essential concepts for building community capacity, while the micro theory of symbolic interactionism is important for creating or strengthening solidarity. There are obvious tensions inherent in these classical theories. The dualism of macro versus micro characterizes much of the theoretical thinking in sociology. Sharing the same goal of picturing the social reality, these schools choose to proceed from the opposite directions. The macro thinkers attempt to draw a holistic picture and lay down the workings of "society," whereas the micro theorists hope to arrive at the same results by scrutinizing what happens "in" and "between" the individual people. Neither approach is entirely successful in producing a complete and exhaustive picture for community development practice. In a more recent development, efforts have been made at a "micro-translation," seeking to visualize social reality as made up of individuals interacting with one another and forming "larger interaction ritual chains" (Collins, 1988).

However, it has also been recognized in the recent theory that the issue of social agency itself, pointed out above as a key concern for community development, represents a concern that needs to be theoretically addressed in a way that transcends the established orientations in modern social theory and the whole macro-micro split. In his structuration theory, Anthony Giddens (1984; 1989) offers a perspective that is more fluid and process-oriented than either the macro or the micro approaches. Giddens introduces a third dimension, or an "in between" level of analysis, which is neither macro nor micro. It has to do with the cultural traditions, beliefs, and norms of society, and how the actors draw upon them in their behavior (Collins 1988, p. 399). For Giddens, those normative patterns of society exist "outside of time and space" (Collins, 1988, pp. 398–399), meaning they are neither properties of the empirical social system, nor of the individual actors. Their actuality consists in the moments when individuals reach up to that level of society's traditions and norms in their behavior. People also draw upon and act upon thought patterns or cultural "molds," for example, the notion of reciprocity – getting something in return for something else. Cultural traditions and patterns become modalities by virtue of placing them on Giddens's analytical scheme. They represent a third level, which is in between individualistic behavior and the macro structures. Even though the reality of modalities may be only momentary, when people actually reach up to them in their behavior, we can better visualize the social process and the role of culture and normative patterns. "Actors draw upon the modalities of structuration in reproduction systems of interaction" (Giddens, 1984, p. 28). Social structure is upheld and existing divisions of society carry on through those "mental molds."

The laying out of society on three theoretical levels serves to better visualize the issue of agency compared to either the macro or the micro theories (see Figure 10.2). The relationship between those three levels is not necessarily unidirectional or mechanical. Rather, it is a fluid process in which all three levels interact with each other. Individuals represent the agency whereby interactions between levels take place.

Thus, it becomes easier to grasp how macro structures have an independent existence outside of individuals, people are pictured as free agents exercising their motives and agendas, and yet society continues to exercise an influence on individuals. The notorious problem of Marx's theory and several radical thinkers informed by it, of people being the "puppets of the macrostructure," becomes circumvented.[2]

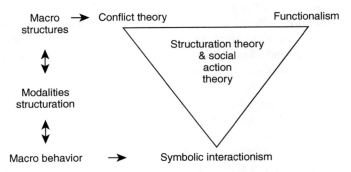

FIGURE 10.2 Gidden's Modalities: The Link to Social Change at the Macro and Micro Levels

Coming back to the community development profession and its key concerns, Giddens's model is perhaps best suited to grasp how social agency is exercised and solidarity established amid and often against the existing structural divisions of society. Modalities represent the level whereby solidarity is established by people following the symbolic norms and patterns available to them, based on their cultures and traditions. Behavior is neither haphazard nor merely a reflection of the existing social structure and its divisions, but it follows certain paths (modalities) established and available to people through the cultural patterns. Similarly, new rules of behavior also occur through the medium of modalities, in this instance their creative redefinition. This is how the existing divisions can be overcome and new bonds between people forged. For this to take place, a genuine social creativity is necessary, meaning that people come up with solutions and ideas that simultaneously draw on their cultural traditions (a common reference point) and transcend, as a basis for new bonds, the new patterns of solidarity to be put into place. Modalities serve not only as the rules for the reproduction of the social system, but also for its transformation (Turner, 1998, p. 494).

Giddens's concept of modalities is the link between macro and micro theories. Modalities are part of the analytical scheme in a particular place. For example, individualism in the United States is a strong modality and can keep citizens from becoming united to take action. The notion of a common good is another American modality, which can be used to transform a divided community into a greater sense of solidarity. Modalities can be used to influence the macro or micro level of social change. There are several substantive analyses of the social processing and the dynamics of social transformation that have been carried out, at least in part, on the level of modalities, looking at cultural patterns and systems of ideas and how they mediate the social process. Gaventa (1980) examines the modalities of Appalachia with a focus on rebellion and quiescence. He analyzes how power is used in the region to prevent or implement decisions. The use of force and threat of sanctions are discussed, along with less intrusive aspects such as attitudes that are infused into the dominant culture by elites and internalized by non-elites. For example, there are perspectives such as "you can't change anything around here" or "you don't have to be poor if you want to really work." Gaventa argues there are other modalities in which Appalachian culture has resisted the penetration of dominant social values. Those with less power can develop their own resources for analyzing issues and can explore their grievances openly. He views the "myth of American democracy" as another modality that can set the stage for greater openness and transparency in local government.

Staniszkis (1984) provides further insights about modalities through her ideas about how workers' solidarity emerged in Poland. She saw the working class under the communist regime as a unified bloc, both in a positive hegemonic way and negatively, as subject to the party's control and manipulation. These modalities were taken by Solidarity and its charismatic leader Lech Walesa and transformed through references to workers' common identity as opposed to the party apparatus. Walesa forged workers' strong Christian identification into this new self-understanding and

Theory and Community Development Practice **175**

self-image of the workers in Poland to further create a sense of solidarity and unity in opposition to the communist party and the system. Through her consistent attention to symbolic meanings and their interplay with the social structure, Staniszkis's work on the transformation of workers' collective identity represents an apt demonstration of how a transformation of modalities may take place.

Analytically, Giddens's structuration theory stands as the middle ground between the micro and the macro theories, where we have also placed the issue of agency and solidarity (see Figure 10.2). The theory suggests that the micro theories associated with symbolic interactionism can influence cultural and traditional norms and patterns (modalities) and vice versa. While the symbolic interactionist tends to ignore structure, Giddens's mid-level theory about modalities is a crucial link between symbolic interactionism and the macro conflict and "structural functionalist theories" (Giddens, 1984).

Max Weber's social action theory was originally cast at an "in-between level." If his theory was not explicit, it was at least implicit in his intentions.[3] Weber attempted to view society as a fluid process, for analytical purposes dissecting it into various components (Turner, 1998, p. 17) much like Giddens does. Although Weber never attempted an analytical model of society along those lines, some observers have categorized Weber as a micro-theorist because of his subjective interpretation of behavior and its meaning to the actor. Others argue that Weber is a strong macro-theorist. Our understanding is that his intentions actually lie closer to Giddens's perspective that a three-tiered model is better suited to grasp the complexities of social action and the interplay between the symbolic meaning and the structural forces of society. Weber's writings suggest he is constantly preoccupied with the interplay between the symbolic meaning and the structural forces of society. This is especially obvious in his attempts to explain the rise of modern capitalism through the interplay of social structural conditions and the religious beliefs of Protestantism. He followed similar analyses for non-Western societies in his sociology of religion volumes.

What Giddens lays down in theory, Weber actually performs in his works, bridging the macro and micro dimensions by his attention to society's traditions and norms and how they become transformed, independently of the macro structural forces of society, through people interpreting and reinterpreting them. Similarly, Gaventa and Staniszkis demonstrate how one can connect communities or groups to structure in a way that is not fixed or mechanical.

In contrast to debates about whether structure shapes action to determine social phenomena or the reverse, Giddens believes that structure exists in and through the activities of human agents. He views it as a form of "dualism" in which neither can exist without the other. When humans express themselves as actors, and when they engage in the monitoring of the ongoing flow of activities, they are contributing to structure and their own agency. He contends that social systems are often the result of the unanticipated outcome of human action. Giddens viewed time and space as crucial variables. Many interactions are face-to-face, and hence are rooted in the same space and time. However, with the advent of new technologies, there can be

176 R. Hustedde and J. Ganowicz

interaction across different times and spaces. Community developers are likely to feel some kinship with Giddens because he has a dynamic rather than a static concept of the world. He recognizes the interplay of humans in shaping and being shaped by structure. Critics are likely to argue that he has oversubscribed to the concept of the power of human agency. Our space limits the response to such critiques; we cannot provide a fuller exploration of Giddens's theoretical insights.

How Can Giddens's Structuration Theory Guide Community Development Practice?

Structuration theory provides many theoretical insights (see Ritzer, 1996, p. 433) for those engaged in community development because it links disparate macro theories about structure and conflict with micro theories about individual and group behavior and symbols (symbolic interactionism). Giddens's concept of modalities is essential for community development practice.

Let us revisit the case of the Appalachian community group that is opposing the construction of a road through a nearby state forest. They believe they are overpowered by the Department of Transportation (DOT) that wants to build the road. The community finds it difficult to argue against the DOT report, which contains sophisticated economic, social, and natural resource information. Here is what the community developer practitioner did. First, the community's residents identified the strengths of their local traditions – particularly storytelling and the arts – as a venue for building a sense of solidarity about the integrity of the forest. They examined the modalities of storytelling and the arts as a way to make an impact through the media to the public and elected leaders in the region. The community's strong respect for the local Cooperative Extension Service was identified as another modality that could mobilize the broader informational resources of the land-grant university. The developer was able to draw upon the services of professional economists, sociologists, foresters, and others without spending much money; these professionals developed an alternative to the DOT report that was widely disseminated. Storytelling, the local arts, and links with the local Extension Service influenced broader structures and led to fewer power imbalances. Eventually, the DOT decided to permanently "postpone" the development of the road. Because the community developer understood the power of modalities (local cultural traditions and patterns), the community was able to develop a sense of shared meaning which led to greater influence on structure and resolution of the conflict.

How do Giddens's structuration theory and the concept of modalities relate to the three classical theories: structural functionalism, conflict theory, and symbolic interactionism?

When one looks at functionalism through the Giddens lens, one sees how structures shape and can be shaped by modalities. From a Giddens perspective, community change agents are not powerless when faced with powerful structures. Cultural patterns can be transformed to influence or break down structural constraints that inhibit solidarity or capacity building.

Giddens's structuration theory illuminates conflict theory because it suggests that communities can influence power imbalances through cultural norms and patterns. It also means that external power can shape behavior.

On the basis of a Giddens perspective, the micro theories associated with symbolic interactionism can influence cultural and traditional norms and patterns (modalities), and vice versa. While the symbolic interactionists tend to ignore structure, Giddens's mid-level theory about modalities is a crucial link between symbolic interactionism and the macro "conflict" and structural functionalist theories.

Limitations of Giddens's Structuration Theory

Giddens's writing is analytical and abstract to the point of being vague and imprecise. He rarely gives concrete examples, which can be frustrating to those community developers who are more empirically grounded. Giddens's analysis is also difficult because it involves a constant moving between the levels of modalities and societal institutions and the actual actions of individuals.

In spite of these limitations, we believe it is especially useful to community developers because of the potent role of symbolic norms and cultural patterns (modalities) in creating new structures, influencing power differences, and shaping individual behavior into a sense of solidarity.

Conclusion

We have defined community development by its intention to build solidarity and agency (capacity building). There are three classical theories that are essential for community development practice. They comprise the macro theories of structural functionalism, conflict theory that relates to capacity building, and symbolic interactionism that is associated with solidarity building. We have provided some case studies that illustrate the importance of these theories to community development practice.

We have focused on Anthony Giddens's structuration theory because Giddens links macro and micro theories through his concept of modalities that represent the level where social solidarity is established. Modalities are symbolic norms and patterns that can be found in community cultures and traditions. Modalities are shaped by structures and power differences. However, they can also be transformed to influence structure and address power differences. For example, a community can transform its belief about the common good to build a stronger sense of unity and to take appropriate action steps rather than feel powerless. Our discussion of modalities is interspersed with examples from Appalachia and Poland.

This article is about reaching across the conceptual divide between theory and action. It is about stimulating dialogue and further discussion about essential theory for community development practice. We believe that Giddens and other synthesizers have reenergized interests in classical theory by linking theoretical camps in a novel way.

Notes

1 There are several exceptions, such as the text *Community Economics* by Ron E. Shaffer (1989). It is theoretically driven. However, it focuses on one aspect of community development, namely economic development.
2 We argue that structuration theory represents an improvement over conventional micro theories (i.e. those of symbolic interactionists) which also visualizes behavior on two levels, the "me" and the "I." The "me" is reminiscent of Giddens's modalities but the micro theorists miss the significance of the social structure and its divisions, which Giddens treats as the analytical third level.
3 Talcott Parsons's original 1937 formulation of his theory was cast at a similar level, with the dimension of "culture" representing a bridge between personality and the social system, but subsequently it got lost as the social system swallowed up the micro dimension in Parsons's theorizing (Collins, 1988).

References

Bhattacharyya, J. (1995). Solidarity and agency: Rethinking community development. *Human Organization* 54(1): 60–68.

Biddle, W., with L. Biddle (1965). *The Community Development Process*. New York: Holt Rhinehardt and Winston.

Blumer, H. (1969). *Symbolic Interactionism: Perspective and Method*. New York: Prentice-Hall.

Chaskin, R.J., P. Brown, S. Venkatesh, & A.Vidal (2001). *Building Community Capacity*. Hawthorne, NY: Aldine De Gruyter.

Christenson, J., & J. Robinson (eds) (1989). *Community Development in Perspective*. Iowa City: University of Iowa Press.

Collins, R. (1988). *Theoretical Sociology*. New York: Harcourt Brace Jovanovich.

Coser, L. (1956). *The Functions of Social Conflict*. New York: The Free Press.

Dahl, R.A. (1971). *Polyarchy: Participation and Opposition*. New Haven, CT: Yale University Press.

Dahrendorf, R. (1959). *Class and Class Conflict in Industrial Society*. Stanford, CA: Stanford University Press.

Ejigiri, D. (1996). The value of local knowledge and the importance of shifting beliefs in the process of social change. *Community Development Journal* 31(1): 44–53.

Flora, C.B., J.L. Flora, & R.J. Tapp (2000). Meat, meth and Mexicans: Community responses to increasing ethnic diversity. *Journal of the Community Development Society* 31(2): 277–299.

Foucault, M. (1965). *Madness and Civilization: A History of Insanity in the Age of Reason*. New York: Vintage.

Foucault, M. (1975). *The Birth of the Clinic: An Archeology of Medical Perception*. New York: Vintage.

Foucault, M. (1979). *Discipline and Punish: The Birth of Prison*. New York: Vintage.

Foucault, M. (1980). *The History of Sexuality, Volume 1, An Introduction*. New York: Vintage.

Foucault, M. (1985). *The Use of Pleasure. The History of Sexuality, Volume 2*. New York: Panthenon.

Galbraith, J.K. (1971). *The New Industrial State*. Boston, MA: Houghton Mifflin.

Gaventa, J.L. (1980). *Power and Politics: Quiescence and Rebellion in an Appalachian Valley*. Urbana: University of Illinois Press.

Giddens, A. (1984). *The Constitution of Society*. Berkeley: University of California Press.

Giddens, A. (1989). A reply to my critics. pp. 249–301 in D. Held & J.B. Thompson (eds), *Social Theory of Modern Societies: Anthony Giddens and his Critics*. Cambridge, UK: Cambridge University Press.

Theory and Community Development Practice **179**

Goffman, E. (1959). *The Presentation of Self in Everyday Life*. Garden City, NY: Anchor.

Goffman, E. (1986). *Frame Analysis: An Essay on the Organization of Experience*. Boston, MA: Northeastern University Press.

Horton, H.D. (1992). A sociological approach to black community development: presentation of the black organizational autonomy model. *Journal of the Community Development Society* 23(1): 1–19.

Jeffries, A. (2000). Promoting participation: A conceptual framework for strategic practice, with case studies from Plymouth, UK and Ottawa, Canada. *The Scottish Journal of Community Work and Development,* Special Issue, 6(Autumn): 5–14.

Mead, G.H. (1982). The *Individual and the Social Self: Unpublished Work of George Herbert Mead*. Chicago, IL: University of Chicago Press.

Merton, R.K. (1968). *Social Theory and Social Structure*. Rev. ed. New York: The Free Press.

Mills, C.W. (1959). *The Power Elite*. New York: Oxford University Press.

Nash, K. (2000). *Contemporary Political Sociology: Globalization, Politics, and Power*. Maiden, MA: Blackwell Publishers.

Parsons, T. (ed.) (1960). Some reflections on the institutional framework of economic development. In *Structure and Process in Modern Societies*. Glencoe, IL: Free Press.

Parsons, T., & E.A. Shils (eds) (1951). *Toward a General Theory of Action*. New York: Harper & Row.

Perkins, D.D. (1995). Speaking truth to power: Empowerment ideology as social intervention and policy. *American Journal of Community Psychology* 23(5): 569–579.

Ritzer, G. (1996). *Sociological Theory*. 4th ed. New York: McGraw-Hill.

Rothman, J., & L.M. Gant (1987). Approaches and models of community intervention. pp. 35–44 in D.E. Johnson, L.R. Meiller, L.C. Miller, & G.F. Summers (eds), *Needs Assessment: Theory and Methods*. Ames, IA: Iowa State University Press.

Schellenberg, J.A. (1996). *Conflict Resolution: Theory, Research and Practice*. Albany, NY: State University of New York.

Shaffer, R.E. (1989). *Community Economics: Economic Structure and Change in Smaller Communities*. Ames, IA: Iowa State University Press.

Staniszkis, J. (1984). *Poland's Self-Limiting Revolution...* Princeton, NJ: Princeton University Press.

Turner, J.H. (1998). *The Structure of Sociological Theory*. 6th ed. Belmont, CA: Wadsworth Publishing Company.

Wallerstein, I. (1984). The development of the concept of development. *Sociological Theory* 2: 102–116.

Weber, M. (1947). *The Theory of Social and Economic Organization*. A.M. Henderson & T. Parsons (Trans.). New York: Oxford University Press.

11

A FRAMEWORK FOR THINKING AND ACTING CRITICALLY IN COMMUNITY

Jeffrey C. Bridger, Paloma Z. Frumento,
Theodore R. Alter, and Mark A. Brennan

While the chapters in this book are diverse, they all underscore the extent to which historical and contemporary forces complicate our understanding of community and community development. The pace of change on the ground has far exceeded that of both academic theory and professional practice. Our task in this chapter is to sketch a framework for thinking and acting critically in the diverse settings that are today's communities. In particular, we emphasize the importance of the relationship between community, community development, and democracy. The principal goal of this chapter will be to suggest ways that community development scholars and practitioners can better facilitate a dialogue between abstract theoretical and ideological lenses and what Harvey (1996) terms the concrete, localized 'structure of feeling' inherent in lived experience. By strengthening this linkage, scholars and practitioners can foster democratic governance that helps communities address critical problems and issues.

The rate of environmental, economic, social, and technological change has introduced a new level of complexity to issues of community development. For this reason, experts across a range of social and natural scientific disciplines have increasingly been called on to provide technical advice and skills that are beyond the capacity of ordinary citizens. This is problematic because, as Fischer (2000, p. 23) explains, "... the lack of access to such knowledge hinders the possibility of an active and meaningful involvement on the part of the large majority of the public" and creates an environment that depresses citizen participation in crucial decisions that impact them. The exclusion of citizens from the sphere of public policy and decision-making militates against solidarity and agency, which are the central components of community development (Bhattacharyya, 2004). Things are further complicated by the fact that the most pressing issues facing communities can increasingly be described as what Rittel and Weber (1973) call 'wicked problems.' These are problems that are difficult to define and do not have 'correct' or 'best'

Conclusion and Future Directions **181**

technical solutions. In fact, they typically only have temporary solutions that require trade-offs. Especially at the community level, wicked problems require an explicit discussion of competing interests and values in order to make decisions that are acceptable to the relevant publics.

In addressing wicked problems, the abstract plans and generic rules that dominate technical and empirical knowledge fall short. Scott (1998), for instance, provides several examples of the ways in which grand schemes to improve life tend to fail without the active participation of those impacted. In reference to 'scientific cities' based upon rational planning and high modernism, he writes:

> Just as the stripped-down logic behind the scientific forest was an inadequate recipe for a healthy, 'successful' forest, so were the thin urban-planning schemata of Le Corbusier an inadequate recipe for a satisfactory human community. Any large social process or event will inevitably be far more complex than the schemata we can devise, prospectively or retrospectively, to map it. (p. 309)

In his highly influential treatise on what he terms 'phronetic' social science, Flyvbjerg (2001) advocates an epistemic shift in theory, practice, and policy that captures the importance of context for prediction, decision-making, and implementation. He argues:

> The problem in the study of human activity is that every attempt at a context-free definition of action, that is, a definition based on abstract rules or laws, will not necessarily accord with the pragmatic way an action is defined by the actors in a concrete social situation. … The rules of a ritual are not the ritual, a grammar is not a language, the rules for chess are not chess, and traditions are not actual social behavior. (pp. 42–3)

The central, foundational role of context to the social sciences, and particularly to community development, necessitates the devolution of power in knowledge creation, dissemination, and legitimation. In particular, we need to move beyond the expert-driven model in which legitimate knowledge is portrayed as technical, instrumental, value-neutral, and divorced from particular times and places. The rise to power of experts in local decision-making processes was predicated upon precisely this technocratic paradigm. Community development professionals must reconceptualize the expert–citizen dichotomy and develop new patterns of communication that replace the unidirectional transfer of knowledge from expert to citizen. In the remainder of this chapter, we argue that the relationship between experts and citizens can be most productive when it is conceptualized as a deliberative democratic partnership, in which both actors participate in a mutual learning process.

This dynamic co-production of knowledge is still absent from most popular conceptualizations of scholarship and expert knowledge. For instance, Peters et al. (2010)

outline three normative traditions for engaged scholarship in the academic profession: the service intellectual tradition, the public intellectual, and the action researcher/public scholar/educational organizer. Each tradition acts on a different model for the purpose and role of the professional in the public sphere. Peters et al. (2010, p. 51) seek to bring to the forefront the fundamental, epistemic issues that structure these models: "professional and cultural identities and norms, bets and assumptions about what works, and academic professionals' (and others') public philosophies and political theories – that is, their conceptions about the nature and meaning of democracy, politics, civic agency, citizenship, freedom, and public life." These are critical issues that have remained largely unchallenged in engagement, community, and community development literatures.

The first tradition, that of the service intellectual, posits a professional who is unbiased, disinterested, and neutral and serves to provide scientific and technical information and products (as the authors write, "i.e. the 'truth'") to external constituencies and clients only when solicited (Peters et al., 2010, p. 28). Experts in this tradition favor quantitative data above other types of information and knowledge. In contrast, Peters et al. define the service intellectual against two 'purposivist' traditions which blur the boundaries between expert and citizen identities: the public intellectual and the action researcher/public scholar/educational organizer. The public intellectual holds that scholars play an important role in influencing how public issues and problems are framed, discussed, and addressed through their role as social critics. Like the service intellectual, however, the public intellectual remains distanced from the public by the unidirectional dissemination of knowledge through various forums and media outlets.

The action researcher/public scholar/educational organizer, instead, directly collaborates with external partners in the co-production of knowledge, in specific, localized settings. This model is uniquely process-oriented: "[It] is not only about achieving instrumental or material ends. It is also aimed at facilitating inquiry, learning, and growth; at developing people's knowledge, relational power, leadership potential, civic skills, spirit, and capacities ..." (Peters et al., 2010, p. 59). A growing number of scholars have come to argue that this kind of social learning, in the context of complex interdependencies among stakeholders, including academic professionals and community members, is a necessary component of community development.

Problematizing the concept of engaged scholarship is a critical theoretical move because it provides the opportunity to explicitly reconsider and restructure the decision-making milieu, both in theory and in practice. To this end, Bridger and Alter (2010) argue in favor of an egalitarian relationship between experts and citizens. However, Mathews (2009) suggests that most professionals continue to uncritically conceptualize their role as that of an expert or guide tasked with serving communities through the provision of knowledge, as in the models of the service and public intellectual. He uses the analogy of 'ships passing in the night' to describe what he views as a disconnect between academic and grassroots community-level efforts to foster engagement: "It would seem that two civic engagement movements,

Conclusion and Future Directions **183**

occurring at the same time and often in the same locations, would be closely allied – perhaps mutually reinforcing. That doesn't seem to be happening very often" (p. 10). Ultimately, Flyvbjerg (2001, p. 60) suggests all professionals are responsible for answering a set of inherently value-laden questions: "Where are we going? Is it desirable? What should be done? And who gain and who loses; by which mechanisms of power?" These questions suggest a need for a more widespread critical reexamination of values, norms, and power as they manifest in a wide range of academic and other professional and institutional engagement paradigms.

We advocate in favor of the action researcher/public scholar/educational organizer model, which requires active citizen participation (Peters et al., 2010). Lane (2005) argues that citizen participation can only be understood and evaluated for effectiveness in terms of the theoretical context in which it is embedded. To this end, he traces the intellectual history of the concept of 'public participation' in planning. Active public participation is firmly located in the literature on communicative theory, structured largely by the work of Habermas (1984) and Giddens (1984). This theoretical perspective emphasizes unfettered discourse and intersubjective argumentation. According to Lane, the key contributions of communicative theory to planning are to focus attention on the interests and perceptions of participants, and to recognize multiple forms of rationality (other than scientific, technical, and economic) that they employ in decision-making.

The influence of this model is clear in Fischer's (2000, p. 125) analysis of public participation in the environmental movement, more specifically NIMBY, or 'not in my backyard,' activities addressing the location of landfills, prisons, power plants (nuclear or otherwise), industrial parks, housing for the homeless, treatment facilities for drug addicts, and hazardous waste facilities. He notes that arguments forwarded by NIMBY advocates are typically viewed as 'irrational' by policy makers and professionals who seek to orient location decisions around scientific risk assessment. However, these arguments do not exemplify irrationality, but instead a different form of rationality. Citizens often form arguments on the basis of 'cultural rationality' which "is geared to – or at least gives equal weight to – personal and familiar experiences rather than depersonalized technical calculations" (Fischer, 2000, p. 132). The challenges for scholars focusing on participation and decision-making, he argues, are to better understand the interactions between these forms of rationality and to integrate them more systematically.

Complicating this research agenda, we argue that multiple forms of rationality, including economic, scientific, and cultural, may be employed simultaneously by a single actor. This calls for a more nuanced analysis of how and in what circumstances stakeholders may privilege one form of rationality above another or attempt to reconcile multiple rationality frameworks. This task is particularly important because expert and citizen identities are not mutually exclusive. Sullivan (2005) calls for a more explicit merging of the two identities in his conceptualization of a 'civic professional,' which he contrasts with the 'technical professional.' The civic professional is committed to disciplinary excellence, but not at the expense of a larger public focus. Sullivan's (2005, p. 181) goal with this framework is to advance a professionalism that stands "on the boundary of interaction between systems of technical capacity and the moral of political processes that aim to integrate these powers into humanely valuable forms of life."

To create this interaction, several key theorists referenced throughout this book advocate for the creation and maintenance of networks of ties across diverse groups as a critical component of community development. This is particularly evident in Wilkinson's (1991) concept of the community field and Putnam's (2000) concept of bridging social capital, which is drawn in part from Granovetter's (1973) work on weak ties. These theorists agree that healthy community social structures require robust and consistent boundary spanning to address problems and foster collective action. This is a hermeneutic task involving what Gadamer (1975) calls the 'fusion of horizons' or the bringing together of diverse viewpoints in a productive exchange that blurs the boundaries between distinctive roles and expands the perspectives of all actors. Johansson (2004) argues that this 'fusion of horizons,' which he terms the intersection, is the source of insight, creativity, and innovation in society. The intersection exists wherever there are connections between people from different fields, with fields being defined as "disciplines, cultures, and domains in which one can specialize through education, work, hobbies, or other life experiences" (p. 16). As opposed to a directional innovation in a specific field, an intersectional innovation is an unusual combination of concepts across fields that forges an entirely new path. Particularly in the face of increasingly complex, multi-dimensional wicked problems, policies which cultivate intersectional innovation support the ability of communities to continually innovate for environmental and economic sustainability – and to, in effect, themselves become more sustainable communities.

In order to stimulate this type of intersectional innovation, it is not enough simply to bring people together. They must have the opportunity for the open and equitable sharing of ideas. It is with this in mind that a number of contemporary scholars have returned to, further developed, and championed what is called either participatory or deliberative democracy, a form of what Barber (2003) terms strong democracy. In his elaboration of the concept, Barber emphasizes that strong democracy is predicated upon diversity: "the politics of conflict, the sociology of pluralism" (p. 117) or "the way that human beings with variable but malleable natures and with competing but overlapping interests can contrive to live together communally not only to their mutual advantage but also to the advantage of their mutuality" (p. 118). However, Barber does not take an idealistic view of the realities of intractable conflict, nor of the potentiality for privileged and/or extreme voices to dominate debate and decision-making (see also Fiorina, 1999 and Schlozman et al., 1999). Ultimately, he asserts, strong democracy does not seek to eliminate, repress, or tolerate conflict, but rather "aspires to transform conflict through a politics of distinctive inventiveness and discovery" (Barber, 2003, p. 119). The parallels here between Barber's argument regarding social and political structures and Johansson's ideal conditions for innovation are quite clear, in that both underscore the importance of bringing together diverse parties as a means for fostering creative new ideas and policies (see also Ostrom, 2010).

Conclusion and Future Directions **185**

Boyte (2004; 2008; 2009) has been a central advocate for both deliberative democracy and innovative policy solutions generated through collaboration between experts and citizens. In particular, he addresses the need for "middle spaces, not owned by academics or professionals, but open to academic and scientific knowledge, where different ways of knowing and acting intermingle in creative ways" (Boyte, 2009, p. 2). He provides as examples of such vital public spaces everything from farmers' markets to libraries and local schools with community orientations (Boyte, 2004, p. 28). Ultimately, any physical setting can take the form of a 'public space' provided it allows for interaction between diverse segments of the population: "Public space is a quality of human interaction among diverse individuals, and also a cultural dynamic" (Boyte, 2008, p. 112).

A discussion of public spaces is especially relevant now, given that opportunities for interaction are increasingly disappearing as income inequality in many parts of the world reaches a level not seen in decades. Some have suggested that technology may allow for new, virtual forms of public space. A prominent example is that of Wikipedia, an online encyclopedia to which anyone can contribute knowledge. Wikipedia began with the mission, stated on the homepage, to "write a complete encyclopedia from scratch, collaboratively" (quoted in Gleick, 2011, p. 381). Gleick (2011) writes: "It exposed the difficulties – perhaps the impossibility – of reaching a neutral, consensus view of disputed, tumultuous reality. The process was plagued by so-called edit wars, when battling contributors reversed one another's alterations without surcease" (p. 382). Because the content of Wikipedia is constantly changing, sometimes literally from one minute to the next, it highlights for users the socially constructed nature of knowledge and the need to recognize other viewpoints.

Simply providing spaces for interaction is a necessary but not sufficient condition for bridging difference; it is also important to create communicative forms that foster productive discourse. Fisher (1985) calls us homo narrans – the species that tells stories. Brooks (1984, p. 3) captures the essence of this phrase when he writes: "We live immersed in narrative, recounting and reassessing the meaning of our past actions, anticipating the outcome of our future projects, situating ourselves at the intersection of several stories not yet completed." For this reason, much of communication is narrative in form; this is as true of public discourse as it is of private communication. In other words, narrative construction is an inherently social process. Thus narratives are a particularly useful tool for exploring difference because they can be used to address multiple perspectives specifically grounded in both space and time, in ways that more technical and empirical forms of knowledge alone cannot. Fischer (2009, p. 197) notes:

> It is through storytelling that people access social positions in their communities, understand the goals of different social groups, and internalized social conventions. Narrative stories do this by imposing a coherent interpretation on the whirl of events and acts that surrounds us. Threading these sequential components together through storylines, narratives place social phenomena in the larger patterns that attribute social and political meaning to them.

> In the process, the storyline is at the same time an invitation to moral reasoning.

In this way, narratives become an indispensable foundation for making decisions and taking action in communities. Boyte (2009, p. 6) suggests that the theory and practice of community development cannot be separated from narrative: "Community organizing, at its deepest level, is best understood not as a method of civic action but as a philosophy based on a narrative view that recognizes each person to be unique, dynamic, and immensely complex." This role of narrative is underscored by Moore's (2002) research, which focused on how practitioners used theory or developed theory to guide their practice. Through a set of in-depth interviews with practitioners working in a number of global settings, he found that they often used visioning, storytelling, and metaphors as planning and communication tools. They also employed many of these elements in describing their own work. For this reason, narrative is also a useful tool for helping practitioners to be reflexive about their own frames and biases.

Although application of post-positivist perspectives that draw heavily on narrative have been applied to analyses of national environmental disputes and international policymaking, community development still remains the province of what Fischer (2009) calls empiricist scholarly work. This is problematic, given that local communities still form the mesostructural level where most people meet their daily needs, and it is at least partially through the interactions that occur at this level that people develop a social definition of the self and beliefs about the way the larger society operates. Hustedde and Ganowicz (this volume, chapter 10) note that communities provide the setting in which individuals interact with the modalities that shape agency within larger macro structures. As Fine (2012, p. 128) argues, it is through the small groups that comprise communities, and the acts of framing and mobilizing in which these groups engage, that it is possible to create citizens and "… produce identities that embed individuals in larger entities, such as the nation." Even though its boundaries are fluid, the local community is still central to individual and social well-being.

Despite the continued relevance of community, the ability of residents to address issues and challenges is limited by the gap between community development professionals and the people with whom they work. For instance, de Souza Briggs (1998) observes that community planners often struggle to communicate; he suggests that professionals cannot truly incorporate the broader community in their work unless they understand residents' vocabulary, politics, and narratives. Based on a close analysis of speech during a large-scale planning process in five densely populated, high-poverty, predominantly African-American and Latino neighborhoods in a single city, the author argues that professionals must learn how to talk with others in a way that "leads to constructive learning on both sides" (p. 3). "Such competence," he suggests, "is critical for doing democracy and building community in a diverse and rapidly changing world" (p. 11). Although de Souza Briggs's focus is on urban planning, his argument is just as valid in other community settings marked by significant diversity and power differentials.

Conclusion and Future Directions **187**

It is equally important that community development professionals are able to facilitate authentic communication between other experts and citizens. At the most basic level, community development professionals must work with other experts to translate technical jargon into language that citizens can understand and also to represent their perspectives to the experts. In some instances, this may require creating environments where dialogue can occur, such as the 'middle spaces' identified by Boyte (2004; 2008; 2009). In other instances, this may require that a community development professional should take on an advocacy role and serve more directly as a representative on behalf of citizens to experts, especially when experts devalue local participation and knowledge. At the level of deliberation and decision-making, community development professionals should, according to Fischer (2009, p. 233), guide public discourse in such a way that "participants develop their reflective capacities to identify and interpret different, often competing. perspectives from alternative theoretical points of view." These participants include all stakeholders, experts and citizens alike.

We often assume that citizens are lacking in this capacity while experts, because of their specific knowledges and education, have the capacity to engage in this kind of discourse. But as Flyvbjerg (2001) argues, while experts may have strong analytical skills, they are often less versed in the moral reasoning that is central to effective deliberation and decision-making in settings that are typically characterized by diverse viewpoints and conflicting values. Moreover, experts – including community development professionals – often face challenges unique to their educational socialization and professional prospects. Fischer (2009, p. 241) notes:

> Although they are the ones who have to provide the leadership (or perhaps more appropriately here, the guidance) in critical learning, such people can often suffer from inflated egos and from their own exaggerated and sometimes distorted views of their own expertise. Moreover, their commitment to social causes can be quite fragile in the face of new attractive career opportunities higher up the professional ladder. All of this illustrates just how difficult it is to question the very hierarchy upon which professional education itself is based.

For this reason, Fischer argues that community development professionals (and other experts for that matter) must be trained, not only for higher quality interpersonal skills and the ability to develop tacit, practical knowledge in a range of settings, but also to be particularly self-aware and reflective, and to recognize the personal biases and motivations that color their interactions with others and, by extension, their professional work.

Conceptualizing community development professionals as facilitators, organizers and educators suggests that community development practice is a more labor-intensive, complicated process than it is typically described in the literature, especially textbooks. Community development is often presented as a linear, stage-dependent process that begins with the identification of some problem and then continues with a set of tasks designed to solve that problem. However, as Mathews (this volume, chapter 9) suggests, the 'democratic practices' he elaborates have multiple, overlapping functions and often occur simultaneously. They are not necessarily temporally dependent upon one another. Furthermore, community development professionals often enter into discussions and action processes that citizens have already initiated. In such situations, it would make no sense to follow a predetermined script. Mathews (1999, p. 123) writes: "If people are already engaged in a kind of politics, the challenge is not to draw them out of their supposed apathy to become advocates in politics as usual. The challenge is to connect politics as usual to the politics that people already practice." Successful capacity building, then, is characterized by an emphasis on process rather than specific outcomes or objectives.

As Wilkinson (1991) argues, simply trying to achieve goals is enough. Failure to achieve goals relating to development in the community – for example, recruiting an industry or developing a local business park – is bound to occur. However, failure can be a key source of learning and innovation at the intersection of difference, particularly if in mobilizing around these goals community members are able to build relationships across groups and interest lines, especially lasting relationships that could be leveraged in future projects. Chaskin (2001, p. 318) writes: "Community capacity tends to be spoken of as a unitary thing, as a generalized characteristic of a neighborhood social system. But it resides in a community's individuals, formal organizations, and the relational networks tying them to each other and to the broader systems of which they are a part." Capacity building is not a conflict-free process, but community depends upon all kinds of relationships – including conflictual ones.

Although it may seem as though we are discussing best practices with this general framework for thinking and acting critically in communities, the processes and professional values we describe are best practices only in the broadest sense of the term. In the context of issues such as the growing mobility of people and ideas, the economic restructuring brought about by globalization, the environmental challenges related to climate change, and the rapid social and technological changes that characterize the information age, the concept of best practices for community development does not make sense. The problems brought about by these changes are complex and interconnected. For this reason, they require similarly complex and fluid solutions. These solutions will not and cannot happen at the local level alone. However, as we have tried to show in this chapter, community development should aim to facilitate the capacity for individuals and communities to discuss values, make decisions, and take meaningful action at the local level. Essentially, it should foster stronger governance structures and networks that bring together local realities and global frameworks for innovative approaches. Harvey (1996, p. 44, emphasis in the original) puts it best when he writes: "*Theoretical practice* must be constructed as a continuous dialectic between the militant particularism of lived lives and a struggle to achieve sufficient critical distance and detachment to formulate global ambitions." By acting as the bridge between these two levels, community practitioners can work with citizens to help to foster this dialectic.

References

Barber, B.R. (2003). *Strong democracy: Participatory politics for a new age* (Twentieth-anniversary ed.). Berkley, CA: University of California Press. (Original work published 1984.)

Bhattacharyya, J. (2004). Theorizing community development. *Community Development Society Journal*, 34(2), 5–34.

Boyte, H.C. (2004). *Everyday politics: Reconnecting citizens and public life*. Philadelphia, PA: University of Pennsylvania Press.

Boyte, H.C. (2008). *The citizen solution: How you can make a difference*. St Paul, MN: Minnesota Historical Society Press.

Boyte, H.C. (2009). Repairing the breech: Cultural organizing and the politics of knowledge. *Partnerships: A Journal of Service-Learning and Civic Engagement*, 1(1), 1–21.

Bridger, J.C., & Alter, T.R. (2010). Public sociology, public scholarship, and community development. *Community Development*, 41(4), 405–416.

Brooks, P. (1984). *Reading for the plot*. New York, NY: Alfred A. Knopf.

Chaskin, R.J. (2001). Building community capacity: A definitional framework and case studies from a comprehensive community initiative. *Urban Affairs Review*, 36(3), 291–323.

de Souza Briggs, X. (1998). Doing democracy up-close: Culture, power, and communication in community building. *Journal of Planning Education and Research*, 18(1), 1–13.

Fine, G.A. (2012). *Tiny publics: A theory of group action and culture*. Russell Sage Foundation series on trust. New York, NY: Russell Sage Foundation.

Fiorina, M.P. (1999). Extreme voices: A dark side of civic engagement. In T. Skocpol & M.P. Fiorina (Eds.), *Civic Engagement in American Democracy* (pp. 395–425). Washington, DC: Brookings Institution Press.

Fischer, F. (2000). *Citizens, experts, and the environment: The politics of local knowledge*. Durham, NC: Duke University Press.

Fischer, F. (2009). *Democracy & expertise: Reorienting policy inquiry*. Oxford: Oxford University Press.

Fisher, W.R. (1985). The narrative paradigm: An elaboration. *Communication Monographs*, 52, 347–367.

Flyvbjerg, B. (2001). *Making social science matter: Why social inquiry fails and how it can succeed again*. Cambridge: Cambridge University Press.

Gadamer, H.G. (1975). *Truth and method*. New York, NY: The Crossroad Publishing Corporation.

Giddens, A. (1984). *The constitution of society: Outline of the theory of structuration*. Berkeley, CA: University of California Press.

Gleick, J. (2011). *The information: A history, a theory, a flood*. New York, NY: Pantheon Books.

Granovetter, M. (1973). The strength of weak ties. *American Journal of Sociology*, 78(6), 1360–1380.

Habermas, J. (1984). *The theory of communicative action: Reason and the rationalization of society* (T. McCarthy, Trans.). Boston, MA: Beacon Press. (Original work published 1981.)

Harvey, D. (1996). *Justice, nature & the geography of difference*. Malden, MA: Blackwell Publishing.

Johansson, F. (2004). *The Medici effect: Breakthrough insights at the intersection of ideas, concepts & cultures*. Boston, MA: Harvard Business School Press.

Lane, M.B. (2005). Public participation in planning: An intellectual history. *Australian Geographer*, 36(3), 283–299.

Mathews, D. (1999). *Politics for the people: Finding a responsible public voice* (2nd ed.). Urbana, IL: University of Illinois Press. (Original work published 1994.)

Mathews, D. (2009). Ships passing in the night? *Journal of Higher Education Outreach and Engagement*, 13(3), 5–16.

Moore, A.B. (2002). Community development practice: Theory in action. *Community Development Society Journal*, 33(1), 20–32.

Ostrom, E. (2010). Beyond markets and states: Polycentric governance of complex economic systems. *American Economic Review,* 100(3), 641–672.

Peters, S.J., Alter, T.R., & Schwartzbach, N. (2010). *Democracy and higher education: Traditions and stories of civic engagement.* Transformations in higher education: The scholarship of engagement. East Lansing, MI: Michigan State University Press.

Putnam, R.D. (2000). *Bowling alone: The collapse and revival of American community.* New York, NY: Simon and Schuster.

Rittel, H.W.J., & Weber, M.M. (1973). Dilemmas in a general theory of planning. *Policy Sciences,* 4(2), 155–169.

Schlozman, K.L., Verba, S., & Brady, H.E. (1999). Civic participation and the equality problem. In T. Skocpol & M.P. Fiorina (Eds.), *Civic Engagement in American Democracy* (pp. 427–459). Washington, DC: Brookings Institution Press.

Scott, J. (1998). *Seeing like a state: How certain schemes to improve the human condition have failed.* New Haven, CT: Yale University Press.

Sullivan, W.M. (2005). *Work and integrity: The crisis and promise of professionalism in America* (2nd ed.). San Francisco, CA: Jossey-Bass.

Wilkinson, K.P. (1991). *The community in rural America.* New York, NY: Greenwood Press.

INDEX

Introductory Note

References such as '178–9' indicate (not necessarily continuous) discussion of a topic across a range of pages. Wherever possible in the case of topics with many references, these have either been divided into sub-topics or only the most significant discussions of the topic are listed. Because the entire work is about 'community' and 'community development', the use of these terms (and certain others which occur constantly throughout the book) as an entry point has been restricted. Information will be found under the corresponding detailed topics.

abandoned agency 47, 91–2
academic literature 26, 123–4, 127, 133–4, 157
academics 1, 28–9, 157–8, 185
action: collective *see* collective action; community *see* community action; concerted 49, 74; individual 28, 50, 54, 89, 177; social 22, 173, 175
active communities 44, 52, 94
activeness 54, 73, 102
actors 42–3, 45, 72–3, 134, 173, 175, 181; collective 129, 131–2; individual 7, 168, 173; local 47, 51, 67; rational 99, 115
adaptive capacity 55, 86
agency 6, 45–6, 50, 55, 164–6, 173, 175; abandoned 47, 91–2; authentic 94–5; community 43, 50, 54–5, 82, 85–7, 91–2, 110; emergence 87, 93–4; incomplete 92–4; minimal 88–9; ritualized 47, 89–91; social 172, 174
agendas 82, 88, 95, 129, 158, 173

agent-centred community-based collective action 124, 135
agreements 80–1, 87, 113
agricultural adaptation 34, 37
agriculture 15, 27–8, 35, 64, 75, 100, 125; civic 35; exurban 35; small-scale 126; United States 63–4
alcoholism 145, 147, 149, 151, 154
alliances 90, 92, 107
America: North 16–17 *see also* United States: rural 41, 63–5, 75
analytical scheme 173–4
Ancient Order of Hibernians (AOH) 107
anthracite 5, 103–5, 109, 111–13, 115; industry 104, 110, 112, 115; market 103–4, 109; Pennsylvania 110, 112; region 101, 104–6, 110–11, 113
apathetic citizens 146, 170
Appalachia 52, 89–90, 168, 174, 177; communities 169, 176; culture 174

192 Index

apparel industry 110
Aristotle 158, 160
assets, local 67–8
associations 42, 72, 85, 131, 134, 140–1,
    154–5
attachment, community 4, 28, 57
Audirac, I. 25–7, 29, 32, 37
Aurand, H.W. 106, 110
authentic agency 94–5
authority 6, 80–1, 141, 158, 168; legal 152
Avril, T. 113
Ayres, J. 53

Barber, B.R. 184
barriers 6, 50–1, 76, 84; to place-based
    competitiveness 67–9
baseball 151
Bayou La Batre 139–40, 158
bedspreads 65
behaviors 7, 16, 43, 71, 81, 84, 173–5;
    group 166, 176
beliefs 16, 56, 68, 81, 84, 89, 92
Bell, D. 15
Berthoff, R. 103–4, 106
Berube, A. 26–7, 29–30
best interests 47, 91–2
Bhattacharyya, J. 7, 12, 16, 164, 180
black lung 106–7
bonding social capital 5, 15–17, 20–2, 69,
    100, 102, 106
bonds 12, 71, 83, 174
Boulding, K.E. 82
boundaries 1–2, 107, 158, 168, 182,
    184, 186
Boyte, H.C. 159, 185–7
Brooks, D. 25–6, 28–9, 37, 185
Brooks, P. 185
business leaders 83, 104, 115
business proprietors 55–6
businesses 4, 35, 50, 63–5, 93, 126, 166

California 17–18, 68
calls to action 2–7
campaigns 103, 108, 141
capacity 35–6, 48–52, 72–4, 79–80, 85–7,
    89–92, 164–7; adaptive 55, 86; building
    4, 75, 90, 93–5, 164–7, 176–7, 188;
    civic 140; collective 79, 85–6, 88–9,
    92–3; community 51, 55, 95, 166–7,

171–2, 188; local see local capacity;
    social 50, 55
capital, social see social capital
capitalism 168
census 30–1, 33, 64, 111
centrality 129–30, 133
Chang, S. 15, 18
Change: community 7, 15, 25, 47, 117,
    154; economic 164–5; political 1, 90,
    128; social 2, 4–6, 79–80, 82–3, 90–2,
    94–5, 173–4; structural 5, 90, 130;
    technological 1, 15, 180, 188
character 34–5, 42, 123–4, 129, 133, 172
characteristics: community 12, 48;
    population 26, 66; structural 47, 101
Chaskin, R.J. 165, 188
choice 47, 50, 85–6, 88–9, 91–4, 131; of
    power 88; setting 88–9; work 149, 157
cities 5, 12, 14–15, 19, 29–33, 35, 131–2;
    creative 22; global 14; industrial 13–14
citizen identity 182–3
citizen participation 6, 180, 183
citizens 4–6, 91–3, 99–100, 111–12,
    138–60, 180–3, 185–8; apathetic 146,
    170; couch potato 144; local 87, 89,
    91–2, 94–5, 169; work 139, 141–3, 156
civic agriculture 35
civic capacity 140
civic engagement 3–4, 79–80, 94, 144, 146,
    157, 182; strategies 79, 150
civic entrepreneurs 23
civic groups 153, 155
civic projects 144, 153
civic resources 143, 151
civic work 141–2, 144–7, 152–3, 157–9
class 51, 83, 100, 106, 114, 144, 168–9;
    social 102, 104, 166; structure 71, 104
classical and revised concepts of community
    12–14
classical theoretical framework 7
classical theory 172, 176–7
clients 141, 182
coal 5, 52, 90, 101, 103–14, 116; ash 113,
    115–16; companies 103, 106, 113;
    industry 110–11, 115; miners 105, 113;
    mining 106–7; rights 103
coalitions 83, 90, 94, 155
collaboration 36, 114, 116, 185; and
    government reform 36

Index   193

collaborative efforts 53–4, 81
collective action 4–5, 22, 42, 51–2,
  114–15, 129–30, 135; agent-centred
  community-based 124, 135; effective
  129–31; rural underdog 129–30
collective actors 129, 131–2
collective bargaining, age of 110
collective capacity 79, 85–6, 88–9, 92–3
Columbus 30–3; Metropolitan Area
  32–3
commitment(s) 44, 52, 93, 127, 141,
  143–4, 156
common goals 15, 49, 51, 53
communication(s) 2, 4, 14–15, 17, 21,
  48–9, 51; channels 95; open 4, 42, 48,
  51, 56–7
communicative theory 183
communion 42, 49, 52, 56–7
community *see also Introductory Note and
  detailed entries*: classical and revised
  concepts 12–14; definition 2, 11–23;
  loss of 12
community action 4–5, 21, 36, 42–6,
  48–51, 53–4, 74–5; and structure
  dimensions 50–2
community agency 43, 50, 54–5, 82, 85–7,
  91–2, 110
community building 12, 18, 93, 98, 186
community development *see also Introductory
  Note*: activities 44, 51, 54, 57; definition
  44, 164–5, 177; and democracy *see
  democracy, and community development*; literature 4, 50, 53, 158, 166, 182;
  perspective 21, 93; politics of rural 124,
  135; populist 5, 124; practices 6, 42, 51,
  163, 165–9, 171–3, 175–7; practitioners
  55–7; process 42, 44, 93; profession 163,
  174; professionals 1, 181, 186–8; research
  163–4, 171; researchers 171; rural 5,
  123–36; texts 164; theory 1–7, 98,
  163–77; underdog 5, 124, 135
Community Development Society 1, 163
community history 98, 101–3, 114, 116
community identity 16, 21, 42, 116
community interaction field 41–3, 45;
  theory 3–4, 41–57
community leaders 41, 46, 55, 110, 152,
  157; role 46, 55
community participation 17, 46, 57

community power 5, 46, 54, 78–95;
  emergence 4, 88; field theoretical
  approach to 85–8
community resilience 55, 156
community without propinquity 11–12,
  14–15, 17
commuters 18
companies 103, 105–6, 110
competitiveness 65–7, 75; place 4, 65, 67–9
complementary acting 6, 143, 152–4
compliance 80–1, 129
conceptualization 1, 6–7, 72, 78, 99,
  124, 135
concerted action 49, 74
concrete goals 43, 53
conflict theory 7, 166–70, 172–3, 176–7;
  and community development practice
  169–70; and power 167–70
conflicts 80–1, 85–6, 104–7, 124–6,
  167–70, 175–7, 184; and consensus
  80–1; labor 109–10, 115
connections, social 27–8
consensus 4, 6, 12, 27, 47, 65, 80–1; and
  conflicts 80–1; models 5, 80
consequences of power 88
consolidation 35, 63, 104, 110, 115
constituencies 126, 129, 131–2, 140,
  157, 159
contacts 3, 17, 70–1
contemporary communities 15, 94, 103
contemporary decision making 98, 116
contemporary power literature 124, 135
control 34, 46, 66, 69, 84, 89–91, 140–2;
  social 15–16
conversations 11, 110, 143, 147, 154, 156
cooperation 49, 91, 102, 107–8, 141,
  153, 172
Coser, L. 81–2, 168
couch potato citizens 144
councils 112–13, 153
counteracting power 129–30, 135
countryside 123, 125–6, 128, 131–2
courses of action 114, 147
crisis conditions 126, 132
cultural patterns 7, 174, 176–7
cultural rationality 115, 183
cultural traditions 68, 115, 173–4, 176
cultures 3, 16, 66, 68, 165–6, 168–9,
  173–4; community 55, 177

194 Index

Dahl, R.A. 79, 81, 168
Dahrendorf, R. 80, 168
Dalton, Georgia 65–6
Daniels, T.L. 28, 34
Dayton, Ohio 30
decision-making 6, 38, 91, 143, 186;
contemporary 98, 116; deliberative 143;
local 2, 5, 80–2; processes 51, 80, 87, 91,
100, 110, 114–15; sound 149–50
decisions: contemporary 98, 114, 116;
deliberative 144, 150–1, 156–7
deliberations 6, 143, 147, 149–52, 155–7,
159, 187; public 143, 149–51, 157, 159
democracy 6–7, 138–41, 150, 154, 156,
158, 160; and community development
6, 138–59; concept 140–1; deliberative
6, 184–5; strong 184; theory of 142
democratic framework 142, 147
democratic participation 2, 5
democratic practices 6, 133, 141–3, 156–8,
188; Suggsville 144–56
democratic processes 51, 80
Department of Environmental Protection
(DEP) 113
Department of Transportation (DOT)
169, 176
developers, community 3, 23, 46, 54–5,
163–5, 169–71, 176–7
development: community *see* community
development; in the community 52–3;
economic *see* economic development;
exurban 3, 29, 34; interactional approach
to 72–3; leadership 74; local 52–3, 87,
128; place-based *see* place-based,
development; projects 4, 54, 116; rural
see rural development; rural, policies 75;
rural manufacturing 41, 52; workforce
66–7, 72, 74
dimensions of power 81–2, 129
disadvantaged places 131
disaffection 86–8, 90, 93, 114
disagreements 46, 93–4, 138, 143–4, 147–8
disasters 138, 140
diseases 106–7
disenfranchised groups 51
dispersed power 94–5
distances 17, 27, 29, 64, 66, 71
distributive justice 4, 42, 48, 50, 56–7, 87
diverse groups 102, 184
diversification 102–3

diversity 3, 16, 49, 51, 94, 102, 184
divisions of society 173–4
dominance 80, 130
domination 78, 90–1, 94, 116, 129;
power over 129, 135; urban 125–6, 130
DOT *see* Department of Transportation
downturn, economic 3, 34–5, 101, 109
dualism 172, 175
Dublin, T. 104, 106, 108–11, 113
Duncan, C. 71, 91, 94
dynamic theories 1

earnings 64
ecology, local 48
economic activities, small-scale 125, 131
economic benefits 112, 169
economic change 164–5
economic development 22, 35, 64–5, 98,
100, 116–17, 146–7; activeness 5, 98,
100–1, 117; policies 4, 66; and social
capital *see* social capital, and economic
development; strategies 51, 68
economic downturn 3, 34–5, 101, 109–13;
national trends 109–10; Schuylkill
County 110–12; Tamaqua 112–13
economic growth 68, 74–5, 93, 115
economic interests 108, 114, 125–6,
130–2, 169
economic issues 114, 116
economic niches 66–7
economic power 50, 82, 128
economic rationality 115–16
economic trends 67, 74
economy 12, 15, 29, 74–5, 89, 93, 146–7;
global 41, 64; local 86, 103, 142; political
34, 36; rural 64, 130
education 1, 12, 48, 66, 91, 111, 138–41;
level of 102, 111
effective collective action 129–31
efficacy 54–5, 83, 101
Eicher, J.B. 26, 29
electricity 140, 157
electronics industry 22
elites 5, 47, 54, 79, 84, 87–92, 94–5; local
4, 82, 84, 87, 89–92; political 128;
power 46, 79, 83, 88–9, 91, 93; ruling
78, 82–4, 92
elitism 79–80
emergence of community 3, 78, 83, 85,
87, 93

emic terms/level 134, 136
employment 2–3, 22, 63, 104, 110–11, 170–1
empowerment 75, 89, 95, 166; local 79, 88
engagement 158, 182–3; civic *see* civic engagement
Engels, F. 125
entrepreneurs 23, 103, 167; civic 23
entrepreneurship 41, 51, 74
environment 4, 27, 64, 71, 84, 88–92, 95; changing 43; geographical 2, 4; political 133, 148
equality 7, 123–4, 128, 130, 135, 159
equalization 108–9, 113
equity 56, 87, 140
equity-in-exchange 48, 87
essence of community 15–16, 20, 45
ethnic fractionalization and labor organization *see* labor organization, and ethnic fractionalization
ethnic groups 105–6, 116, 168
ethnic tensions 108, 114
EU (European Union) 75
events 6, 16, 52, 90–1, 114, 164–5, 170–2; community 16, 90, 170
expenses 82, 84, 93, 168, 183
experiments 37, 139, 156–7
expert identity 182–3
expertise 187; professional 142–3, 150; technical 67, 158
experts 5–6, 65, 68, 150, 180–3, 185, 187
exurban agriculture 35
exurban areas 26–7, 29, 34, 36
exurban change 29–34, 36
exurban community 35–6
exurban development 3, 29, 34
exurban governments 34, 36
exurban growth 28–9, 34, 36
exurban locales 36
exurban population 29
exurban research 3, 25, 26–9, 34–5
exurban residents 3, 27–8, 32
exurbanites 27
exurbanization 28–9, 38; process 27
exurbia 3, 25–6, 28–9, 32, 36–7; and community sociology 3, 25–37
exurbs 25–9, 35, 37

faces of power 81–2
facilities: physical 43; processing 64

factories 14–15, 22, 104
failure 2, 79, 88, 92–4, 133, 155, 188
fairness 123, 135, 148
families 13, 15–16, 70, 91, 105, 138–9, 149–50
farm-dependent counties 64
farmers 35–6, 63, 125–6, 146, 171, 185
farming 34, 125, 145
farmland 28, 34, 171
farms 26, 63–4
Fear, F. 158, 160
federal government 50, 168
Feldstein, L.M. 100
Fischer, F. 115, 180, 183, 185–7
Fisher, W.R. 185
Flora, C.B. & J.L. 48, 51, 170
food 18, 34–5, 48, 111, 140, 146
forces 5, 69, 73, 126–7, 138, 144, 158; market 69, 126, 168; structural 124–5, 129–30, 135
forest, state 169, 176
foresters 169, 171, 176
forums 143, 152–3, 159–60, 182
Foucault, M. 167–8
foundations 42, 49, 94, 107, 116, 138–40, 157–60
fractionalization 5, 98, 113–14, 116
frameworks 5–6, 54, 74, 79, 147–8, 156–7, 180; comprehensive 53; Mead's 71; theoretical 2, 7, 79, 166, 168, 170; for thinking and acting critically in community 180–8
framing 142–4, 148, 151, 157, 186; of issues 146–8, 151, 159
freedom 7, 140, 148, 182
fringe 27–8, 31; counties 31–2; rural-urban 3, 25–6, 29, 37
functionalism 83, 164, 166–7, 173, 176; structural *see* structural functionalism; and structures 166–7
functions 23, 51, 66, 102, 106; latent 166–7; manifest 166–7
fusion of horizons 184

Gaventa, J. 78–9, 81–5, 89–91, 94–5, 130, 174–5
gay community 12, 16
Gemeinschaft 3, 13, 15, 20
generalized reciprocity 99–101, 114, 116; norms 99–100, 102, 114, 116

196 Index

generalizing structure 4, 42–7, 49–57; and
community context 45–7; concept 42,
45; dimensions 3, 41–57
geography 12, 33, 64–5, 67; political 30, 33
Gesellschaft 13–15
Giddens, Anthony 7, 164, 172–8, 183;
concepts 166, 174, 176; on mid-level
theory 175, 177; on modalities 173, 178;
perspective 175–7; on structuration
theory 172–7
Gleick, J. 185
global cities 14
global community 14, 22
global economy 41, 64
global markets 66–7
global scale 3, 17–18
globalization 4, 63, 69, 82, 95, 163, 188
goals 2, 43–7, 50, 52–4, 73–4, 88–9, 92–4;
common 15, 49, 51, 53; community 47,
51; concrete 43, 53
Goffman, E. 170
goods, public 141
governance 3, 28, 34, 36, 128, 180; local
32, 35, 66, 128; structures 35, 38, 188
government geography, Ohio 33
governments 12, 35–6, 138, 140–1, 151,
153; exurban 34, 36; federal 50, 168;
local 34–8, 51, 106, 110, 113, 128, 174;
reform and collaboration 36
Gramsci, A. 82–4, 92
groups: civic 153, 155; diverse 102, 184;
ethnic 105–6, 116, 168; interest 94, 114,
168; local 79, 94; organized 72, 85;
powerless 88, 90, 125; religious 113,
169; social 114, 185
growth 21, 28–9, 33, 35–7, 54, 68, 74;
economic 68, 74–5, 93, 115; exurban
28–9, 34, 36; machine 88, 94, 167;
management 3, 28, 32, 34; population
25–6, 28, 32–4, 37, 105
Gudelunas, W.A. 107

Harvey, D. 64, 67–8, 180, 188
hegemonic power 129
hegemony, ideological 82, 84, 91–2
Heinz, A.S 53
heritage narratives 68
highways 66, 169
historic structure 171
historical processes 102, 116

history 4–5, 13, 63, 66, 68, 78, 100–1;
community 98, 101–3, 114, 116; local
68, 106, 115–16; and local economic
development 5, 98–116; regional 100,
103, 106, 112; and social capital 5,
98–116
holistic place-based development policy
73–6
horizontal patterns 43, 45–6
human community 141, 181
human interaction 170, 185
Hurricane Katrina 139–40, 142

ideal-typical scenarios 124, 134–5; radical
and pragmatic 130–2
identity: citizen 182–3; community 16, 21,
42, 52, 116; expert 182–3
ideological hegemony 82, 84, 91–2
ideologies, prevailing 87, 90, 92
immigrants 105–6, 108, 139
inaction 78, 88, 91–2, 129
inclusion 54, 56
incomes 27, 43, 48, 63, 67, 72, 74
incomplete agency 92–4
individual action 28, 50, 54, 89, 177
individualism 107, 174
industrial city 13–14
industries: anthracite 104, 110, 112, 115;
apparel 110; electronics 22; new 111,
147, 154
inequality 48, 85, 87, 123–4, 133, 135
infrastructure 22, 37, 41, 67, 93, 113;
improvements 66, 74; social 48–53
innovations 74, 184, 188
instability 103–4, 147
institutions 72, 83–4, 151–2, 154–5, 157–8,
165–6, 168; formal 12, 141; large 138;
local 67, 102, 152, 159
interaction fields 5, 42, 45, 72, 74;
community *see* community interaction
field
interaction theory, symbolic 164, 171
interaction(s): community 12, 46, 87;
human 170, 185; individual 34, 50; local
4, 85, 92; patterns 36, 71; purposive 86,
93; social 2, 12, 15, 36, 48–50, 70–3,
85–6; sustained 41, 43
interactional approach to place-based rural
development 63–76
interactional community 48–9

Index **197**

interactional structure 37, 48, 55
interactional theory 83, 159
interactionism, symbolic *see* symbolic
  interactionism
interest groups 94, 114, 168
interests: common 7, 28, 49, 85, 168;
  community 5–6, 49, 72, 125, 128;
  community-based 127, 132; competing
  170, 181; economic 108, 114, 125–6,
  130–2, 169; international 17, 22; local
  17, 79, 81, 87, 128; local residents 48–9;
  personal 46–7; popular 128; private 43,
  55, 89; public 46–7, 54–5, 57; rural 5,
  128, 130, 132; shared 43, 108, 114, 116;
  special 4, 17, 46; underdog 126, 133;
  urban 125–6, 131
international interests 17, 22
internet 14, 17, 21, 155
intervention, state *see* state intervention
interviews, key informant 98, 101–2, 114
invasion/succession process 3, 28
Ireland 22, 105–6
Irish immigrants 106
Isocrates 158, 160
issues: community 23, 52, 87, 109;
  economic 114, 116; framing 146, 151,
  159; local 79, 86

Jewish community 12, 16
job creation 74, 132
Johansson, F. 184
Johnson, C. 65–6, 158
journalism 139, 156
journalists 28, 157
judgment 141, 150, 158
justice, distributive 4, 42, 48, 50, 56–7, 87

Katrina, Hurricane 139–40, 142
Kentucky *see* Appalachia
Kettering Foundation 6, 138–40,
  146, 159
key informants 102; interviews 98,
  101–2, 114
Kitching, G. 126–7
Kline, C.N. & M. 106, 108, 113
knowledge 25, 37, 157, 164–5, 181–2, 185,
  187; power 82, 91
Kolbe, R.L. 107, 111
Krugman, P. 65
Kurtz, R.A. 26, 29

labor conflicts 109–10, 110 *see also* Molly
  Maguires
labor organization 106, 113; and ethnic
  fractionalization 105–9
laborers, unskilled 105–6
Lancaster County 68
landscapes 66–7, 75
Lane, M.B. 183
languages 16, 146, 163, 170, 181, 187
latent functions 166–7
LC&N *see* Lehigh Coal & Navigation
  Company
Leach, W. 69
leaders 22, 46, 55, 84, 103–5, 160; business
  83, 104, 115; community 41, 46, 55,
  110, 152, 157; local 46, 54, 66, 102,
  104, 116
leadership 50, 57, 67, 74–5, 110, 133, 182;
  community *see* community leaders;
  development 74; programs 51, 74; style
  131, 133
learning 139, 144, 154–6, 182, 188;
  communities 68, 155; public 6, 143,
  154–5, 157
legal authority 152
legitimacy 6, 47, 81
Lehigh Coal & Navigation Company
  (LC&N) 103–4, 108–9, 113
Leonard, J.W. 106–7
Licht, W. 104, 106, 108–11, 113
life 13, 23, 74–5, 89, 111, 136, 140;
  community 52, 95, 100, 116, 127,
  141, 164; everyday 69, 144; local 5,
  48, 72–4, 83, 86, 89–91, 95; public 127,
  142, 158, 182
linkages 4, 43, 70, 72–5, 86, 88, 95
Lipset, S.M. 125–6
literature 2, 4, 26–7, 42–3, 45–6, 138,
  158–9; academic 26, 123–4, 127, 133–4,
  157; community development 4, 50, 53,
  158, 166, 182; power 124, 129, 135;
  theoretical 4, 78
living condition 20
local actors 47, 51, 67
local assets 67–8
local capacity 36, 67, 73–4, 78–9, 87–8, 90,
  93–4; emergence 5, 79
local citizens 87, 89, 91–2, 94–5, 169
local communities 3, 17, 91–2, 95, 125,
  127–8, 186

local conditions 84, 114
local decision making 2, 5, 80–2
local development 52–3, 87, 128
local ecology 48
local economy 86, 103, 142
local elites 4, 82, 84, 87, 89–92
local empowerment 79, 88
local governance 32, 35, 66, 128
local governments 34–8, 51, 106, 110, 113, 128, 174
local groups 79, 94
local history 68, 106, 115–16
local institutions 67, 102, 152, 159
local interaction 4, 85, 92
local interests 17, 79, 81, 87, 128
local issues 79, 86
local life 5, 48, 72–4, 83, 86, 89–91, 95
local participation 41, 75, 86, 187
local people/population 7, 42, 44, 48, 53, 66, 85–7
local power 87–8, 95, 124
local relationships 52, 86
local residents 3, 6, 49, 79, 84–5, 87–9, 92–5; diverse 78, 91, 94; interests 48–9
local society 42, 55, 70, 72, 75, 85, 131
local uniqueness 66–7
local well-being 78, 93
locality 35, 41–6, 48, 50, 52, 70, 85–6
loitering 149
loss of community 12
Lukes, S. 5, 81–2, 129
Luloff, A.E. 41, 50–2, 54, 72–3, 85–8, 91, 93–4
Lyon, L. 15, 25–6, 37
Lyson, T.A. 28, 34–5

McKibben, B. 75
macro level 7, 166, 172–5, 177
macro structures 173
macro theories 7, 172, 175–7
manifest functions 166–7
manipulation 79–81, 91, 94, 129, 174
manufacturing 63–4, 66, 101, 104, 110–11, 126, 147; development, rural 41, 52; operations 104, 111
marginalisation 125–6
market conditions 90, 108
market forces 69, 126, 168
markets: anthracite 103–4, 109; global 66–7

Marsh, B. 111–12
Marx, K. 82, 125, 169
Marxist theory 168–9
Mathews, D. 6, 182, 188
Mead, G.H. 71, 170
meaning: shared 7, 71, 164–6, 170–2, 176; symbolic 172, 175
meat packing 64
meetings 14, 48, 87, 141, 149, 151–4, 167; town 145–6
members, community 80, 84, 151, 182, 188
Merton, R.K. 166
metropolitan areas 29–32, 34, 64
metropolitan counties 32
metropolitan statistical areas (MSAs) 27
Mexico 18, 108
Meyrowitz, J. 69
micro approach 7, 166, 172
micro dimension 175, 178
micro level 7, 79, 83, 172–5
micro theorists 172, 178
micro theory 172–8
middle-class 108, 126
middle spaces 185, 187
Midwestern communities 56
Miller: B. 115; D.L. 105, 109–12
mills 111
mines 103–4, 108–10, 113
mineworkers 103–10
minimal agency 88–9
Mitchell, John 107, 109
mixed-methods approach 98, 100, 116
mobilization 4, 44, 79, 82, 87, 89, 93–4
modalities 7, 173–7, 186; Giddens's 173, 178
model communities 12, 156
models 6–7, 13, 15, 26, 65, 155, 181–3; consensus 5, 80
modernization 12, 14–15, 21
Molly Maguires 106–7, 112
Molotch, H. 46, 68, 73, 94, 114
momentum 53, 64, 143–4, 154
Monk, P.M. 44, 52–3
moral reasoning 158, 186–7
MSAs see metropolitan statistical areas
multiple communities in virtual time-space 17–18
mutual promises 152

Index 199

names 14, 139, 141–2, 145–7, 155–6, 160, 170; professional 142, 146
naming 142, 145, 151, 157; problems 6, 144–6, 156
narratives 101, 114, 116, 185–6; community 114, 170; heritage 68
National Issues Forums 159
natural resources 27, 64, 66–7, 75, 86, 101
negative consequences 89, 91–2, 94, 125, 149, 157
negotiations 109, 170
neighborhoods 12, 19–20, 23, 51, 100, 105, 148
neighbors 70, 102, 140, 142, 145
neo-Marxists 168–9
networks 15–16, 20–3, 51–2, 92, 113, 115, 155; comprehensive 49, 85; far-flung 23, 71; social 2, 15, 20, 70, 80, 99–100, 103
New York City 103, 107
niches, economic 66–7
NIMBY 183
nodes 22–3
nonmetropolitan areas 30, 32
nonmetropolitan counties 63–4
nonplace communities 13–16
normative patterns 173
normative structures 16, 49, 115
norms 16, 21–2, 99, 101–2, 115, 173, 182–3; generalized reciprocity 99–100, 102, 114, 116; shared 3, 16; symbolic 174, 177; traditional 175, 177
North America 16–17 see also United States
North Carolina 31–2
Northeastern United States 109, 111
Nugent, W.T.K. 136

Ohio 3, 25, 37–8; exurban change and significance 29–34; government geography 33; population 31
open-country residents 28
open spaces 34
oppositions 5–6, 49, 108, 115, 123–8, 130, 133–5
oppression 88, 90
organizational structures 29, 44, 49
organizations 41–3, 45–6, 73–5, 83–4, 99–100, 102, 165–9; existing 165, 167; external 46, 167; formal 103, 108, 188;

labor see labor organization; new 165, 167; nongovernmental 50, 151; social 65, 70, 72; voluntary 102

paired communities 101
Panizza, F. 134
Panther Valley 104, 108–9
parks 52, 152–3
Parsons, T. 83, 166–7, 178
participants 44, 47, 49, 74, 147, 170–1, 187
participation 4, 6, 15, 50–1, 54–5, 101–2, 128; citizen 6, 180, 183; community 17, 46, 54, 57; democratic 2, 5; local 41, 75, 86, 187; public 142, 159, 183
participative pro-community state intervention 5, 124, 129–30, 135
partnerships 90
Pateman, C. 51, 91
patterns 32, 64, 67, 98, 103, 173–7; cultural 7, 174, 176–7; horizontal 43, 45–6; interaction 36, 71; normative 173; settlement 26, 37; voting 107
Pennsylvania 5, 31–2, 68, 73, 98, 111; anthracite 110, 112; communities 52, 98, 100
personal interests 46–7
perspectives 1–2, 11–12, 23, 56, 83, 123–4, 187; current 2–7; interactional 50, 72–4, 85
Peters, S. 158, 160, 181–3
Philadelphia 103, 105, 113
Philadelphia & Reading Coal & Iron Company 103
Philadelphia and Reading Corporation (PRC) 110
place, and social well-being 69–72
place-based approach 67
place-based community 12, 16, 21
place-based development 4, 65–6, 73; holistic 73–6; rural 63–4, 66, 68, 70, 72, 74–6
place competitiveness 4, 65, 67–9; barriers to 67–9; as rural development 65–7
planners 12, 26–7, 169, 186
planning 28, 32, 34, 36, 38, 44, 183; land-use 3, 28–9, 32, 34; urban 11, 167, 186
Poland 174–5, 177

200 Index

policies 3, 35, 47, 65–6, 69, 74–5, 184; economic development 4, 66; public 133, 171, 180; rural 64–5
political change 1, 90, 128
political economy 34, 36
political elites 128
political environment 133, 148
political geography 30, 33
political populism 133–4
political science 36, 167
political systems 84, 138, 140
political theory 159, 182
political trust 153
politicians 109, 115, 132, 140, 150
politics 5, 99, 104, 128, 157, 184, 188
popular powerlessness 123–5, 128, 130, 135
population 3–4, 25–7, 29–34, 48, 64, 100–1, 111; characteristics 26, 66; exurban 29; growth 25–6, 28, 32–4, 37, 105; local 42, 44, 48, 53, 72, 85; Ohio 31; rural 27–8, 30–1, 126; total 29–32
populism 5–6, 123–9, 131, 133–6; political 133–4; representational 127–8; and rural community development 123–36; strengths and weaknesses 133–4
populist community development 5, 124
populists 5, 123–5, 127–8, 130–6; opposition 125, 134; pragmatic 131–2; radical 130–2; representational 128; rural 126
post-place communities 2, 11–21; concept 16–17; conundrum 21–3; strength 18–20
Pottsville 103
poverty 6, 27, 83
power 4–7, 46–7, 78–86, 88–9, 127–31, 133–5, 164–71; choice and consequences of 88; community *see* community power; conceptualizing 79–82; and conflict theory 167–70; consequences 88; counteracting 129–30, 135; differences 165, 169, 177; dimensions of 81–2, 129; dispersed 94–5; economic 50, 82, 128; elites 46, 79, 83, 88–9, 91, 93; faces of 81–2; grassroots 88, 91; hegemonic 129; holders 47, 82–3, 89–91, 93–4; imbalances 116, 176–7; knowledge 82, 91; literature 124, 129, 135; local 87–8, 95, 124; over 5, 123–4, 128–30, 135; and powerlessness *see* powerlessness, and power; relations 5, 7, 83, 98, 132; relationships 81–2, 133; and rural

community development 123–36; social 114, 130, 169; structural 123–7, 130, 132, 135; structures 78–81, 84, 90, 92, 102, 115; theoretical perspectives 82–8; threat 81; to 5, 123–4, 128–30, 135; underdog 124–5, 133–6; understanding 79–82; urban 5, 130
power-holding elites 79, 89, 93
powerless groups 88, 90, 125
powerlessness 83–4, 124–5, 127, 130, 133–5; negotiating 128–30; popular 123–5, 128, 130, 135; and power 83–5; oppositions between 125–8; relative 125, 127–8; rural *see* rural powerlessness
practitioners 1, 6–11, 138–9, 163, 165–7, 169–71, 180; community development 55–7
pragmatic ideal-typical scenarios 130–2
pragmatic populists 131–2
pragmatists 131–2
PRC (Philadelphia and Reading Corporation) 110
prevailing ideologies 87, 90, 92
private interests 43, 55, 89
pro-community state intervention 5, 124–5; participative 5, 124, 129–30, 135
production 63–5, 67, 108, 112
professional expertise 142–3, 150
professional names 142, 146
professional routines 142, 151, 157
professional work 139, 145, 158, 187
professionalism 184
professionals 108, 138–9, 141–6, 150, 156–60, 183, 185–6; academic 182; community development 1, 181, 186–8
promises, mutual 152
propinquity 12, 14–15, 17, 21–3; community without 11–12, 14–15, 17
Pryor, R.J. 26
public deliberations 143, 149–51, 157, 159
public goods 141
public interest 46–7, 54–5, 57
public learning 6, 143, 154–5, 157
public life 127, 142, 158, 182
public participation 142, 159, 183
public policies 133, 171, 180
public spaces 22, 185
public terms 145–6, 155–6
public work 160
Putnam, R.D. 17, 30, 98–100, 127, 184

quiescence 81, 83–5, 88–90, 174;
emergence 94–5

race 51, 102, 108, 144, 168–9
radical ideal-typical scenarios 130–2
radical populists 130–2
radicals 131–2
rationality 98, 115–16, 183; cultural 115,
  183; economic 115–16
Reading Anthracite 110, 112
reality, social 1, 166, 170, 172
reciprocity 99–102, 115, 173; generalized
  see generalized reciprocity
redevelopment efforts 111, 114
reforms: and collaboration 36; minor 131–2
regional level 23, 101
regional scale 17, 23
regions 14, 22, 34, 37, 66–8, 103–4,
  107–12
relations 14, 16, 22, 27, 37, 41, 86;
  power 5, 7, 83, 98, 132; social see social
  relations
relationships 3–4, 21, 41–2, 48–9, 69–75,
  180–2, 188; complicated 2, 106; local 52,
  86; power 81–2, 133; social 18, 49, 51
relative powerlessness 125, 127–8
religions 12, 102
religious groups 113, 169
representational populists 128
reputation, negative 134–5
research 1, 3–4, 29, 37–8, 42, 52–4, 140–1;
  community development 163–4, 171;
  empirical 163; exurban 3, 25, 26–9, 34–5
researchers, action 182
residence 12, 21, 70
residents 2–4, 12, 14–15, 30–3, 43–4, 72–3,
  85–6; community 44, 51–2, 56, 169,
  176; exurban 3, 27–8, 32; local see local
  residents 3, 6, 49, 79, 84–5, 87–9, 92–5;
  new 28, 36; open-country 28; rural 27,
  32; suburban 27
resilience, community 55, 156
resources 46, 50–1, 54–6, 82, 86–90,
  142–4, 151; civic 143, 151; external 51,
  67; identifying and committing 6, 143,
  151–2; institutional 151–2;
  natural see natural resources:
  new 22, 71
restaurant 147, 149, 154
retail trade 111

ritualized agency 47, 89–91
rituals 84, 181
roads 99, 140–1, 169, 176
Robinson, J.W. 44, 51, 85, 164
Rokkan, S. 125–6
Rothman, J. 164
routines, professional 142, 151, 157
rules 81, 92, 138, 140, 170, 174, 181
rural America 41, 63–5, 75
rural areas 3–4, 14, 25, 64–5, 70, 75, 125
rural communities 5, 13–14, 41, 51, 64,
  127, 131–2
rural community development 5, 123–36
rural conditions 123–4, 134–5
rural development 74; place-based see
  place-based development, rural: place
  competitiveness as 65–7
rural economy 64, 130
rural interests 5, 128, 130, 132
rural policies 64–5
rural populations 27–8, 30–1, 126
rural populists 126
rural powerlessness 5, 123, 125, 130;
  perceived forms 123, 128; relative
  125, 130
rural residents 27, 32
rural underdog collective action 129–30
rural-urban fringe 3, 25–6, 29, 37
rural world 123, 132

Salamon, S. 12, 14, 28, 36, 52
sanctions 82, 115, 174
Santa Barbara 68
scapegoats 133, 150
scholars 1, 5–12, 14, 28–9, 36, 138–9,
  182–4; community 1, 12, 25, 32, 45, 47;
  public 182; urban 3, 32
scholarship 11, 158, 181; engaged 182;
  exurban 29, 34; public 158
schools 83, 91, 93, 106, 145, 148–9, 151
Schuylkill County 101, 103, 105–7,
  111–13; in early development 103–4;
  economic downturn 110–12; labor
  organizations and ethnic fractionalization
  in 105–8
Schuylkill Economic Development
  Corporation 111
scientific community 12, 16
Scott, J. 83–4, 91, 181
security 64, 142, 145–8

202 Index

self 71, 186
self actualization 48
self-governance 141
self-help approach 51
self-interests 85–6, 95
self-rule 139, 141, 156, 158
services 18, 36–7, 43, 67–8, 75, 168–9, 182
settlement area 29, 37
settlement patterns 26, 37
shared interests 43, 108, 114, 116
shared meaning 7, 71, 164–6, 170–2, 176
shared norms 3, 16
shared values 16, 80
Sharpless, R.E. 105, 109–12
shopping centers 18
Silicon Valley 18, 21–2
skills 74, 82, 91, 141, 151, 157, 180
small-scale agriculture 126
small-town community 14, 26
small towns 13, 15, 23, 28
social action 22, 173, 175
social agency 172, 174
social capacity 50, 55
social capital 5, 15, 17, 23, 66, 98–102,
    114–17; bonding 5, 15–17, 20–2, 69,
    100, 102, 106; bridging 5, 100, 102, 184;
    and economic development 5, 98–116;
    study overview 100–2; theory 5, 98,
    101, 114
social change 2, 4–6, 79–80, 82–3, 90–2,
    94–5, 173–4
social class 102, 104, 166
social connections 27–8
social control 15–16
social disruptions 70
social evening 19
social fields 49, 72, 75, 85–95
social foundations of community 20–1
social groups 114, 185
social infrastructure 48–53
social interaction 2, 12, 15, 36, 48–50,
    70–3, 85–6
social networks 2, 15, 20, 70, 80,
    99–100, 103
social organization 65, 70, 72
social power 114, 130, 169
social practices 165
social processes 11, 43, 71, 173–4, 185
social reality 1, 166, 170, 172

social relations 3, 5, 12, 14–15, 21, 23, 99;
    Tamaqua 108
social relationships 18, 49, 51
social sciences 124, 134, 181
social solidarity 99, 177
social structure 5, 43, 55, 70, 72, 82–3,
    173–5
social systems 34–6, 166–7, 173–5,
    178, 188
social theory 124, 166, 172
social ties 13, 21
social trust 99–101, 114, 116; high levels
    99, 101–2; norms 100, 114, 116
social well-being 4, 7, 42, 46, 48–9, 65,
    72–5; five conditions of 42, 48–9; and
    place 69–72
sociologists 26, 163, 169, 176
sociology 13, 159, 172, 175, 184;
    community and exurbia 3, 25–37
solidarity: building/strengthening 170, 172,
    177; community 21; social 99, 177
spaces 17, 34, 175–6, 185; middle 185, 187;
    open 34; public 22, 185
special interests 4, 17, 46
Spectrosky, A.C. 28–9, 37
Springdale Pit 113, 115–16
stability 69, 83, 167–8
Staniszkis, J. 174–5
state action 5, 123–4, 128–30, 133
state actors 129–30, 134
state forest 169, 176
state intervention 124, 126, 128, 132–3,
    135; pro-community 5, 124–5
Stoker, G. 133
stories 12, 34, 68, 145, 158, 185
storylines 185–6
storytelling 176, 185–6
strategies 4, 6, 28, 47, 54–5, 57, 66–7;
    collaborative 54–6
streets 14, 110, 146–9, 154
structural change 5, 90, 130
structural characteristics 47, 101
structural conditions 86, 175
structural forces 124–5, 129–30, 135
structural functionalism 7, 166–7, 172,
    176–7; and community development
    practice 167
structural power 123–7, 130, 132, 135
structuration theory 7, 172–8

structures: building 41–2, 44, 52–3, 56, 91; class 71, 104; community 4, 23, 43, 45, 53; and community action 50–2; and functionalism 166–7; generalizing *see* generalizing structure: governance 35, 38, 188; historic 171; interactional 37, 48, 55; normative 16, 49, 115; organizational 29, 44, 49; social 5, 43, 55, 70, 72, 82–3, 173–5
suburban communities 14–15
suburban residents 27
suburbs 12, 15, 18, 26–7, 31
success 17, 44, 51–3, 66, 73, 92–3, 154–5
Suggsville 6, 144–5, 147–9, 151–4, 156, 159; democratic practices 144–56; meetings 147, 149, 152, 155
Suggsvillians 145–6, 151, 156
Sullivan, W.M. 183
Summers, G. 88, 93–4
surveys 3, 18–19, 55, 114, 116; community 33, 56, 102; respondents 19, 56, 101–2
sustainable communities 48, 184
sustenance 21, 48
Swanson, L.E. 41, 50, 54, 86–8, 91, 93
symbolic interactionism 7, 166, 170–3, 175–8; and community development practice 171–2
symbolic meanings 172, 175
symbolic norms 174, 177
symbols 18, 165, 170–1, 176

Taiwan 15, 18
Tamaqua 5, 98–116; early development 104; economic downturn 112–13; labor organizations and ethnic fractionalization 108–9; paradox 5, 98–116; social relations 108; train station 113
Tamaqua Iron Works 104
Tamaqua Manufacturing Company 104
task accomplishment 41–2, 44, 46, 52–3
taxes 36, 65, 99, 106, 110, 126, 171
technical expertise 67, 158
technological change 1, 15, 180, 188
tensions 28, 114, 116, 142, 147–51, 155, 172; ethnic 108, 114
theoretical basis 7–11
theoretical directions, future 2–7
theoretical frameworks 2, 7, 79, 166, 168, 170

theoretical groundings 53, 164
theoretical literature 4, 78
theoretical perspectives 2, 5, 78–9, 95, 166, 183; on power 82–8
theorists 44, 163, 166–7, 184; micro 172, 178
threats 47, 81–2, 84, 89, 91, 95, 126; power 81
Thucydides 158
ties: social 13, 21; strong 23, 70
tolerance 4, 16, 42, 51, 56–7, 101, 136
Tonniës, F. 13, 15–16
tools 5–6, 28, 34–5, 55, 78, 82, 91; useful 4, 116, 124, 167, 185–6
town meetings 145–6
towns 12, 69, 104–5, 108, 110–11, 145, 152–4; company 88, 104
townships 29–30, 32–3, 35–8, 107; trustees 35–6
trade, retail 111
tradeoffs 148, 150
traditional community 14, 16
traditional norms 175, 177
traditions: cultural 68, 115, 173–4, 176; society 173, 175
trust 13, 99–102, 115, 144; political 153; social *see* social trust
trustworthiness 99

UMWA (United Mine Workers of America) 106–9
underdog community development 5, 124, 135
underdog identities, construction of 124, 135
underdog interests 126, 133
underdog power approach 124–5, 133–6
underdogs, rural 129–30
unions 90, 104, 109–10, 115
uniqueness, local 66–7
United Mine Workers of America *see* UMWA
United States 18, 31, 34, 36–7, 74–5, 103, 101 *see also individual states/places*: agriculture 63–4; Census of Population 30–1; Department of Agriculture (USDA) 63, 100, 116; Environmental Protection Agency (USEPA) 36; Northeastern 109, 111

Index

unskilled laborers 105–6
urban areas 13, 27, 29–31, 35, 37, 64
urban domination 125–6, 130
urban interests 125–6, 131
urban places 25, 68
urban planning 11, 167, 186
urban power 5, 130
urban scholars 3, 32
Urbina, I. 111–12
US *see* United States
USDA *see* United States, Department of Agriculture
USEPA *see* United States, Environmental Protection Agency
utility 6, 42, 55, 92, 99

values 6–7, 15–16, 65–6, 115, 123, 148–50, 168–70; shared 16, 80
villages 28–30, 32–3, 35, 69, 106
violence 106, 109
virtual time-space, multiple communities in 17–18
voting patterns 107

wages 64, 104–6
Warner, P. 44, 52–3

Warren: M. 158; R. 43, 45–7, 50, 52, 54
water 52, 138, 140
Webber, M. 11–12, 16–17
Weber, M. 81, 175, 180
welfare 41, 43, 46–7, 49, 52, 104, 127
well-being 2, 12, 35, 44–5, 47–50, 70–5, 95; community 44, 73, 86–7, 92; individual 48, 101; local 78, 93; social *see* social well-being
Welsh 105–6
whole community organizing 54
wicked problems 180–1, 184
Wikipedia 185
Wilkinson, K.P. 4, 41–6, 48–9, 51–3, 70–5, 79–80, 85–8
work condition 20
workers 64, 74, 104–7, 109–10, 153, 172, 174–5
workforce 65, 67, 105; development 66–7, 72, 74
worldviews 84, 89, 91
Wright Mills, C. 83

Zekeri, A.A. 52
Zukin, S. 69

CPSIA information can be obtained
at www.ICGtesting.com
Printed in the USA
BVHW070902291118
534271BV00006B/39/P